D1519684

Bioarchaeology of the Florida Gulf Coast

Florida Museum of Natural History: Ripley P. Bullen Series

Florida A&M University, Tallahassee
Florida Atlantic University, Boca Raton
Florida Gulf Coast University, Ft. Myers
Florida International University, Miami
Florida State University, Tallahassee
University of Central Florida, Orlando
University of Florida, Gainesville
University of North Florida, Jacksonville
University of South Florida, Tampa
University of West Florida, Pensacola

Bioarchaeology
of the Florida Gulf Coast

Adaptation, Conflict, and Change

Dale L. Hutchinson

With contributions by Lynette Norr and Mark Teaford

University Press of Florida

Gainesville · Tallahassee · Tampa · Boca Raton

Pensacola · Orlando · Miami · Jacksonville · Ft. Myers

09 08 07 06 05 04   6 5 4 3 2 1

Library of Congress Cataloging-in-Publication Data
Hutchinson, Dale L.
Bioarchaeology of the Florida Gulf Coast : adaptation, conflict, and
change / Dale L. Hutchinson with contributions by Lynette Norr and
Mark Teaford.
p. cm. – (Ripley P. Bullen series)
Includes bibliographical references and index.
ISBN 0-8130-2706-3
1. Palmer Site (Fla.) 2. Indians of North America—Florida—Gulf
Coast—Antiquities. 3. Indians of North America—Anthropometry—
Florida—Gulf Coast. 4. Human remains (Archaeology)—Florida—
Gulf Coast. 5. Ethnoarchaeology—Florida—Gulf Coast. 6. Gulf Coast
(Fla.)—Antiquities. I. Norr, Lynette. II. Teaford, Mark Franklyn, 1951–.
III. Title. IV. Series.
E78.F6H87 2004
975.9'6101—dc22   2003057909

All photographs without attribution are by the author.

The University Press of Florida is the scholarly publishing agency
for the State University System of Florida, comprising Florida A&M
University, Florida Atlantic University, Florida Gulf Coast University,
Florida International University, Florida State University, University
of Central Florida, University of Florida, University of North Florida,
University of South Florida, and University of West Florida.

University Press of Florida
15 Northwest 15th Street
Gainesville, FL 32611-2079
http://www.upf.com

for the Palmer family,
who recognized the importance of archaeological remains

for Ripley and Adelaide Bullen,
who contributed much to Florida archaeology

and in memory of Karen Chavez,
archaeology mentor and friend

Contents

Maps

Tables

Figures

Foreword

In 1959, 1960, and 1962, Ripley P. and Adelaide K. Bullen of the Florida State Museum, today the Florida Museum of Natural History, excavated several archaeological sites on the former Palmer family estate in Sarasota County, Florida, north of the town of Osprey. They prepared a report on the project, *The Palmer Site*, that appeared in 1976 as Publication 8 of the Florida Anthropological Society. Included in that monograph-length study are twelve pages recounting the results of the Bullens's excavation of a sand mound known as the Palmer Mound. The remainder of the publication details their work in various middens and shellworks on the estate, which had been established in 1910 by Bertha Matilde Honoré Palmer, widow of Chicago tycoon Potter Palmer. (Today the sites, including the mound, are within the Historic Spanish Point natural and historical area, which is open to the public [www.historicspanishpoint.org].)

While *The Palmer Site* was in final preparation Ripley was quite ill. At the time I was a newly hired assistant curator at the Florida State Museum and was recruited to assist the Bullens in readying the publication for printing (camera-ready copy was required). Thanks to a generous grant from the Wentworth Foundation, created by A. Fillmore Wentworth, and its president, William M. Goza, we were able to have Publication 8 in print before Ripley died in December 1976.

Because of Ripley's illness, he and Adelaide were not able to prepare as complete a report on the Palmer Mound as they wanted. Their plan to have the large human skeletal collection from the mound analyzed was never carried out. Over the years that osteological collection, one of the largest from any site in Florida, remained unpublished and largely unstudied.

The importance of the Palmer collection did not escape bioarchaeologist Dale L. Hutchinson, who began working in Florida in the 1980s while a graduate student at the University of Illinois. Since that time, Hutchinson has continued his research interest in the bioarchaeology of American Indian populations in Florida and the southeastern United States while a faculty member at East Carolina University and, most recently, at the University of North Carolina. That research led him to the Palmer Mound collection curated at the Florida Museum of Natural History. He was quick to recognize the Palmer Mound population as a potentially significant source of new data for helping us to understand more about Florida's past inhabitants.

In *Bioarchaeology of the Florida Gulf Coast: Adaptation, Conflict, and Change*, Hutchinson has used the analytical approaches and other tools of his trade to interpret the Palmer population, including such topics as health and diet, trauma, and demography. His analysis, which places the Palmer population in the context of what is known about other coastal societies, provides a fresh and detailed view of those pre-Columbian Indians who made their livelihood by hunting, collecting, and fishing, rather than farming. The presentation is exemplary. Of special note are the many excellent illustrations that help tell the story of the Palmer and other coastal people.

Ripley and Adelaide Bullen would have loved to read Dale Hutchinson's comprehensive study of the Palmer Mound population (Adelaide died in 1987); it is a fitting tribute to their own work at that site. I am delighted to have this important contribution to bioarchaeology and Florida archaeology in the Bullen series.

Jerald T. Milanich
Series Editor

Preface

It has long been recognized by prehistorians that the lifestyle practiced by indigenous Florida Gulf coast populations prior to the arrival of Europeans was organized around the use of maritime resources. Perhaps nowhere along the Florida Gulf coast have human ties to the sea been emphasized more than for the south Florida Calusa of the Charlotte Harbor region. At the time of European contact in 1566, the Calusa were a ranked society with a paramount chief, subsidiary chiefs, trade networks, and a subsistence based entirely on foraging.

Agriculture, often seen as a correlate of complex sociopolitical organization, was conspicuously absent among the Calusa. The presence of maize has often been seen as a prime mover in the development of cultural complexity, but its absence has served as both a catalyst for debate and a welcome deviation from an often formulaic and linear evolutionary explanation for the development of socially ranked societies. Indeed, the potential of marine resources to sustain large populations, the chronology of marine resource dependence, and the origin of the ranked chiefdom organization of the Calusa have all served as items of debate for more than 50 years (Goggin and Sturtevant 1964; Marquardt 1986, 1987, 1991, 1992; Widmer 1988).

Far less scholarly attention has been devoted to populations north of Charlotte Harbor. Dietary reconstructions have shown that those populations also relied largely on maritime subsistence items and that they did not practice maize agriculture. In fact, most of the Florida peninsular populations adopted maize much later than populations farther north, some after European contact and the influence of Spanish missionaries and government officials (Hutchinson et al. 1998, 2000; Larsen et al. 2001).

In this book, I examine the human biology of prehistoric and protohistoric populations inhabiting the central Florida Gulf coast, emphasizing the time period A.D. 500–1400. Central to the discussions is the Palmer population, interred at one of the largest systematically excavated coastal mortuary sites in the southeastern United States. Several other large populations from Tampa Bay are used with Palmer to form the nucleus of the study. Comparative populations from the Florida Gulf coast, from the Florida interior, and from coastal and noncoastal areas in the greater Southeast are used to interpret the human biology of the central Florida Gulf coast. The synthesis of data along the Florida Gulf coast can contribute important information regarding the transition from foraging to farming, the emergence of complex social and political networks, and the nutrition and health of Florida coastal and adjacent populations.

Acknowledgments

My first archaeological experience in Florida was brought about through collusion between my master's degree advisor, Clark Spencer Larsen, and the principal investigator of Tatham Mound, Jerald T. Milanich. To both of them I owe tremendous gratitude for including me in a project that has absorbed me for years. I benefited immensely during that first field experience in Florida from the able knowledge of Jeffrey Mitchem and his familiarity with southeastern archaeology. Expeditions to collect data along the entire Florida Gulf coast with Jeff provided a deeper exposure to Florida archaeology, as well as enjoyable companionship.

My name is on the cover of this book as author, along with my two coinvestigators, Lynette Norr and Mark Teaford. Unfortunately, the structure of a nonedited volume does not allow for other authors. I would be negligent if I did not acknowledge those who contributed to the research reported in this volume and to my current thoughts on issues discussed here, or those who labored to help me make a better final written product. In that order, those with whom I have been privileged to collaborate on research for this and related projects include Clark Spencer Larsen, William Marquardt, Jerald Milanich, Jeffrey Mitchem, Lee Newsom, Lynette Norr, Chris Ruff, Katherine Russell, Margaret Schoeninger, Scott Simpson, Mark Teaford, and Karen Walker. In addition, several colleagues at East Carolina University and in Florida have contributed to my knowledge and insights regarding Florida archaeology. They include Ann Cordell, Randy Daniel, Susan DeFrance, Charlie Ewen, Laura Kozuch, George Luer, David Sutton Phelps, Donna Ruhl, Mike Russo, and Brent Weisman. My graduate and undergraduate students have been among my closest colleagues: Lori Higginbotham, Suzanne Johnson, Kristina Killgrove, Larry McSwain, Ferzana Siddiqui, and Bree Tucker. For editing and comments, I thank especially Lorraine Aragon and Kristina Killgrove.

The Palmer burial mound skeletal remains are curated at the Florida Museum of Natural History. I thank Jerald Milanich for permission to analyze the Palmer skeletal materials and his dedication to obtaining photographs and tracking down museum specimens. Elise LeCompte excelled in the role of registrar of the museum, and Theresa Schober assisted in the organization of the remains for analysis. David Hunt provided assistance at the National Museum of Natural History.

Preparation of the stable isotope samples was also facilitated by Theresa Schober. She kept the isotope samples in processing and saw them through to completion. With only a day to collect them, Bobby Knight of the Bokelia Fish Company provided numerous modern samples of fish for isotope analysis. Lee Newsom, Charles Blanchard, and Karen Walker assisted in the collection of plants and animals for stable isotope analysis on Pine Island. Robin and Jan Brown provided isotope samples, personal insights on potential food resources, and lunch on my sudden visit to Fort Myers in 1998. M.G.M. Gilliland and Elizabeth Claus provided their equipment and assistance in obtaining radiographs. Susan Brannock-Gaul was responsible for all of the maps, and her dedication during many years of collaboration is appreciated. Funding for this study was generously provided by the East Carolina Faculty Senate Research and Creative Activities Fund and the National Science Foundation (SBR 9707921).

Writing a book entails numerous late arrivals for breakfast, late nights at the computer, and other periods of solitary confinement away from family. Lorraine and Will, my family, have tolerated those obsessions with patience. They have participated in the study when possible through plant and animal collecting expeditions along the shores and estuaries of the Florida Gulf coast, and visited numerous archaeological sites. My gratitude to them both exceeds any words I could give them.

Author's Note

In 1997, I proposed a study to the National Science Foundation focused on coastal adaptation of late prehistoric populations from North Carolina. I wanted to compare a variety of dietary and pathological indicators of nutrition and health from inner coastal and outer coastal populations inhabiting the estuary system of North Carolina. For comparative purposes, I included the Palmer population in Florida. Because the analysis of the Palmer and the North Carolina populations was undertaken as a single larger study, the research design and data collection are identical.

The course of writing is one of growth and change. Consequently, despite similar themes in the two books—coastal adaptation, the transition to agriculture, and human health—there are enough separate research issues, comparative populations, and independent discussions to warrant the presentation of the data in two separate volumes.

The approach to the background ecology and data analysis in the two books is similar. I first present the ecological and cultural context of the region, then the basic theory behind interpreting skeletal and dental pathology as an indication of nutrition and health and, finally, the results obtained by analysis of the remains. The two books deviate in the next two sections, where the interpretation of the data and comparison with other populations are presented in a synthesis and conclusion. I view the North Carolina volume (Hutchinson 2002a) and the Florida Gulf coast volume (this work) as companion discussions, each with a focus on coastal populations, but each addressing several separate theoretical issues. The reader interested in coastal adaptation would profit by examining both volumes.

1

Introduction

Every area of the world is complicated with regard to its physiography, climate, and cultural heritage, and Florida is no different. However, unlike any other region in the United States, Florida is bounded almost completely by water. The northern panhandle of Florida is contiguous with the terrestrial United States, while the southern peninsula extends south into a maritime environment. Thus there are radically different ecological niches and potential exploitation areas for humans in northern and southern Florida.

Through time, as in many regions of the southeastern United States, the populations inhabiting Florida experienced changes in the way they organized themselves, the ways they made a living, the beliefs they had about death and burial, and numerous other aspects of their lives. Here I present a general overview of those changes for populations inhabiting eastern North America. Chapter 2 explores those changes in detail for Florida.

The earliest humans to inhabit the southeastern United States were Paleoindians (10,000–8000 B.C.) whose camps and resource extraction areas indicate a way of life focused on mobile foraging and hunting, perhaps hunting focused on large mammals as has been demonstrated for the Southwest. The following Archaic period (8000–1000 B.C.) began with the warming trend of the Holocene epoch.

It was during the Archaic period that sea levels rose substantially and populations in the southeastern United States underwent the first dramatic transformation in their lives (Steponaitis 1986:370). Although it was largely a subsistence transformation that expanded the dietary repertoire to include numerous foraged plants and aquatic resources, other cultural changes took place as well. Among these were the formation of larger and more permanent settlements, the construction of earthen mounds and other earthworks, long-distance trade, and burial ceremonialism that incorporated personal utilitarian and exotic adornment items (Bense 1994; Smith 1986; Steponaitis 1986). Apparently some plant cultivation was conducted with gourds and hard-rind squash by 5000 B.C., but the fruits appear to have been used as containers rather than as food (Doran et al. 1990).

Artifact diversity in the Archaic increased over that of the Paleoindian period, and new artifacts made of stone, such as groundstone axes and celts, appeared, as well as more diverse chipped stone point types with notches and stems (Smith 1986; Steponaitis 1986). The use of shell for ornaments and tools became important. Textiles made of plant fibers, including nets, bags, baskets, and clothing, have been found in contexts where preservation is possible, such as submerged sites and dry caves.

The Woodland stage (1000 B.C.–A.D. 1000) represented a time of gradual change with continued emphasis on innovations that began during the Archaic period, such as plant cultivation of seed-bearing plants, increased sedentism, and mortuary ceremonialism (Steponaitis 1986:379). Populations increased in size during the Woodland period, and many clustered in river valleys and along the coast. Pottery manufacture became prevalent and incorporated technological innovations such as coiling, tempering, and shaping of bases. These pottery innovations occurred earliest along the South Carolina and Georgia coastal plain at the termination of the Archaic (DePratter and Howard 1981, 1983). The bow and arrow was an important technological advance for hunting.

Mortuary ceremonialism was particularly important during the Woodland stage and is well documented for the Middle Woodland period (A.D. 1–500), especially for the Adena and Hopewell traditions of Ohio and Illinois (Bense 1994). Burials associated with the Adena and Hopewell traditions were placed in log and stone crypts that were covered by earthen mounds, which were apparently used in ritual cycles of several decades (Hutchinson and Aragon 2002). Objects made of exotic trade materials such as copper, marine shell, galena, and greenstone often accompanied burials (Steponaitis 1986).

The elaborate mortuary traditions of the Adena and Hopewell were transfigured for later cultural traditions; although they continued to emphasize ritual cycles, sometime after A.D. 1000 charnel houses entered into the mortuary repertoire. They were described by the Europeans (Le Page du Pratz 1947) and are documented archaeologically at sites such as Angel (Black 1967) and Fatherland (Neitzel 1965).

In many areas of the eastern United States, horticulture began sometime shortly after A.D. 700, and it was one of the most influential, if not *the* most influential, change that occurred in the economic lives of humans. Plant cultivation of chenopods, amaranths, and cucurbits had undoubtedly occurred prior to that time as indicated at several archaeological sites (Smith 1986), but after A.D. 700 many populations began to focus their attention on domesticated plants, particularly maize (Bender et al. 1981; Dunn 1981; Gremillion 1996; Jeffries et al. 1996; Moore 1985; Reitz 1982, 1988; Scarry 1993a,b; van der Merwe and Vogel 1978; Vogel and van der Merwe 1977; Watson 1989; Wymer 1987a,b; Yarnell and Black 1985).

The "wholesale adoption of maize agriculture" (Steponaitis 1986:388) is particularly well documented for populations inhabiting the interior Southeast from the central Mississippi Valley to the western Appalachian piedmont. In those areas, maize adoption and a suite of other traits that appeared between A.D. 800 and 1000 have been referred to collectively as the Emergent Mississippian (Steponaitis 1986:386–387). After A.D. 1000, beans (*Phaseolus vulgaris*) are commonly found in archaeological contexts as well (Blake and Cutler 1979; Chapman and Shea 1981).

In general, the agricultural transition was associated with larger settlements, denser populations, specialized labor, ranked social systems, and monumental architecture (Smith 1986; Steponaitis 1986). In the eastern United States, these changes were especially marked for Mississippian cultural groups, who predominated in river valleys such as the Black Warrior River (Scarry 1993a,b), the Illinois River (Johannessen 1993; Johannessen and Whalley 1988), and the Ohio River (Wymer 1987b).

Ranked hierarchical sociopolitical systems known as chiefdoms were an important part of the Mississippian transition (A.D. 1000–1500; Bense 1994; Smith 1986; Steponaitis 1986). The emergence of ranked social and political systems required a loss of regional autonomy with concomitant regional integration. The Southern Cult (sometimes called the Southeastern Ceremonial Complex) undoubtedly functioned as the central worship system of the people of the Mississippian stage and provided the fundamental symbolic means for regional integration. The artistic artifacts left behind from the Southern Cult appear to emphasize a few major themes that include ancestor worship (depicted through iconographic images of charnel houses, sacred totems, and mortuary inclusions), war (depicted through decapitated heads and weapons such as axes), and fertility (depicted through statuary such as the Birger stone figurine) (Bense 1994; Prentice 1986).

Many would argue that a correlate of stratified societies is the use of force to enforce legitimacy as well as to gain new territory and human labor (Fried et al. 1968). As demonstrated through the Southern Cult iconography, warfare was at least symbolically important, if not important as well in practice. Other indicators of increased intergroup violence appear to support the symbolism expressed in Southern Cult iconography. For instance, stockades are found at many late prehistoric sites such as Lubbub Creek (Peebles 1987), Cahokia (Milner 1990), and the Savannah River valley (Anderson 1994).

Skeletal indicators of intergroup aggression are present in late prehistory in many areas of the Southeast. These include mutilations such as scalping (Bridges 1996), embedded stone and bone projectile points (Bridges 1996), and parry fractures (Smith 1996). Furthermore, Smith (2003) notes that different kinds of violence characterized different time periods in Tennessee and that only intergroup violence increased during the late prehistoric period.

There are substantial data indicating that human populations experienced a decline in health and nutrition following the increased focus on domesticated plants (Cohen and Armelagos 1984; Larsen 1995). Undoubtedly, some of the changes in health were due to the lower nutritional quality of maize as a vegetable resource, and to decreased dietary breadth that seems to have accompanied the adoption of agricultural products (Cohen and Armelagos 1984; Larsen 1995).

Other factors that were part of the agricultural transition were also influential in health declines, including aggregated settlements, increased population pressure, centralized water supplies, and potentially differential access to food resources based on status, age, and sex. Regardless of the direct causes, at the time that many populations increased their use of agricultural products and became more sedentary, health declines occurred.

However, not everyone in the southeastern United States adopted the Mississippian cultural system. Some societies continued to practice foraging alongside the development of ranked societies and larger urban centers (Bense 1994). For instance, in coastal North Carolina and Georgia, larger population centers appear to have occurred prior to the emphasis on domesticated plants (Anderson 1994; Hutchinson 2002a). Furthermore, it appears that maize horticulture was not a prerequisite for the development of more complex social and political organization.

The Agricultural and Transformational Paradox in Florida

In most of Florida, the agricultural transition did not occur until after European contact (Hutchinson and Norr 1994; Hutchinson et al. 1998, 2000; Larsen et al. 2001; Newsom 1991; Scarry 1999; Scarry and Newsom 1992). In fact, only in the Florida panhandle, located nearest the influence of Mississippian populations in southern interior Alabama and Georgia, did maize agriculture seem to predominate in the subsistence lives of native Floridians (Newsom and Quitmyer 1992; Scarry 1993c). Foraging, it seems, provided most of the subsistence resources for Floridians well into late prehistory.

Undoubtedly, several factors contributed to the persistence of foraging and the absence of farming for Florida populations. Aquatic areas are numerous and provide a range of aquatic resources; furthermore, the multiple habitats adjacent to the coast provide numerous edge areas so important for ecological diversity (Odum 1963). The soils of the southern part of Florida are very sandy and not conducive to maize agriculture (W. Johnson 1990). The sole evidence contrary to that statement is the maize pollen recovered from Fort Center (E. Sears 1982), but that evidence is disputed. Regardless of the combination of factors that resulted in the absence of agriculture in much of prehistoric Florida, the fact that foraging and foraged foods comprised the bulk of the economic activities and dietary regime of indigenous Florida populations provides a marvelous comparative database for agricultural populations from the same time period.

Thus, unlike many of their more northern counterparts, most Florida populations went through the period between A.D. 700 and 1400 without depending on maize agriculture. Yet, the period between A.D. 500 and 1000 was one of cultural transformation in Florida (Milanich 1994). Along the central and southern Florida Gulf coast, multiple lines of evidence suggest that this period was one of emerging social and political complexity accompanied by population growth (Milanich 1994). Settlement density, size of settlements, the accumulation of substantial middens, changes in ceramic technology, and diversity of shell and stone tools are among the supporting evidence. Monumental architecture in the form of large site complexes with multiple mounds is found in both the Tampa Bay and the Charlotte Harbor regions. Burials indicate social ranking, and cultic objects become more common through time, indicating rich belief systems.

If populations inhabiting the central peninsular Florida Gulf coast were not maize horticulturalists, then how might populations inhabiting that region differ from agriculturally dependent populations in the eastern United States? Goggin and Sturtevant (1964) pondered this same question for the Calusa, just to the south in the southern peninsular Gulf coast region. They focused in particular on the ability of the Calusa to develop a chiefdom-level political organization without agriculture and its associated surplus stores. The issue they did not ponder is whether human populations in coastal and interior peninsular Florida suffered the same declines in health noted among many agricultural populations throughout large areas of the eastern United States.

In this study, emphasis is placed on the adaptation and human biology of central Gulf coast Floridians. Nutrition and health of the prehistoric peninsular Floridians is assessed and compared to that of more northern agricultural populations. In order to reconstruct and compare human nutrition and health, a bioarchaeological approach must be employed.

Adaptation and the Bioarchaeological Approach

Adaptation refers to the interaction between phenotype and environment (Moran 2000). Increasingly, discussions of human adaptation include not only environmental factors but also social and behavioral ones. Changes in several aspects of human social organization that include economy, social and political structure, and religion are seen not only as responses to environmental change but as integral components of adaptation that affect human biology.

Bioarchaeologists are interested in the interpretation of nutrition, health, biomechanics, and several other aspects of human biology as reconstructed from human skeletal remains recovered from past populations (Larsen 1997). They are particularly interested in the interactions among the natural environment, human biology, and behavior, and how different human groups vary in their use of natural and cultural resources to ensure adequate food, shelter, and reproductive success.

Culture provides and preserves guiding principles for the selection of dietary items, appropriate types of shelter, fruitful times for planting, optimal number of offspring, and a host of other decisions made by human populations. However, culture is difficult to document for past populations, except through the behaviors that result from cultural ideas and orientations. It is behavior that produces results; it is culture that guides behavior. Behavior is often detectable from the human skeleton because it involves bending, lifting, mobility, mastication, and alteration of dental and skeletal tissues.

Goals and Assumptions of this Study

The incorporation of environmental variables has played a pivotal role in archaeological research on the Florida Gulf coast, especially in the past twenty years and particularly as related to human adaptation (e.g., Marquardt 1992, 1999; Milanich et al. 1984a,b). However, human biology, as an integral component of the adaptive framework, is missing from most discussions of human adaptation for prehistoric Floridians. Biological investigations have generally been related to plant and animal remains as indicators of human diet. When human remains are mentioned at all, they are usually described relative to mortuary practices and how they might inform us about the social and political organization of a society.

In spite of the limited emphasis on human biology, the recovery and analysis of human remains has occupied archaeologists for more than a century. Systematic recovery and recording of human remains began along the Florida Gulf coast during the late nineteenth century, when C. B. Moore made several expeditions along the coast in his paddle wheeler, the *Gopher*, recording and excavating remains from a number of mortuary localities (1892, 1894, 1900, 1902, 1903, 1907). The excavation of mortuary localities was facilitated in the 1930s by the Works Progress Administration (WPA), which supervised several projects (Milanich 1994:9–10). By the 1940s, several government organizations, university departments, and museums were contributing to systematic efforts to record and study human remains from the Florida Gulf coast and elsewhere in Florida (Milanich 1994).

Unfortunately, the recovery and description of human remains has resulted in only a limited and disarticulated set of reports. Few of these separate studies of human skeletal remains have focused on human biology, and fewer still have been integrated into bioarchaeological syntheses oriented toward human adaptation.

The approach taken in this book is to synthesize the skeletal data from several central peninsular Florida Gulf coast populations. The Palmer population from Sarasota County plays a central role in the book for several reasons. With more than 400 human burials, Palmer is one of the largest systematically excavated coastal mortuary sites in the southeastern United States. Furthermore, extended archaeological excavations at Palmer and dietary reconstruction for Palmer individuals have produced detailed subsistence data that are unavailable for most other Gulf coast populations.

Other medium-to-large central peninsular Gulf coast skeletal series that are included are Tierra Verde, Safety Harbor, Weeki Wachee, and

Perico Island. In all cases, I personally conducted the analysis of these populations, ensuring a level of continuity in data collection and interpretation that is often not possible in bioarchaeological syntheses.

The synthesis is organized around three basic themes and four major hypotheses. The first theme is coastal adaptation. Investigations of late prehistoric coastal populations from North Carolina, Georgia, and Florida (Hutchinson 1990, 1992, 1993a,b, 1999, 2002a; Hutchinson and Larsen 1988, 1990, 2001; Hutchinson and Mitchem 1996; Hutchinson and Norr 1994; Hutchinson and Weaver 1998; Hutchinson et al. 1998, 2000, n.d.) have demonstrated that several skeletal and dental lesions are commonly found in high frequencies among coastal populations, including dental chipping, alveolar infection, porotic hyperostosis, and external auditory exostoses. They appear to be associated with a variety of behaviors oriented around coastal foraging and marine foods and food preparation methods.

The second theme, related to the first, is that Florida is unique in the pervasiveness of the coastal environment among nearly all populations. The maritime environment is a major component of human ecology for at least half of the populations inhabiting Florida. Yet, it is neither a static environment nor is it homogeneous. Contained within a lengthy record of sea level rise and fall, changes in oceanic currents, shifting sand bars, and fluctuating inlets are myriad local habitats.

The third theme, related to the first two, is that Florida populations began extracting a living from the sea very early during the Archaic and maintained that way of living until the influence of Europeans. Centuries after many populations in the eastern United States had dedicated themselves to the agricultural lifeway, Florida populations continued to restrict their subsistence activities to foraging (Hutchinson et al. 1998, 2000; Larsen et al. 2001). Thus, they are unique in their late adoption of maize horticulture.

A number of health changes have been documented following the adoption of maize, including increased frequencies of dental disease and infectious disease. Although those health changes can be attributed in part to a decrease in dietary breadth and to the role of maize specifically as a poor dietary staple, other changes that accompanied the agricultural lifeway are also implicated. Among those changes are increased sedentism, more aggregated populations, social stratification, and contamination of community water supplies.

Florida populations also experienced many of these changes through time without the influence of maize horticulture. Furthermore, the high frequencies of pathological lesions often used to demonstrate declines in health among populations adopting maize horticulture were found in even higher frequencies in nonhorticultural populations inhabiting the outer coast of North Carolina (Hutchinson 2002a).

In order to explore those three themes, I formulate four hypotheses (fig. 1.1) about the human biology of the coastal dwellers of central peninsular Gulf coast Florida between A.D. 500 and 1600. I assess differences and

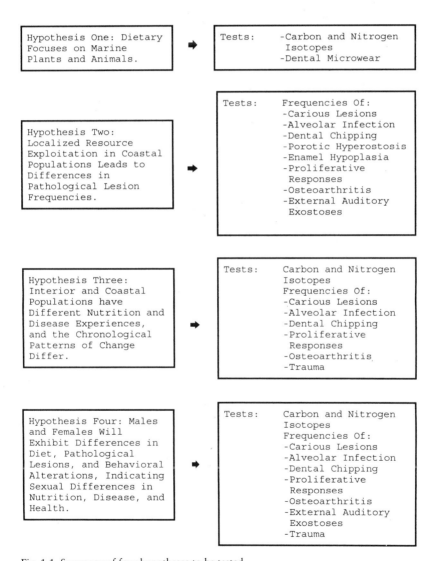

Fig. 1.1. Summary of four hypotheses to be tested.

similarities in their adaptation through time by comparison of their dietary focus and pathology frequencies with those of populations located farther south and north on the Florida Gulf coast. The diet and pathology comparisons are extended to interior Florida populations in order to address similarities and differences between coastal and interior dwellers. Finally, diet and pathology comparisons are made for interior and coastal populations throughout the southeastern United States concentrating on those populations inhabiting the modern states of Alabama, Georgia, and North Carolina.

The dietary focus will be established through the use of stable isotopes of carbon and nitrogen assessed from the organic and mineral portions of human bones and through dental enamel microwear analysis. Several pathological lesions and behavioral alterations will be used to measure human health and adaptation (fig. 1.1). The theory and method for the dietary analyses as well as that for intepreting the pathological lesions and behavioral alterations of the skeleton are reported in chapter 4.

Pathological lesions that are directly linked to diet and/or masticatory behavior include carious lesions, alveolar infection, premortem tooth loss, dental chipping, and dental enamel microwear. Pathological lesions resulting from metabolic disruption are porotic hyperostosis and enamel hypoplasia. These lesions can be due to deprivation of nutrients, disease, or some combination of malnutrition and disease. Lesions that provide information about the presence of an infection but are not specific as to the type of infection are termed "nonspecific infectious lesions" and include periosteal reactions and osteomyelitis. The location and patterning of those lesions is often informative about specific disease processes such as syphilis or tuberculosis. Pathological lesions related to lifestyle and activity include osteoarthritis, external auditory exostoses, and trauma.

The *first hypothesis* is that the diet of central peninsular Gulf coast populations after 500 B.C. was focused largely on animals and plants foraged from marine and estuarine contexts. Thus, maize did not form any appreciable portion of the diet for central Gulf coast Florida populations. Our previous analyses (Hutchinson and Norr 1994; Hutchinson et al. 1998, 2000; Larsen et al. 2001; Norr et al. n.d.) have shown that maize was only adopted in the northwestern Florida panhandle prior to European contact.

The Palmer population, with an early date of A.D. 500–800, lived prior to the adoption of maize in much of the southeastern United States. However, later populations in the central peninsular Gulf coast such as Tierra Verde (A.D. 1400) are expected to show that (1) maize was not a significant dietary resource even in late prehistory, and (2) no major dietary shifts occurred between A.D. 500 and 1400. Stable isotopes of carbon and nitrogen obtained from the organic and mineral portions of human bone will be used to reconstruct human diet and will be compared with the isotopic signatures for modern local dietary resources. Dental microwear will be used to assess the abrasion and pitting caused by the dietary constituents. *T*- tests will be used to assess statistical differences in diet.

Hypothesis two is that coastal populations will exhibit differences in pathological lesion frequencies that can be attributed to localized resource exploitation. The Florida coastline exhibits considerable ecological difference, brought about by barrier islands, size and depth of bays, wave action, and water temperature (see more extended discussion in chapter 2). Consequently, heterogeneity is expected with regard to pathological lesion frequencies and dietary focus. We found that local variations in diet characterized North Carolina populations between A.D. 1200 and 1450 (Hutchinson 2002a; Norr 2002; Teaford 2002), which we attributed to the exploitation of very localized habitats. The exploitation of different habitats is manifested both in dietary focus and in mechanical impact.

I expect that populations inhabiting different areas of Gulf coast Florida (e.g., the coastal strand and adjacent shallow Gulf waters as compared with large sheltered bays such as Tampa Bay) will exhibit differences in lesions reflecting diet and masticatory behavior (carious lesions, alveolar infection, and dental chipping), metabolic disruption (enamel hypoplasia and porotic hyperostosis), infectious disease (proliferative responses), and lifestyle (osteoarthritis, external auditory exostoses). Chi-square and Fisher's Exact tests will be used to assess statistical differences between populations.

Hypothesis three is that interior populations (25 km or more from the coast) had a different dietary focus and different nutritional and disease experiences than did central peninsular Gulf coast populations. Furthermore, after A.D. 500 increased population size and settlement density placed more stress on interior populations than on those inhabiting the coast. Coastal populations, because of the availability of maritime resources, did not experience resource shortages that occur for inland dwellers.

Dietary focus will be assessed using stable isotopes of carbon and nitrogen for the organic and mineral portions of human bone and will be compared with the isotopic signatures for modern local dietary resources. Lesions indicating diet (carious lesions, alveolar infection), metabolic disruption and deprivation (enamel hypoplasia, porotic hyperostosis), infectious disease (periosteal reactions and osteomyelitis), and activity and lifestyle (osteoarthritis, trauma) will be used to test hypothesis three. T-tests will be used to assess stable isotope differences in diet. Chi-square and Fisher's Exact tests will be used to assess statistical differences for pathological lesions and behavioral alterations between populations.

Hypothesis four is that males and females will exhibit differences in dietary focus, pathological lesions, and behavioral alterations indicating sexual differences in nutrition, disease, and health. Studies worldwide show that foragers and farmers generally have a sexual division of labor (see Kelly 1995; Larsen 1997). Increasingly, the importance of examining nutrition and health by sex has become apparent (Grauer and Stuart-Macadam 1998; Lukacs 1995). Analyses that employ sex as well as age as influential variables have resulted in several insights regarding the role of biological as well as cultural differences between men and women.

For instance, discussions of male and female adaptive differences have been conducted for dental health (Grauer et al. 1998; Higginbotham 1999; Larsen 1998; Lukacs 1996), bone quality (Weaver 1998), diet (Cook and Hunt 1998), activity (Larsen 1998), and immunity and infection (Ortner 1998; Roberts et al. 1998; Storey 1998). Dietary differences between males and females will be tested using stable isotopes of carbon and nitrogen obtained from the organic and mineral portions of human bone. They will be tested for statistical significance using t-test of the mean.

Pathological lesion and behavioral alteration frequencies for males and females will be assessed for diet (carious lesions, alveolar infection, premortem tooth loss), masticatory behavior (dental chipping), metabolic disruption and deprivation (porotic hyperostosis and enamel hypoplasia), infectious disease (periosteal reactions and osteomyelitis), and activity and lifestyle (osteoarthritis, external auditory exostoses, trauma). Chi-square and Fisher's Exact tests will be used to determine those differences in pathological lesion and behavioral alteration frequencies between males and females that are statistically significant.

Chapter Organization

I review the archaeology and bioarchaeology of Gulf coast Florida in chapter 2 with emphasis on subsistence behavior, social organization, and bioarchaeology. I focus in chapter 3 on the archaeological research and excavations conducted at Palmer in the last 125 years and on the demography and taphonomy that affect the interpretation of the Palmer skeletal remains. The methods and results of the assessment of diet, nutrition, pathology, disease, and health are presented in chapter 4, in the context of a reconstruction of nutrition and disease of the Palmer population. Comparisons of nutrition and disease for Florida Gulf coast populations are conducted in chapter 5 with particular emphasis on geographic and temporal variation. Comparisons are also extended to coastal and noncoastal populations in the greater Southeast, principally in Georgia, Alabama, Tennessee, and North Carolina. Finally, in chapter 6 I review the conclusions reached regarding nutrition, health, and prehistoric population dynamics of regional Florida Gulf coast populations.

2

Environment, Culture History, and Archaeology of the Florida Gulf Coast

Archaeologists have noted that populations living in Florida after 500 B.C. "tended to live within one major environmental or physiographic zone and each developed an economic base and other aspects of lifestyle that were well suited to life in that particular region" (Florida Anthropological Society 2000:10). Nine post–500 B.C. regions are identified by Milanich (1994:xix; map 2.1); all but two contain both extensive coastal and interior land areas. Each of the regions contains diverse ecological zones that include some combination of uplands of pine and hardwood forests intermingled with dry prairies, freshwater wetlands in the form of swamps, marshes, lakes, rivers, and springs, and coastal ecosystems comprising mangrove swamps, inshore marine habitats, salt marshes, dunes, and maritime forests (Myers and Ewel 1990). To complicate matters, the regions were inhabited by people who may have had rather different cultural traditions and adaptive strategies.

In short, even populations inhabiting relatively close geographic areas were exploiting potentially different environments and resources, were using different technology, and were guided by different cultural values. These differences in environment and behavior undoubtedly contributed to differences in their life experiences and, particularly for our interests, differences in their health. In order to fully understand the variation exhibited geographically and temporally by Florida prehistoric Gulf coast populations, I summarize in this chapter the environment, culture history, and archaeology of the Florida Gulf coast.

Environment of Gulf Coast Florida

Florida is a large platform of sedimentary rock that has been deposited over a period of 200–300 million years in a warm shallow sea (Fernald

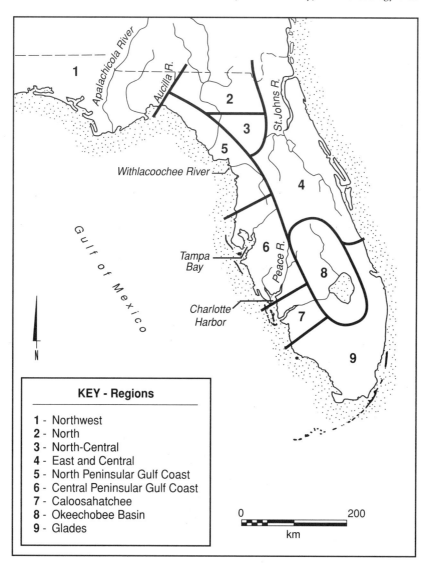

Map 2.1. Florida, showing archaeological regions.

1981; Livingston 1990). On the Atlantic coast the submerged portion of the platform is relatively narrow, but on the Gulf coast it is broad. As one comes onto land on either coast, there is little topographic relief—most coastal areas and the Everglades have elevations of less than two meters above sea level (Livingston 1990). Low topographic relief in the interior combined with almost constant influence of coastal areas is what characterizes Florida. In fact, Florida has the longest shoreline in the United States at 13,676 km, with massive areas of open estuaries and tidal marshes along the Gulf coast (Livingston 1990).

Tampa Bay and Charlotte Harbor (map 2.1) form two of the numerous large bays that provide more protected aquatic areas with abundant resources. In addition, many other estuarine areas in central Gulf coast Florida lie behind a broken chain of barrier islands (maps 2.1–2.5). These narrow estuarine lagoons combine with shallow oceanic waters on the other side of the barrier islands (fig. 2.1) to form inshore marine habitats that are important high-productivity, low species-diversity biological ecosystems, and they are essential to most of Florida's aquatic species. The continual wind and tide currents and multiple sources of nutrients make possible a rich environment for the production of microorganisms.

In addition, the freshwater and saltwater wetlands and submerged aquatic vegetation all contribute to a rich food web. Many freshwater and saltwater species, such as blue crabs (*Callincectes sapidus*), oysters (*Crassostrea virginica*), and spotted seatrout (*Cynoscion nebulosus*) spend at least part of their lifetime in the near-shore marine environment (Living-

Fig. 2.1. Fishing from Casey Key, looking toward the mainland.

ston 1990). Additionally, many marine species migrate in or near the shore during their larval and juvenile stages (Livingston 1990).

The inshore marine habitats of the southern and central Gulf coast are lined with red mangrove (*Rizophora mangle*), black mangrove (*Avicennia germinans*), and white mangrove (*Laguncularia racemosa*) communities (fig. 2.2). Red and black mangroves are distributed according to the inter-tidal zone, with red mangrove dominating the middle and lower portions and black mangrove dominating the upper portion (Odum and McIvor 1990). Mangrove communities provide essential habitats for a number of species of invertebrates, fishes, amphibians, reptiles, birds, and mammals (Kaplan 1988; Odum and McIvor 1990).

The mangrove root systems, which extend both above and below water, form an extensive and complicated habitat zone. The most important contribution of the mangroves is the large amount of detritus produced

Fig. 2.2. Mangrove community on Sanibel Island.

each day, forming the base of an extensive food web (Kaplan 1988:179). Odum and coworkers reviewed the numbers of species reported from Florida mangrove systems and found listings for 220 species of fishes, 24 species of reptiles and amphibians, 18 species of mammals, and 181 species of birds (Odum and McIvor 1990:542–543; see also Kaplan 1988).

Sea grass beds are a particularly important and productive feature of inshore marine habitats. They provide nutrients, oxygen, and shelter, and serve to filter larger particulate matter by slowing wave velocity, thus facilitating the deposition of nutrients on the bottom (Kaplan 1988). Sea grass beds are used by a wide range of species for refuges from predation, as nurseries, and as feeding areas (Livingston 1990). Important species that occur along the southern and central Gulf coast include turtle grass (*Thalassia testudinum*), shoal grass (*Halodule wrightii*), and widgeon grass (*Ruppia maritima*).

Salt marshes are composed of nonwoody, salt-tolerant plants that are located in intertidal zones at least occasionally inundated with salt water (Montague and Wiegert 1990; fig. 2.3). Thus, they have qualities of terrestrial and marine ecosystems. The principal salt marsh plants are black needlerush (*Juncus roemerianus*) and smooth cordgrass (*Spartina alterniflora*), although many other salt marsh plants can be found in Florida (see Montague and Wiegert 1990: table 14.1). Smooth cordgrass grows closest to the edges of tidal streams as it is the only grass that can withstand the daily inundation by salt water (Kaplan 1988).

Because the utilization of salt marshes requires the mitigation of alternating terrestrial and aquatic environments, species diversity in salt marshes is low, but for those species able to adapt to the conditions, the number of individuals is abundant (Montague and Wiegert 1990:495). Raccoons (*Procyon lotor*) are the most common mammal, but others include marsh rabbits (*Sylvilagus palustris*), cotton rats (*Sigmodon hispidus*), and cotton mice (*Peromyscus gossypinus*) (Montague and Wiegert 1990). Fiddler crabs (*Uca* spp.) are especially common, feeding on the detritus from the dead grasses. Snails, such as the marsh periwinkle (*Littorina irrorata*), the olive nerite (*Neritina reclivata*), and the eastern melampus (*Melampus bidentatus*), provide a stable source of food for ducks (Kaplan 1988).

Muddy flats generally line the salt marshes where slow-moving tidal flows meander through them. A centimeter under the surface layer of detritus lies an anaerobic zone of decay. Intrusion frees a gas smelling like rotten eggs, hydrogen sulfide produced by bacteria that metabolize sulfur compounds in the absence of oxygen (Kaplan 1988:37). In the

Fig. 2.3. Salt marsh, St. Catherines Island, Georgia.

mud flats live a variety of worms and bivalves that serve as food for other animals.

The rich biotic environment of the Gulf coast has potential as a dependable subsistence base for the human inhabitants living along the coast. The protected waters of the lagoons that lie behind barrier islands afford substantial food resources, as do the near-shore environments of the barrier islands. Adjacent terrestrial areas include grasslands and pine forests that are both home to and foraging areas for numerous mammals, birds, reptiles, and amphibians. It appears that humans have utilized these resources at least since the beginning of the Archaic period (8000 B.C.).

Archaeological Context of Central Gulf Coast Florida

Paleoindian and Archaic Periods

Although prehistoric use of the coastline can be documented as far back as the Archaic period, human habitation of Florida preceded the Archaic by several centuries, when Paleoindian hunters stalked large mammals. Paleoindians first began to inhabit Florida after 11,000 B.C. (Borremans 1993a). Their bone and stone tools, as well as the animals they hunted, are often found at the bottoms of rivers or in sinkholes at sites such as Warm Mineral Spring (8SO19; Cockrell and Murphy 1978), Little Salt Spring (8SO18; Clausen et al. 1979), Harney Flats (8HI507; Daniel 1987), Silver

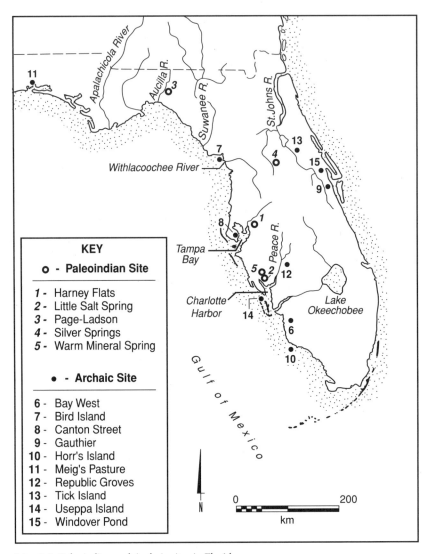

Map 2.2. Paleoindian and Archaic sites in Florida.

Springs (8MR59; Neill 1958), and Page-Ladson (8JE591; Dunbar et al. 1989) (map 2.2).

By 8000 B.C., a wider variety of stone tools of different sizes and shapes as well as more attention to aquatic resources indicate the beginning of the Archaic period. Technological innovations during the Archaic include pins, points, awls, and a throwing stick known as the *atlatl*.

It appears that human populations grew in size throughout the Archaic period, as testified by larger and more numerous sites such as Bay West (8CR200; Berriault et al. 1981), Canton Street (Bullen et al. 1978), Gauthier (8BR193; Maples 1987), Harney Flats (8HI507; Daniel 1987), Horr's Island (8CR37–42; McMichael 1982; Russo et al. 1991; Newsom 1991), Meig's Pasture (8OK102; Curren et al. 1987), Republic Groves (8HR4; Wharton et al. 1981), Tick Island (8VO24; Bullen 1962), Useppa Island (8LL51; Marquardt 1992, 1999; Milanich et al. 1984a), and Windover (8BR246; Doran 2002; Doran and Dickel 1988; Doran et al. 1986; Hauswirth et al. 1988; Stone et al. 1990; Tuross et al. 1994) (map 2.2).

Most known Archaic sites are in the interior highlands, although some are also located in lower elevation riverine and coastal habitats. Because of continued sea level rise during the Archaic, however, many sites are probably submerged on the continental shelf (Russo and Quitmyer 1996). There is a diverse set of site types ranging from small lithic scatters to camps, and presumed villages. At least five types of mortuary sites have been located: wet and dry cemeteries, midden burials, mound burials, and burials in solution pockets (Russo 1993).

The wet cemetery sites (Bay West, Republic Groves, and Windover) are particularly fascinating. One of the most remarkable of these sites is Windover Pond in Brevard County, where human burials and their associated grave goods date to 5000 to 6000 B.C. (Doran 2002; Doran and Dickel 1988; Doran et al. 1986). Human burials (168 individuals were recovered) were secured with stakes in the peat at the bottom of the pond. Associated with the burials were shark, dog, and wolf teeth hafted with pitch to wood for use as tools; bone and antler awls, points, and pins; and plant and animal remains that suggest wide dietary diversity. Stable isotope data indicate a diet focused on riverine, freshwater marsh, and terrestrial resources (Tuross et al. 1994). The preservation of human brain tissue permitted the cellular and molecular analysis of these early humans (Doran et al. 1986; Hauswirth et al. 1988). Other well-known cemeteries include Bay West, Gauthier, Tick Island, and Horr's Island (map 2.2).

Hunting and fishing appear to have been frequent subsistence activities during the Archaic period. Hunting is indicated by terrestrial animals found at Archaic sites that include whitetail deer (*Odocoileus virginianus*), raccoon, and several species of waterfowl. Fishing was common as well, although current evidence suggests variety in the type of fishing practiced across time and geographic region (Russo 1993). From sites such as Horr's Island (McMichael 1982; Russo et al. 1991), Useppa Island (Milanich et al. 1984a), and Meig's Pasture (Curren et al. 1987), we know that Archaic people used a range of fishing techniques that included nets, hooks, gigs, and traps to take both small and large fish (Russo 1993). Shellfish were also heavily utilized, varying by species dependent on settlement location (e.g., Atlantic coast, Gulf coast, St. Johns River; Russo 1993).

There is less information about foods that were gathered during the Archaic, but it seems clear that gathering was a predominant part of the subsistence regime. Animals that would have been gathered, such as snakes and turtles, have been recovered in Archaic middens (Russo 1990). Several plants have been found as well, such as hackberry (*Celtis laevigata*), cabbage palm (*Sabal palmetto*), hickory (*Carya* sp.), acorns (*Quercus* sp.), and bottle gourd (*Lageneria* spp.) (Russo 1993). Fibers found at Windover have been interpreted as material to be used for manufacturing clothing and baskets (Andrews et al. 1988).

In sum, during the Archaic period subsistence was oriented toward smaller mammals rather than the large mammals hunted during the Paleoindian period, and aquatic resources such as fish and shellfish became much more common in the diet. Although seasonal movements were undoubtedly important for Archaic people, shellfish gathering may have provided an initial stimulus for more permanent settlements.

Woodland and Mississippian Periods (Post-Archaic Periods)

By the end of the Late Archaic period at 500 B.C., the appearance of many distinct types of pottery in Florida signal more regional populations with distinctive cultures. Nine of these distinct regions have been described by Milanich (1994: xix). While all of the regions are of importance for understanding the prehistory of Florida, I will emphasize the central peninsular Gulf coast and the two regions that lie adjacent to it: the north peninsular Gulf coast and the Caloosahatchee region (map 2.1).

The Caloosahatchee Region

The Caloosahatchee region extends from roughly the mouths of the Peace and Myakka Rivers at the north to just south of Estero Bay, with an eastern boundary halfway between Charlotte Harbor and Lake Okeechobee (Walker 1990; map 2.3). Charlotte and Lee counties are completely contained in the region. A rich set of estuarine habitats exists in the region. Especially important are the expansive mangrove and sea grass biological communities described earlier that enable high biotic productivity in Charlotte Harbor and adjacent bay areas.

From ethnohistoric sources we know that the Caloosahatchee region

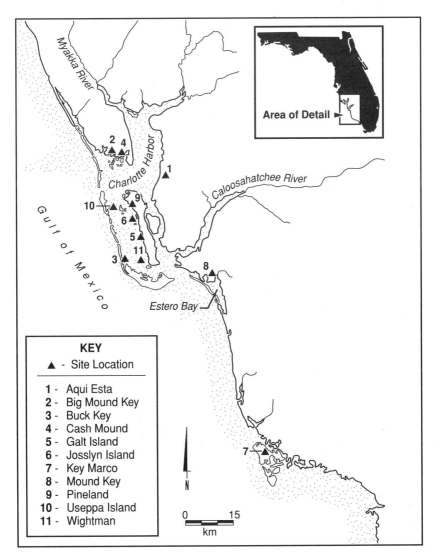

Map 2.3. Caloosahatchee region archaeological sites.

was the historical territory of the Calusa. The Calusa have captured the attention of anthropologists for decades, principally through their achievement as a ranked, nonagricultural society (Goggin and Sturtevant 1964; Hann 1991; Marquardt 1986, 1992; Milanich et al. 1984a; Newsom 1991; Scarry and Newsom 1992; Walker 1992a; Widmer 1988). Marquardt (1991:xv) captures the fascination nicely:

The Calusa constitute one of the great enigmas of anthropology. When Europeans arrived in southwest Florida in the early sixteenth century, they found a complex and powerful society. The Calusa were divided into nobles and commoners, supported an elite military force, and demanded tribute from towns hundreds of kilometers away. They possessed a complex belief system that encompassed daily offerings to their ancestors and a notion of the afterlife. Their elaborate rituals included processions of masked priests and synchronized singing by hundreds of young women. They painted, carved, and engraved. Inside their great temple, the walls were covered by carved and painted wooden masks. The head chief's house was said to be able to hold 2,000 people without being crowded.

Archaeological interest in the Caloosahatchee region began in the nineteenth century, no doubt stimulated by the discovery of the Key Marco site about 50 kilometers south of the Caloosahatchee region (Cushing 1896; Gilliland 1975, 1988; map 2.3). Preservation at Key Marco was excellent, due to the anaerobic conditions (Cushing 1896). Wood and cordage artifacts were abundant there and included woven fiber, toy canoes, stools, statues and figure heads (fig. 2.4), carved tablets, handles, net floats, painted boards, bowls, and masks (Cushing 1896; Gilliland 1975, 1988; Milanich 1998; Purdy 1996). Early explorations and excavations in the Caloosahatchee region were conducted by Collins (1929), Hrdlička (1922), Moore (1900, 1905, 1919), and Stirling (1931, 1935).

Most recently, a large multidisciplinary project under the direction of William H. Marquardt and Karen J. Walker of the Florida Museum of Natural History has focused on reconstructing the environment and prehistoric human use of the Charlotte Harbor region. They have conducted extensive excavations on several sites including Buck Key (8LL55, 8LL721, 8LL722), Galt Island (8LL27, 8LL81), Josslyn Island (8LL32), Pine Island (8LL33, 8LL34, 8LL36, 8LL37), and Useppa Island (8LL51; Marquardt 1984, 1986, 1987, 1992, 1999; Walker and Marquardt 2003).

As would be expected given the focus on maritime resources, most known sites in the Caloosahatchee region occur along the coast (map 2.3). Shell middens are the predominant site type and more than 100 have been recorded from Lee County (Walker 1990). At the larger village complexes, mounds were constructed by refuse accumulation or by relocation of shell midden materials. Among the larger and better documented mound and shell midden sites are Big Mound Key (8CH10; Luer et al. 1986, Marquardt 1992), Buck Key (8LL55; Hutchinson 1992; Marquardt 1992), Cash Mound (8CH38; Bullen and Bullen 1956; Marquardt 1992),

Fig. 2.4. Carved wooden feline figure from Key Marco. (From Purdy 1996: fig. 24. Reprinted with permission of the University Press of Florida.)

Pineland (8LL33, 8LL34, 8LL36, 8LL37; Marquardt 1992), Josslyn Island (8LL32; Marquardt 1984, 1992), Galt Island (8LL27, 8LL81; Marquardt 1992), Useppa Island (8LL51; Griffin 1949; Marquardt 1992, 1999; Milanich et al. 1984a), Wightman (8LL54; Fradkin 1976; Wilson 1982), Key Marco (8CR48; Cushing 1896; Gilliland 1975, 1988), and Mound Key (8LL2, 8LL3; Lewis 1978).

Much less is known about interior Caloosahatchee sites. Austin (1987) found a number in Lee County with many concentrated above the mouth of the Caloosahatchee River. He reported three basic site types: sand burial mounds with shell and dirt middens, small dirt middens occurring in dry areas associated with freshwater marshes, and one canal (8LL756) cutting through Cape Coral (Luer 1989).

The extensive near-shore marine habitats, combined with the estuaries, mangrove, and sea grass habitats, provided ample subsistence opportunities for the Caloosahatchee residents. Most of the animal remains recovered from archaeological sites in the region are from shellfish and fish, although other birds and mammals are also present. Walker (1992a: fig. A3) estimates that 60–90% of the meat biomass consumed by inhabitants of the Charlotte Harbor region consisted of bony fish, sharks, and rays. Most were acquired through fishing with nets, spears, hook and line, and tidal traps.

Shellfish from archaeological sites in Charlotte Harbor appear to have been collected on a local scale (Walker 1992a). Shellfish commonly recovered from archaeological sites include oyster, Atlantic ribbed mussel (*Geukensia demissa granosissima*), whelk (*Busycon* spp.), conch (Melongidae spp.), tulip (*Fasciolaria* spp.), and scallop (*Argopecten* spp.) (Walker 1992a). Stone crabs (*Menippe mercenaria*) are also commonly recovered from archaeological contexts.

Common fish recovered from archaeological sites include pinfish (*Lagodon rhomboides*), hardhead catfish (*Ariopsis felis*), sheepshead (*Archosargus probatocephalus*), spotted seatrout, jack (Carangidae), red drum (*Sciaenops ocellatus*), mullet (*Mugil* spp.), striped burrfish (*Chilomycterus schoepfi*), flounder (*Paralichthys* spp.), gafftopsail catfish (*Bagre marinus*), black drum *(Pogonias cromis)*, pigfish (*Orthopristis chrysoptera*), toadfish (*Apsanus* spp.), bonnethead shark (*Sphyrna tiburo*), Atlantic sharpnose shark (*Rizoprionodon terraenovae*), and lemon shark (*Nagaprion brevirostris*).

Birds commonly recovered include red-breasted merganser (*Mergus serrator*), bay ducks (*Aythya* spp.), and other ducks (Anatidae) that favor shallow sea grass meadows (Walker 1992a). Reptiles found in archaeological contexts include snapping turtle (*Chelydra serpentina*), mud turtle (*Kinosternon* spp.), gopher tortoise (*Gopherus polyphemus*), and box turtle (*Terrapene carolina*) (Walker 1992a). Among the mammals commonly recovered are whitetail deer, raccoon, and cotton rat.

Plants commonly found in Charlotte Harbor archaeological contexts include fruits such as hackberry, seagrape (*Coccoloba uvifera*), mastic (*Mastichodendron foetidissimum*), prickly pear (*Opuntia* sp.), cabbage palm, saw palmetto (*Seronoa repens*), gourd (*Cucurbita* sp.), and hog plum (*Ximenia americana*) (Scarry and Newsom 1992). Plants that may have been used for seeds and/or greens that have been found in archaeological contexts include chenopod (Chenopodiaceae), purslane (*Portulaca* sp.), and poke (Phytolaccaceae) (Scarry and Newsom 1992).

There is no evidence for corn (*Zea mays*) in any of the samples from

Charlotte Harbor sites or elsewhere in the Caloosahatchee region prior to the influence of Europeans. Although corn pollen was recovered from contexts dated to A.D. 300 at Fort Center on the west side of Lake Okeechobee (E. Sears 1982), the presence of pre-Columbian maize in the region has been highly disputed. The soils in south Florida are not suitable for growing corn (W. Johnson 1990), and attempts to demonstrate corn consumption directly by stable carbon analysis (see chapter 3 for an explanation of the theory and methods) have not been successful (Keegan 1987; Norr et al. n.d.).

It is possible that other plants were used as a starchy food resource instead of maize. Fontaneda (1944:27–28) mentions that roots were used to make a bread by populations inhabiting the Caloosahatchee region, and there is some speculation that coonti (*Zamia integrifolia*) was the particular root used. Widmer (1988) doubts, however, that widespread use of coonti occurred prior to Spanish colonization.

Archaeological remains from Caloosahatchee sites are numerous and varied. Shell dippers, cups, spoons, pendants, awls, beads, pins, and points are made from a number of gastropods. Shell hammers and hoes are made from whelks (fig. 2.5). Walker (1989, 1992a) and Marquardt (1992b) have been active in reinterpreting the function of many of these artifacts for the prehistoric fishing industry. Perforated limestone weights and plummets are common (Griffin 1988). Bone artifacts include projectile points, pins, daggers, drilled teeth, beads, and net-mesh gauges (Walker 1992b).

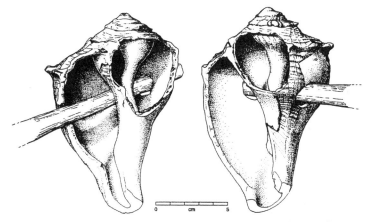

Fig. 2.5. Whelk hammer from Charlotte Harbor. (From Marquardt 1992: fig. 7. Reproduced with permission of William H. Marquardt.)

Monumental architecture is found at several of the Caloosahatchee sites. Although large mounds are known from sites farther north on the Gulf coast and interior such as Safety Harbor (Griffin and Bullen 1950), Crystal River (Weisman 1995), and Fort Jackson (Jones 1982), the size and magnitude of the mounds as well as the associated site complexes are far larger at Calusa sites. Mound Key, for instance, is 70–80 acres in extent and reaches an elevation of 31 feet (Goggin and Sturtevant 1964:183). The Pineland site complex on Pine Island includes roughly 200 acres with enormous mounds and large canals that transect the site. The canals that typify south Florida Caloosahatchee sites are not found farther north. Several uses for the canals have been speculated, including navigation and the transport of fresh water.

That the Calusa, at the time of European contact in the sixteenth century, were a chiefdom-level society is not in question. All of the principal ethnohistoric accounts (Fontaneda 1944; Solís de Merás 1964; Zubillaga 1946) describe the Calusa as a society with a paramount chief named Carlos and chiefs or local headmen in charge of subordinate towns. The office of paramount chief appears to have been hereditary and had several ornamental and symbolic badges of office, such as a gold forehead symbol and a wooden stool.

Widmer (1988:7) states, "Warfare was prevalent, if not a chronic condition, among the Calusa." However, at the time of European contact in Florida, similar statements can be applied throughout many of the areas visited by the Spaniards. The accounts of the Calusa state that the Tocobaga and Serrope were at war with the Calusa (Hann 1991; Widmer 1988). The Calusa attempted to have the Spanish help them in their war with the Tocobaga, although such requests were often made by indigenous groups throughout Florida.

In fact, the ethnohistoric accounts state that indigenous populations were constantly allying with Europeans, and generally the most recent European arrival was most in favor with the indigenous populations. For instance, the Saturiba attempted to enlist the French to fight with them against their enemy Outina (Bennett 2001:112). The engravings of DeBry (Lorant 1965) depict numerous acts and consequences of war in northern Florida.

Mortuary practices in the Caloosahatchee region are not well documented, but Widmer (1988:94–97) has presented a brief summary of those that are known. Continuous-use sand burial mounds containing flexed primary and secondary burials were used between A.D. 700 and 1200 (Caloosahatchee II period). Among these mounds are Captiva

Mound (8LL57; Collins 1929:151–153), the Pine Island 8 site (8LL40; Moore 1900:363), and Calusa Ridge on Pine Island (Hutchinson 1999; Torrence 1999).

Similar mounds occur between A.D. 1200 and 1513, although they contain Safety Harbor and Englewood ceramics (Walker 1990). Mounds from this period include the Pine Island 8 site, Buck Key (Hutchinson 1992; Marquardt 1992), and Aqui Esta (Hutchinson 2002b; Luer 2002). Only a few skeletons have been analyzed from the Caloosahatchee region from populations inhabiting Aqui Esta (Hutchinson 2002b), Buck Key (Hutchinson 1992), Galt Island (Hutchinson 1990), Useppa Island (Hutchinson 1999; Hutchinson et al. 1997), and Pine Island (Hutchinson 2003).

The North Peninsular Gulf Coast

The north peninsular Gulf coast reaches northward from just north of Tampa Bay to the Aucilla River and includes the coastal counties of Pasco, Hernando, Citrus, Levy, Dixie, Taylor, and Lafayette (map 2.4). This region is not well documented archaeologically and generalizations are difficult, partially because of the environmental and cultural heterogeneity of the region (Borremans 1993b).

The region comprises a mixture of habitats, including interior upland hammocks and ridges, low-lying wetlands, and coastal estuaries (Myers and Ewel 1990). Toward the north of the region, the mangroves that predominate in many areas of the central Gulf coast are not found, and salt marshes are more extensive (Myers and Ewel 1990).

There is very little in the way of ethnohistoric documentation that can be used to reconstruct the lives of the populations inhabiting the north peninsular Gulf coast region at the time of European contact. The expedition of Narváez went through part of the region, and one of the members, Cabeza de Vaca, kept a journal, but the descriptions provide only glimpses of the natives and their way of life (Smith 1966).

Archaeological research in the region has been limited as well. Only a few regional surveys have been undertaken in the Cove of the Withlacoochee (Weisman 1986), the Crystal River area (Bullen and Bullen 1953, 1963), the Cedar Key area (Borremans 1993a), Gulf Hammock in Levy County (Jones and Borremans 1991, cited in Milanich 1994), and the Dixie County area (Kohler and Johnson 1986) (map 2.4). One of the most significant early archaeological sites located in the northern peninsular Gulf coast region is Crystal River (8CI1; A.D. 1–1200; Bullen 1951;

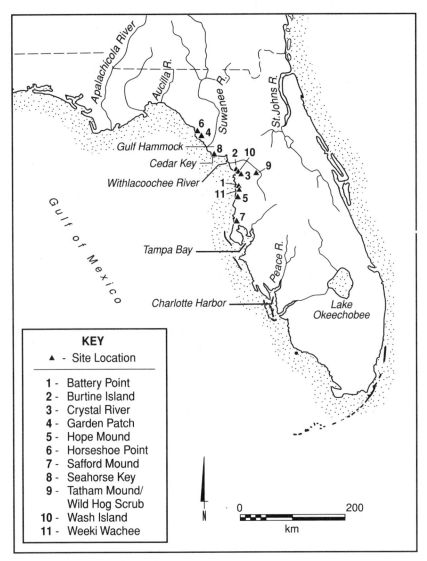

Map 2.4. North peninsular Gulf coast sites.

Moore 1907; Weisman 1995). Comprising several mounds containing burials, Crystal River contains some of the earliest ceremonial artifacts on the Florida Gulf coast.

The interior Cove of the Withlacoochee has been extensively surveyed (Weisman 1986), and two of the known archaeological sites have been extensively excavated: Wild Hog Scrub (Powell's Town; 8CI198; Weisman

1989) and Tatham Mound (8CI203; Hutchinson 1991, 1996, n.d.; Mitchem 1989). Both sites contain components dating to the European contact period that have contributed substantially to our knowledge of European and indigenous American interactions.

Kohler (1975:13–16) defined five types of habitats available for settlement along the north peninsular Gulf coast: shallow Gulf waters, estuarine salt marsh/tidal creek, pine flatwoods, mesic hammocks, and sandhills. The available subsistence data indicate that local resource use characterized populations from at least Weeden Island (A.D. 200–1000) and probably through the sustained influence of European missionization. In coastal contexts, marine resources appear to have been the predominant source of meat. For instance, at the Garden Patch site (8DI4; A.D. 1–500, Timothy Kohler, pers. comm., 2 March 2002) in Dixie County, Kohler (1975) estimates that 75% of the meat came from marine and shallow inshore habitats of the Gulf.

Examination of the animal bone and shell recovered from that site indicate extensive use of the shallow Gulf waters and adjacent estuarine salt marsh and tidal creek areas, but little incorporation of the hammocks and flatwoods areas. Fish that constitute more than 10% of the MNI at Garden Patch included toadfish (*Opsanus* spp.), sheepshead, sea catfish (*Arius felis*), and mullet. White-tailed deer contributed the most meat weight from the hammocks habitat. Vertebrate remains from other coastal sites include sharks, rays, catfishes, mullet, trout, sea bass (*Centropristis* spp.), pinfish, pigfish, sheepshead, jacks, drums, sea turtle, alligator (*Alligator mississipiensis*), and deer, among other vertebrates (Borremans 1993b).

Shell midden sites are common in the north peninsular Gulf coast and are composed primarily of oyster shell, although clam, scallop, whelk, and conch are present as well (Borremans 1993b). The large maritime shell middens generally represent a long and continual use of the region from Deptford (500 B.C.–A.D. 200) through Weeden Island (A.D. 200–1200) periods (Milanich 1994). Borremans (1993b) reports that zooarchaeological evidence indicates intensive maritime adaptation and permanent, year-round occupation. Shell midden sites are also found in brackish water and freshwater locations such as Gulf Hammock in Levy County (Borremans 1993b). Blue crab and stone crab have commonly been found at coastal sites.

Inland, riverine resources appear to have been common, and many sites are located along rivers. Thus, both the coast and interior rivers appear to have been the primary settlement locations for permanent villages. However, in some areas such as the Cove of the Withlacoochee, there appears to have been a transition from permanent river locations to upland seasonal localities following A.D. 500, potentially indicating the beginnings of horticulture (Weisman 1986: 20).

A detailed analysis of four column samples and two features was conducted for Bayonet Field (8CI197) in Citrus County. Extensive wetlands characterize the region and the site is located close to the Withlacoochee River in a scrub and sand pines environment. The major contributors to meat weight were largemouth bass (*Micropterus salmoides*), gar (*Lepisosteus* sp.), and whitetail deer (Fitzgerald 1987). All fauna recovered were from terrestrial and freshwater habitats; no saltwater taxa have been recovered.

There is virtually no available research for plant utilization. The only plant remains recovered from the Garden Patch site were carbonized wood and hickory fragments (Kohler 1975). No indication of plant cultivation has been found in the region (Milanich 1994), although cob-marked pottery has been found at sites in Dixie County (Kohler 1991; Kohler and Johnson 1986).

Ceramics are commonly found at north peninsular Gulf coast sites and include Swift Creek; Alachua cob marked, cord and fabric marked; Carabelle incised; Lochloosa punctated; and Weeden Island punctated, incised, and zoned red ceramic types. Shell artifacts include gorgets, beads, hammers, scrapers, adzes, cups, dippers, and pendants. Stone artifacts include celts and points, bone pins, and perforated shark and canine teeth (Borremans 1993b; Milanich 1994).

Little is known about the social and political systems of the inhabitants of the north peninsular Gulf coast prior to contact. The size and complexity of the Crystal River mortuary area suggests a ranked, hierarchical social system, as does the appearance of mounds at several sites just prior to and during the Weeden Island period. If social ranking were present, then warfare might be expected, but there is no supporting evidence in the ethnohistory or the archaeological remains. No discernible weapons have been recovered.

Multiple burial mounds are associated with the larger north peninsular Gulf coast sites and generally date to the Weeden Island (A.D. 200–1200) period. Isolated mounds are also found on the coast and inland along the rivers (Moore 1903, 1907, 1918; Walker 1880; Willey 1949). Willey (1949) reported that most mounds were circular and about one to three meters in height. There appear to have been a range of burial treatments that included secondary burials, single skulls, and primary flexed and extended interments (Borremans 1993b). Few grave goods appear to have been placed with individual burials, but ceramic sherds and other artifacts were often found in mound fill (Willey 1949). Unfortunately, most mounds had been looted prior to systematic excavations and contextual information is generally not available (Willey 1949).

The most elaborate burial complex from the region occurred at the Crystal River site. Excavations between 1903 and 1985 have demonstrated that the site was used from at least 500 B.C. until A.D. 1500 (Milanich 1994; Weisman 1995). The burial complex (features C–F) appears to span the time periods from the Santa Rosa-Swift Creek (A.D. 100–300) through Weeden Island II (A.D.750–1000), although it appears that the majority of burials were placed in the mounds between A.D. 1 and 400 (Milanich 1998; Weisman 1995).

One early Weeden Island burial mound (post–A.D. 300) has been excavated in the region. Hope Mound (8PA12), located in western Pasco County, was excavated by members of the Pepper-Hearst expedition in 1896 (Smith 1971). It appears that a single interment was placed on the primary mound, perhaps in a crypt, and then several secondary burials were interred in an upper stratum (Smith 1971).

Tatham Mound (8CI203) was an undisturbed mound located in the Cove of the Withlacoochee (Hutchinson 1991, 1996, n.d.; Hutchinson and Mitchem 2001; Mitchem 1989; Weisman 1986). It was completely exavated between 1985 and 1986. Tatham had two components, a contact period component dating to A.D. 1525–1550, and a precontact component dating between A.D. 1200 and 1450 (Pinellas Phase of Safety Harbor; Mitchem 1989). The contact component contained 339 individuals with hundreds of associated grave goods, including glass and metal beads, silver objects, a brigandine iron plate, and chain mail.

The precontact component at Tatham Mound contained 28 burials, some associated with objects such as a copper plate with repoussé decoration, a copper plume, a copper ear spool, and ceramics. Burials in the precontact stratum of the mound appear to have been a combination of primary and secondary burials, while those in the contact stratum were largely secondary (n = 244) although many primary burials (n = 95) were also present (Hutchinson 1991, n.d.; Hutchinson and Mitchem 2001; Mitchem 1989).

The skeletal remains from Crystal River have been the subject of bachelor's and master's student theses (Green 1993; Katzmarzyk 1998), and have been included in a review of the evidence for pre-Columbian treponemal infection (Hutchinson et al. 2003a), but little else has been published.

Analysis of the Tatham Mound skeletal remains has been published by Hutchinson and coworkers (Hutchinson 1991, 1993a, 1996, n.d.; Hutchinson and Mitchem 2001; Hutchinson and Norr 1994).

The Central Peninsular Gulf Coast

The central peninsular Florida Gulf coast extends from Pasco County in the north through the Tampa Bay region in the south and reaches inland nearly to the Peace River. It encompasses Pinellas, Hillsborough, Manatee, and Sarasota counties (Milanich 1994:221; map 2.5).

The principal European accounts for the central Florida Gulf coast come from the De Soto expedition (Milanich 1995; Robertson 1993; Worth 1993) in 1539 and from Pedro Menéndez de Avilé's voyage to Tampa Bay in 1566 (Hann 1991), although Cabeza de Vaca also describes the populations living around Tampa Bay in 1528 (Smith 1966). It appears that the most powerful group were the Tocobaga, who inhabited the village of the same name near modern Safety Harbor on Tampa Bay. There are several descriptions of mound and temple complexes that suggest village plans with central plazas. One of the complexes was described by the Gentleman from Elvas, a member of the Hernando de Soto expedition: "The town [Ucita] consisted of seven or eight houses. The chief's house stood near the beach on a very high hill which had been artificially built as a fortress. At the other side of the town was the temple and on top of it a wooden bird with its eyes gilded" (Robertson 1993:57). It seems from descriptions of Tocobaga (Smith 1966) that it and other towns around Tampa Bay had similar temples in the main village.

The central peninsular Gulf coast region was inhabited between 500 B.C. and A.D. 800 by populations of the Manasota culture (Luer and Almy 1979, 1982). The Safety Harbor period began after A.D. 900 and grew out of the late Weeden Island period cultures (Milanich 1994; Mitchem 1989). It continued until the arrival of Europeans during the first half of the sixteenth century. Willey (1949) originally defined Safety Harbor based on information from Moore's (1900, 1903) early work as well as excavations by the Federal Emergency Relief Agency in the 1930s. The most informative treatise on the Safety Harbor culture was written by Mitchem (1989), and it remains the most thorough discussion of Safety Harbor sites in the central Gulf coast region.

C. B. Moore's (1900, 1903) excavations in the region were not as intensive as those he conducted in other areas such as Moundville or Crystal River, but nonetheless Moore excavated some of the earliest archaeologi-

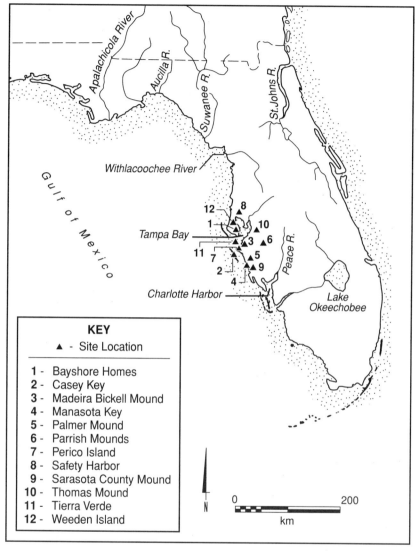

Map 2.5. Central peninsular Gulf coast sites.

cal materials from the region. In 1923–24, Jesse W. Fewkes of the Smithsonian Institution excavated the Weeden Island site on Tampa Bay (Fewkes 1924). Although not extensively published, the excavation and recovered materials served as the basis for the Weeden Island culture and provided an important interest for the Bureau of American Ethnology.

The interest sparked by Weeden Island was an important stimulus for undertaking archaeological excavations in Florida when the Civil Works Administration was organized in 1933 by Franklin D. Roosevelt. Matthew Stirling organized Federal Emergency Relief Administration excavations at nine sites, among them Perico Island (8MA6), Thomas Mound (8HI1), and Englewood Mound (8SO1). These excavations were followed by relief-financed archaeology under the direction of J. Clarence Simpson of the Florida State Archaeological Survey (Willey 1949). He conducted additional excavations at Thomas Mound, and also excavated at the Spender (8HI8), Cagnini (8HI9), Branch (8HI10), Lykes (8HI11), Snavely (8HI5), Jones (8HI4), and Picnic (8HI3) mounds (Bullen 1952; Willey 1949). Willey (1949) summarized all available data for the archaeology of the Florida Gulf coast in his comprehensive *Archeology of the Florida Gulf Coast* in 1949.

In 1949, John W. Griffin and Ripley P. Bullen continued excavations at the Safety Harbor site that Matthew Stirling had begun in 1929–30. Stirling had excavated the greater portion of the burial mound, removing more than 100 burials that were later examined by Hrdlička (1940). He had also excavated in the village area (Griffin and Bullen 1950). Griffin and Bullen worked in three main areas, primarily testing to determine archaeological significance for the public park named Phillippi Park, which is still in operation. The large Safety Harbor mound is still present and protected, and the site is suspected to be that of Tocobaga (Griffin and Bullen 1950).

Ripley Bullen continued the work by excavating several other Safety Harbor period sites, such as Terra Ceia (Bullen 1951), Picnic Mound (Bullen 1952), Branch Mound (Bullen 1952), and others (Bullen 1952, 1955). The excavations mentioned above and many since have produced some of the richest and most complete archaeological data for Florida, and our knowledge of the prehistoric people who lived along the central peninsular Gulf coast is more complete than for populations in the north peninsular Gulf coast.

The majority of Manasota sites, although numbering fewer than 50 in the Florida site files (Milanich 1990), are found adjacent to the narrow bays that lie behind the barrier islands and along Tampa Bay, a location providing ample resources in the form of fish and shellfish (Luer and Almy 1982:39–40). Manasota sites are often extensive shell middens that have been interpreted as village locations. Smaller sites without extensive shell middens may have been special use sites and are often located inland on higher terrain (Austin and Russo 1989). For instance, Luer and coworkers (1987) report that a dirt midden was found at the more inland Myakka-hatchee site.

Most Safety Harbor period sites are also located along the coast, although some are located farther inland (Milanich 1994). In the Tampa Bay region, at least 15 archaeological sites with platform mounds adjacent to plazas with surrounding shell midden deposits have been found, suggesting settled village areas (Bullen 1955; Griffin 1951; Luer and Almy 1981). These larger platform and plaza sites are all coastal or on Tampa Bay, usually along rivers (Milanich 1994:396). Although burial mounds are found farther inland, mound and plaza complexes are not found inland.

Several burial mounds from the Manasota, Weeden Island, and Safety Harbor cultures have been excavated in the region since the last half of the nineteenth century (table 2.1). Limiting discussions to the modern counties of Hillsborough, Manatee, Pinellas, and Sarasota, and to the time period between 500 B.C. and A.D. 1500, burial mounds include Terra Ceia, Thomas, Prine, Safford (8PI3), Bayshore Homes, Sarasota County, Bickell, Palmer, Englewood, Safety Harbor, and many others (see table 2.1 for site numbers and other details).

As defined originally by Luer and Almy (1982), Manasota culture is

Table 2.1. Burial mounds in the central Gulf coast region

Site	Number	N[a]	Primary	Sec.	Cremation	References
Hillsborough County						
Bayshore Homes	8Hi	115+	y	y		Sears 1960; Snow 1962
Branch Md.	8Hi10	6	y	y	y	Bullen 1952
Buck Island	8Hi6			28+		Bullen 1952; Willey 1949
Cagnini Md.	8Hi9			92[b]	2	Bullen 1952; Simpson 1939; Willey 1949
Cockroach Key	8Hi2		186	38		Willey 1949:158–172
Fort Brooke Md.	8Hi13	1				Mitchem 1989
Henriquez Md.	8Hi1077	34–39				Mitchem 1989
Jones Md.	8Hi4	179	135	18	1	Bullen 1952:42–61; Simpson 1939; Willey 1949:337)
Lykes Md.	8Hi11	34	y	y		Bullen 1952
Picnic Md.	8Hi3		33	45	1	Bullen 1952; Willey 1949
Snavely Mds.	8Hi5/42			1		Bullen 1952; Willey 1949
Thomas Md.	8Hi1	419[c]	y	y	y	Bullen 1952; Moore 1900; Willey 1949
Quad Block	8Hi998	126				İşcan and Miller-Shaivitz 1983

continued

Table 2.1 continued

Site	Number	N[a]	Primary	Sec.	Cremation	References
Manatee County						
Ellenton Md.	8Ma44	25				Moore 1936, cited in Mitchem 1989
Glazier Md.	8Ma32					Tallant, in Mitchem 1989
Harbor Key Md. (Bishop Harbor)	8Ma14	127	18	80		Bullen et al. 1952; Burger, cited in Mitchem 1989
Johnson Md.	8Ma83e	some	y			Bullen 1951; Moore 1900
Mobley Scrub	8Ma58	77				Tallant, in Mitchem 1989
Ogleby Creek #1	8Ma70	some				Tallant, in Mitchem 1989
Parrish Mds. 1–5	8Ma1–8Ma5		y	240	41	Willey 1949:156–158
Perico Island	8Ma6					Willey 1949:172–182
Pillsbury Md.	8Ma30	134				Luer and Almy 1981:134
Prine Md.	8Ma83c		y			Bullen 1951
Redding Md.	8Ma37	28			2	Burger 1982
Terra Ceia Md.						Bullen 1951
Wingate Creek Md. (Myakka River 1)	8Ma57	some				Tallant, in Mitchem 1989
Pinellas County						
Bay Pines	8Pi64	24				Gallagher and Warren 1975
Cobb Md.	8Pi879	some				Mitchem 1989
Johns Pass Md.	8Pi4		y	y		Walker 1880:401–403; Moore 1903
Maximo Point	8Pi13					Moore 1900; Walker 1880:419
Point Pinellas	8Pi18	some				Walker 1880
Safety Harbor	8Pi2			100+		Griffin and Bullen 1950; Hrdlička 1940; Moore 1900; Stirling 1931; Walker 1880; Willey 1949:134–142
Safford Md.	8Pi3		y	y	y	Bullen et al. 1970; Cushing 1896: 352–354; Moore 1903; Smith 1971; Willey 1949:331–332

Table 2.1 continued

Site	Number	N[a]	Primary	Sec.	Cremation	References
Seven Oaks	8Pi8		y	76		Walker 1880; Willey 1949:333
Tierra Verde	8Pi51	48	y			Hutchinson 1993b; Moore 1900; Sears 1967; Warren et al. 1965
Weeden Island	8Pi1					Bushnell 1926; Fewkes 1924; Willey 1949:105–113
Sarasota County						
Brookside Md.	8So2332	some				Luer 1995
Casey Key	8So17					Bullen and Bullen 1976:47–48
Englewood Md.	8So1	263	16+	y		Willey 1949:26–135
Laurel Md.	8So98	98	y			Luer and Almy 1987
Myakkahatchee (Myakka Valley)	8So397	some				Luer et al. 1987
Ranches Md.	8So401	some				Mitchem 1989
Pool Hammock	8So3	some				Mitchem 1989
Sarasota Bay Md.	8So44	some	y			Grismer 1946; Monroe et al. 1982, cited in Mitchem 1989
Sarasota County		some				Bullen 1971
True Mound	8So5	≈50	y			Luer and Almy 1987; Willey 1949
Yellow-Bluffs Whittaker Md.	8So4	10	7	1		Milanich 1972
Walker Site		some	1			Luer and Almy 1979
Weber Md.	8So20	some				Bullen 1950
Whitaker Md.	8So81	8+				Bullen 1950; Monroe et al. 1982, cited in Mitchem 1989

a. N = total number of burials, usually reported when no specific categories are indicated.

b. One secondary burial was an urn burial.

c. The total count (*n* = 419) is an approximate count tabulated by Willey 1949:116 from all excavations (Moore, Holder, Simpson).

characterized by an economy based on fishing, hunting, and shellfish gathering, with shell predominating as a tool-making source. Manasota middens at several sites have contained floral and faunal remains used to interpret subsistence patterns. Based in part on Luer's excavations at the Roberts Bay (8SO56) and Old Oak (8SO51) sites near Sarasota, Luer and Almy (1982:43) note that 15 species of fish and 10 species of sharks and rays have been identified. They note that a variety of different habitat preferences is reflected in the species of fish recovered, suggesting that a diverse set of fishing strategies was employed. Other faunal remains include deer, wolf, dog, opossum, raccoon, rabbit, rat, red-breasted merganser, and bald eagle. Fifteen species of shellfish have been recovered from Manasota sites, the most common being oyster (Luer and Almy 1982:43; see also Milanich 1994:225).

Subsistence of the Safety Harbor people appears to have been a continuation of the previous Manasota and Late Weeden Island periods, with aquatic resources forming the bulk of food remains at archaeological sites. Kozuch (1986) examined five faunal samples from Safety Harbor sites near Tampa Bay and found that a variety of marine molluscs, freshwater and marine turtles, crabs, sea birds, alligators, rays, sharks, and a wide variety of marine fish predominated in the samples. Terrestrial animals included deer, turkey, and freshwater wading birds.

There is some evidence that the Tocobaga practiced maize agriculture (Milanich and Hudson 1993). Pánfilo de Narváez's men found corn at Tocobaga (Cabeza de Vaca, in Smith 1966), but whether occasional consumption or dependence characterized their use of corn is unclear. Although corn was noted sporadically along the route of De Soto in central Florida, it was not a dietary staple in the sixteenth century, as demonstrated at Tatham Mound in Citrus County (Hutchinson and Norr 1994; Hutchinson et al. 1998, 2000).

Virtually no detailed analysis of floral remains has been published for the central peninsular Gulf coast. "As yet, evidence for any type of agriculture is lacking, and it is doubtful if any extensive farming ever took place in the region from Tampa Bay south" (Milanich 1994:225). Milanich's statement draws upon several types of evidence that include floral remains found in archaeological contexts from sites south of Tampa Bay (Newsom 1991) and soil types (W. Johnson 1990).

The social and political organization of the groups that the Europeans observed living around Tampa Bay was clearly that of ranked societies, probably chiefdoms. When Menendez visited the Tampa Bay region in

1566, it seemed clear that the chief at Tocobaga commanded a lot of authority: "To demonstrate both his power and his willingness to cooperate with the Spaniards, Chief Tocobaga summoned twenty-nine vassal chiefs, some of whom lived up to two days' travel away. The chiefs, along with one hundred principal men, assembled at Tocobaga's town, where fifteen hundred warriors armed with bows and arrows paraded before the Spaniards in a show of strength" (Milanich 1995:74).

The Tocobaga were heavily engaged in warfare with the Calusa when the Spaniards first came to the area (Milanich 1995). They did not limit their aggressions to indigenous populations, however, and De Soto's entrada had several skirmishes with native populations while they were camped along Tampa Bay (Robertson 1993; Worth 1993). The size of the army described above suggests that the Tocobaga, and perhaps other groups in the region, had well-organized military forces with substantial battle experience. It is unknown how long such an organized military structure had been in place, however.

Because of the large number of burial mounds that have been excavated in the central peninsular Gulf coast region and the ethnohistoric records of mortuary temples, there are a number of observations that can be made regarding mortuary ceremonialism. Luer and Almy (1982:46–47) have suggested that Manasota burial ceremonialism was characterized in its earliest times (500 B.C.–A.D. 100) by flexed, primary interments in shell middens or cemeteries. Mound ceremonialism followed, with the incorporation of secondary burials. By the post–A.D. 700 period, late Weeden Island burial mounds were present that contain Wakulla Check Stamped and St. Johns Check Stamped pottery (Milanich 1994).

The temples described in European accounts (Robertson 1993; Smith 1966) would indicate that storage of the dead prior to final burial was common, as it was for mid-Atlantic populations (Hutchinson 2002a). The temples, or charnel houses, would be used for a lengthy period of time, perhaps a couple of decades, and then a large, community-wide ritual event would culminate in the final burial of the disarticulated remains (Hutchinson and Aragon 2002). The predominance of secondary burials at many Safety Harbor period mounds suggests that charnel houses were being used for several centuries prior to European contact.

Most published reports on the mound excavations and recovered materials include descriptions of the artifacts and the burials, but little systematic osteological analysis has been performed. Few skeletal series have been extensively reported from the central peninsular Gulf coast region, and most consist of fewer than 50 individuals (Hutchinson 1991, 1993b; Snow 1962). Thus, at present, the human biology of the people inhabiting the central peninsular Gulf coast region is not well understood.

Summary

Humans have taken advantage of the diverse habitats that lie along the Florida Gulf coast since the beginning of the Archaic period in 8000 B.C. Maritime resources, subsidized by terrestrial plants and animals, appear to have provided human populations along the Gulf coast with a dependable resource base until at least A.D. 1600.

In much of the southeastern United States, such unfaltering dependence on one major set of resources was not seen. After roughly 4000 B.C. seed-bearing plants begin to appear in archaeological contexts in the interior. Their use intensified after 1000 B.C., and sometime after A.D. 300 the first maize was grown. Between A.D. 800 and 1000, many populations from the central Mississippi valley to the western Appalachian piedmont began to exhibit characteristics of Mississippian culture; in those areas this time is referred to as the Emergent Mississippian phase. Among the material characteristics were rectangular wall-trench houses and shell-tempered pottery. Charred maize became much more frequent in archaeological contexts at this time. These traits along with an increased reliance on maize agriculture became hallmarks of the Mississippian period between A.D. 1000 and 1500.

Social and political correlates of societies practicing maize horticulture included ranking, status differentiation, warfare, and at some sites, large urban settlements with plaza and mound complexes (Smith 1986; Steponaitis 1986). Health declined for most of these populations during the period between A.D. 1000 and 1500, as demonstrated by numerous assessments of their skeletal remains (Cohen and Armelagos 1984; Larsen 1995).

It appears from multiple lines of evidence that social ranking, status differentiation, warfare, large settlements with plaza and mound complexes, and burial ceremonialism all occurred along the Florida peninsular Gulf coast as well. It also appears that, unlike the interior Southeast, these traits appeared without the adoption of maize horticulture. Whether nutrition and health declined as they did for interior agricultural populations is unknown; assessing the similarities and differences in nutritional and health changes during the period between A.D. 500 and 1600 will serve to reassess current interpretations for both agricultural and nonagricultural populations.

Unfortunately, the bioarchaeology of the Florida peninsular Gulf coast is generally limited to discrete studies of small populations, and no regional bioarchaeological synthesis has been conducted. One of the largest systematically excavated mortuary sites in the southeastern United States is Palmer burial mound, located in Sarasota County. With more than 400 individuals, the Palmer burials represent a potentially significant contribution to our understanding of the human biology of the central peninsular Gulf coast. The Palmer burials have never before been systematically studied and they have remained silent until now on several questions regarding the lifeways of pre-Columbian native populations inhabiting the region between Tampa Bay and Charlotte Harbor. The process of analyzing the Palmer population thus offers an opportunity to examine multiple facets of their biology during a critical time of cultural transition. In the next chapter, I provide details on the history and results of archaeological excavations at the Palmer site, focusing on what was found there and on subsequent reconstructions of subsistence and demography.

3

Archaeology and Bioarchaeology at the Palmer Site

The prehistoric significance of the Palmer site has been known for more than a century. Much of it is now contained within a 29-acre tract known as Historic Spanish Point, located near the modern city of Osprey on Little Sarasota Bay (map 3.1). The earliest recorded interest in the prehistory of the site is accorded to John G. Webb, who sent collections of human bones, pottery, and tools on several occasions to the Smithsonian Institution shortly after he homesteaded the property in 1867 (Almy and Luer 1993:2).

The first of the human skeletons found by Webb was sent to the Smithsonian with a note: "I have discovered in digging in my hammock a perfect skull. It was unfortunately broken in digging it out, but I shall send all the pieces and you will find no difficulty in gluing it into pefect shape" (Hrdlička 1907:53). The second deposit of human bones sent to the Smithsonian by Webb in 1872 was found about ten minutes' walk north of the first find, and is now referred to collectively as the North Osprey Bones (Hrdlička 1907:54). Both sets of bones were examined by Aleš Hrdlička, a physical anthropologist at the National Museum of Natural History who was interested in the antiquity of humans in the New World.

Hrdlička visited the site in 1906, accompanied by Dr. T. W. Vaughan of the U.S. Geological Survey. They excavated a trench near the original location of the skull sent by Webb (known as the Osprey Skull). Based on his examination of the bones and the excavation, Hrdlička concluded in his 1907 report, *Skeletal Remains Suggesting or Attributed to Early Man in America,* that "when compared with ordinary recent Indian skeletons, it is found that not a single piece of the North Osprey bones exhibits any characteristic that is beyond the range of normal variation of modern specimens. . . . There is again possible only one conclusion, namely, that there is absolutely nothing in these bones which would suggest great or even considerable antiquity, geologically speaking" (Hrdlička 1907:59).

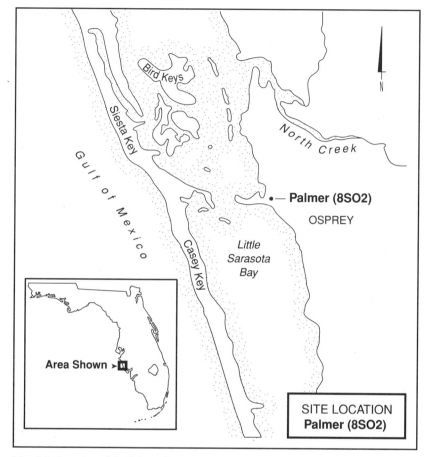

Map 3.1. Location of the Palmer site.

Hrdlička again visited the property in 1918 and collected materials, undoubtedly as part of his research published in 1922 in *The Anthropology of Florida*. The 1918 Hrdlička collection, along with the collection of materials found by Webb, was reported by Gordon Willey in his 1949 volume, *The Archaeology of Gulf Coast Florida* (1949:342–343).

The Bullen Excavations (1959–1962)

In 1911, Mrs. Potter Palmer of Chicago purchased the property that is now Historic Spanish Point for her winter residence, preserving the natural vegetation and minimizing her disturbance of the prehistoric middens and burial mound (Almy and Luer 1993:2).

Archaeology and the State of Florida also owe a debt to Mrs. Potter Palmer of Chicago and Sarasota, grandmother of Gordon Palmer, for the preservation of the site. She purchased the land in 1910, built several houses on the grounds, and did extensive landscaping but maintained the integrity of the aboriginal structures. . . . This situation is different from that at most Florida Indian sites where shell middens have been removed for fill and burial mounds vandalized by unthinking, usually trespassing, pothunters. The Palmer site at the Oaks, as the estate is named, is the only sizable prehistoric Indian Village complex on the Gulf coast south of Crystal River and north of Fort Myers which is substantially as left by its prehistoric inhabitants (Bullen and Bullen 1976:2).

The most extensive excavations of materials from the Palmer site were inaugurated by Mr. Gordon Palmer, grandson of Mrs. Potter Palmer. His request for archaeological investigations on the property was eventually transferred to Ripley P. Bullen, then curator of social sciences at the Florida State Museum (Bullen and Bullen 1976). Between 1959 and 1962, Bullen carried out excavations at five localities on the Palmer property assisted by graduate students and the Palmer Nurseries personnel: (1) the Archaic period (2500–1000 B.C.) Hill Cottage Midden, (2) the Shell Ridge, which extended into Little Sarasota Bay, (3) the Shell Midden (300 B.C.–A.D. 150), (4) the Burial Mound, and (5) the North Creek Area middens. Absolute chronology for the site came from 11 radiocarbon dates obtained from shell; extensive ceramic collections also yielded comparative dates (Bullen and Bullen 1976:1; table 3.1). The excavations were presented in some detail in the report published on the site (Bullen and Bullen 1976). Summary descriptions of the areas excavated are presented directly below and the burial mound is also discussed in more detail later in this chapter.

The Hill Cottage Midden is dated by five radiocarbon dates to the late Archaic period (table 3.1). At the time of the Bullens' excavations, it was the first systematic examination of an Archaic site in Florida. The duration of the midden accumulation is estimated at 1,000 years (Bullen and Bullen 1976:20), with little change exhibited during that time in the tools deposited. The vast majority were shell hammering tools, as well as chisels and celts.

The Shell Ridge was a short distance south of the Hill Cottage Midden and dates to the Middle Woodland period (table 3.1). Undecorated pottery, shell adornments, and shell tools were found in the ridge. The Shell

Table 3.1. Radiocarbon dates obtained from the Palmer excavations

Location	Sample number	Material utilized	Reported B.P. date[a]	Calibrated date[b]	ENAm period[c]
Hill Cottage Midden	G-596	Busycon	3350±120	1657 B.C.	Archaic
Hill Cottage Midden	G-597	Venus	3225±120	1515 B.C.	Archaic
Hill Cottage Midden	G-598	Busycon	3575±120	1918 B.C.	Archaic
Hill Cottage Midden	G-599	Busycon	4050±125	2508 B.C.	Archaic
Hill Cottage Midden	G-600	Busycon	4100±125	2622 B.C.	Archaic
Shell Ridge, Test H	G-601	Busycon	1880±150	A.D. 128	MW
Shell Ridge, Test H	G-604	Strombus	2250±110	269 B.C.	Archaic
Shell Midden, Test F	G-605	Busycon	1800±110	A.D. 238	MW
Shell Midden, Test F	G-606	Busycon	950±105	A.D. 1143	Miss
Burial Mound, Upper	G-602	Venus	1100±105	A.D. 910	LW
Burial Mound, Lower	G-603	Busycon	2350±110	400 B.C.	EW

a. Bullen and Bullen 1976.

b. Calibrated using Calib, version 4.3, Stuiver and Reimer 1993, Standard Calibration.

c. EW = Early Woodland; MW = Middle Woodland; Miss = Mississippian

Midden was located to the southeast of the Shell Ridge. Radiocarbon dates (table 3.1) and check-stamped pottery indicate that it is later in date than the Shell Ridge, and was probably used from the Middle Woodland through Mississippian periods. It was undoubtedly the midden of the village that built the burial mound (Bullen and Bullen 1976:33). The two North Creek middens were located to the north of the Hill Cottage. The Bullens (1976:35) indicated that they were late in date and probably used only casually as there were not great accumulations of shell.

The burial mound was excavated during the 1959 field season, the 1960 field season, and completed during the 1962 field season (fig. 3.1). Two radiocarbon dates were obtained for the mound. The first, from a *Venus mercenaria* clam shell (G-602), is 1100 ± 105 B.P., or about A.D. 910 (calibrated, Calib 4.3, Stuiver and Reimer 1993). The second date (G-603) from *Busycon* shells is 2350 ± 110 B.P., or 400 B.C. (calibrated, Calib 4.3, Stuiver and Reimer 1993), much too old for the ceramic contexts of the site (table 3.1). The first radiocarbon date is more consistent with the artifacts: ceramics (predominated by Belle Glade Plain, St. Johns Plain, Sand-tempered Plain, St. Johns Check-Stamped), *Busycon* dippers and hammers, shark vertebra beads, shark teeth, plummets, lithics, and, most interestingly, a flute made from a human femur (Bullen and Bullen 1976: 43 and fig. XXIII). Nonetheless, it seems a bit too late for the site.

Fig. 3.1. Burial mound excavations at initiation. Reproduced with permission of the Florida Museum of Natural History.

It is clear that the Bullens' intent in the 1976 report was to summarize the archaeology of the mound and to provide a separate human skeletal analysis in the future:

> This report covers the archaeology of the Palmer site. Food remains from the middens in the form of animal bones have been deposited in the zooarchaeological collections of the Florida State Museum and will become the subject of a separate report. They will receive only cursory mention here. The human skeletal remains are also in the research collections of the Florida State Museum. Kinds of interment and burial locations are included here. Reports on various aspects of interest to Physical Anthropologists will be published elsewhere. The first of these, an article on pathology by Adelaide K. Bullen, "Paleoepidemiology and Distribution of Prehistoric Treponemiasis (Syphilis) in Florida," has already appeared in *The Florida Anthropologist* (A. K. Bullen 1972).

However, Ripley was ill, and the report barely made it into print before he died in December 1976; the reports on faunal remains and other aspects of the Palmer excavations were never completed by the Bullens. Information regarding diet and subsistence, however, was renewed through continued archaeology at the site, beginning with planning for the establishment of the current historic park known as Historic Spanish Point.

The 1974 and 1979–1980 Surveys

In 1974, a survey of the 400-acre Palmer tract was conducted by James J. Miller and David Swindell under a contract between the Florida Division of Archives, History and Records Management and the Gale Organization in conjunction with proposed residential development of the property (Miller 1974). Four new sites (8SO27 through 8SO30) were reported consisting of three shell middens and a previously undisturbed burial mound.

In 1979 and 1980, a review of previous archaeological work and limited additional investigations were conducted in order to plan a program of public interpretation and museum development. The work was oriented toward identifying archaeologically sensitive areas on the 29-acre tract of land called Spanish Oaks (Historic Spanish Point), identifying archaeological features that could be presented to the public, identifying artifacts from the site at the Florida Museum of Natural History and the Smithsonian Institution, and inquiring about potential loans to the museum that would be located at Spanish Oaks. The 1974 survey and the 1979–80 review of previous archaeological projects formed the basis for the establishment of the current Spanish Oaks historical site and interpretation center.

The 1991 Excavations

In 1991, Corbett Torrence, George Luer, and Marion Almy, assisted by members of the Time Sifters Chapter of the Florida Anthropological Society, undertook excavations at the Shell Ridge to prepare an exhibit at Historic Spanish Point titled "A Window to the Past" that features a profile of the shell mound (Kozuch 1998). Environmental archaeological studies of selected contexts of those excavations were undertaken by Laura Kozuch (zooarchaeology), Irvy Quitmyer (molluscan seasonality), and Lee Newsom (archaeobotany), all from the Environmental Archaeology Laboratory of the Florida Museum of Natural History.

Kozuch (1998) analyzed one sample from the 1991 excavations drawn from a dark organic layer and incorporated the extant faunal material from the Bullens' 1959–62 excavations. She noted that the material from the Bullens' excavations consisted of larger fauna, indicating sample bias due to the use of larger gauge screen sizes (Kozuch 1998:179). From the 1991 sample she recovered deer, rabbit, turtles, sharks, 33 species of bony fishes, 11 species of gastropods, and 19 species of bivalves. Pinfish, sea trout, and hardhead catfish predominated the bony fish sample.

Kozuch notes that most of the fish recovered can be found in the sea grass community adjacent to the site; the pinfish in particular is one of the most abundant fish in sea grass beds in the Gulf of Mexico (Kozuch 1998:183). All of the fish recovered inhabit near-shore environments and most were probably taken by net, although they could have been caught by hook and line. Scallops were regularly utilized, and are also inhabitants of the sea grass bed community. Two shark species were commonly represented (Atlantic sharpnose; bonnethead). Kozuch (1998:183) indicates that the sharks had been caught by some means as several articulated centra were found and sharks rarely wash up to shore. It appears that the skin and teeth were utilized as tools (Kozuch 1998:184).

The faunal data from the 1991 excavations as well as the Bullen excavations indicate that the subsistence strategy included few terrestrial species and numerous aquatic species found adjacent to the Palmer site. Most aquatic species are either fish or molluscs. Kozuch (1998:184) speculates that molluscs were gathered at low tide and that fish were potentially captured by these methods: (1) nets with small mesh sizes to catch schooling fish, (2) nets with large mesh sizes to capture medium-sized fishes, and (3) hooks and lines or weirs to capture sharks and larger fishes.

Quitmyer (1998) reviewed the zooarchaeological materials from the 1991 excavations to determine the seasons in which aquatic animals had been taken. He found that Little Sarasota Bay, within close proximity to Palmer, probably was used during all seasons of the year (Quitmyer 1998: 204), with an emphasis on the sea grass beds (scallops and clams) and adjacent solid substrates (oysters).

Newsom (1998) reported that at least 16 types of plants are represented among the Shell Ridge midden samples. From wood she identified pine (*Pinus* sp.), live oak (*Quercus virginiana*), red mangrove, black mangrove, buttonwood (*Conocarpus erecta*), gumbo limbo (*Bursera simuaruba*), and palm, probably cabbage palm. Seed identifications included hickory nut, hackberry, false mastic (*Mastichodendron foetidissimum*), acorn, cabbage palm, and saw palmetto. All of these plants are local early season and summer-fall plants (Newsom 1998:221).

When all of the environmental data collected from the 1991 Shell Ridge excavations are synthesized, several summary statements can be made. First, the faunal remains are largely composed of inshore fish and shellfish from sea grass communities. Quitmyer's (1998) seasonality study of scallops, quahog clams, and loons shows that they were collected during all times of the year. Terrestrial animals are far less common in the faunal assemblage, in number of species as well as in counts of individuals. It appears that plant use was focused on a few species of wild terrestrial plants, with local forests providing wood, nuts, and fruits collected during the early summer and the fall (Newsom 1998). There is no evidence of horticulture in the archaeological remains from Palmer, a fact consistent with several other archaeological reports of subsistence remains from the central and southern Gulf coast region (W. Johnson 1990; Newsom 1991).

The Palmer Burial Mound

At the time of excavation, the burial mound was "a very unassuming, dome-shaped, sand mound rising 4 feet above the surrounding land" (fig. 3.1; Bullen and Bullen 1976:35). Two water pipe trenches had been cut through the mound, but it appeared otherwise undisturbed except for the growth of cabbage and royal palm trees (Bullen and Bullen 1976:fig. 14). Although a chicken coop had once been located on the mound surface, it appeared that only debris from its construction and maintenance had affected the mound.

Three major zones were delineated during excavation: a fairly thin, dark humic zone that included debris of recent origin and a few burials described as "badly decayed" (Bullen and Bullen 1976:38), a middle zone that contained most of the burials, pottery, and features, and a lower zone of dark earth that included charcoal, a few ceramic sherds, and some very badly preserved burials. No pottery cache was found during excavation. It appeared to the Bullens that the mound had been used rather continuously throughout the time it was an active burial site. The stratigraphy, ceramic concentrations, and other artifact inclusions are mentioned in some detail in the Bullens's report (1976:35–47).

Five animal interments were recovered from the mound: four dogs (fig. 3.2) and one ceremonial interment of an alligator (fig. 3.3). Their locations are indicated in figure 3.4. The ceremonial alligator burial is particularly interesting. Two strings of sawfish (*Pristis* sp.) vertebrae were placed parallel to the alligator's body, possibly indicating "some type of totemic relationship" (Bullen and Bullen 1976:46).

Comments regarding the human burials were limited to discussion of the burial form. "Of the nearly 400 burials with sufficient data for classification 75 percent were flexed, 6.5 percent bundled, 5.6 percent isolated

Fig. 3.2. Dog burial recovered from Palmer Mound. (From Bullen and Bullen 1976: plate XVI. Reproduced with permission of Florida Museum of Natural History.)

Fig. 3.3. The alligator burial. (From Bullen and Bullen 1976: plate XVII. Reproduced with permission of Florida Museum of Natural History.)

skulls, and the balance disturbed or indeterminate interments except for 1 sitting and 2 torso only burials" (Bullen and Bullen 1976:46; fig. 3.4). A few photographs are shown of "typical" burials (Bullen and Bullen 1976: plates XIX–XXII).

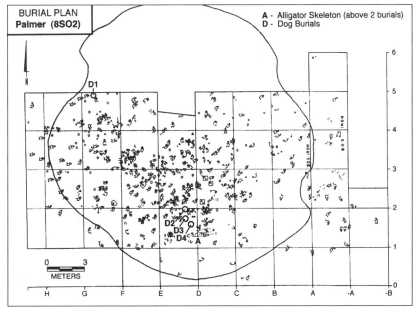

Fig. 3.4. Plan map of the Palmer burial mound. (Adapted from Bullen and Bullen 1976: fig. 17.)

Analysis of Palmer Population Structure: Minimum Number of Individuals (MNI), Taphonomy, and Preservation

The majority of the Palmer burials were distinct primary burials interred in a flexed position shortly after death (Bullen and Bullen 1976). Of all the burials I examined, only 52 contained the remains of a second individual, and the second burial usually comprised only a few skeletal and/or dental elements. Only seven burials contained the remains of more than two individuals.

Assuming that burial numbers were assigned sequentially during excavation, there were 120 burial numbers generated in the field that had no associated skeletal materials at the time of my analysis and 14 sets of skeletal remains with museum accession numbers that had no burial number assigned. Because most burials were the discrete remains of one individual, the minimum number of individuals (MNI) was based primarily on the burials distinguished by Bullen and then secondarily on those remains of multiple individuals found in the laboratory analysis. This resulted in a final MNI of 429 individuals. The dental inventory is presented in appendix A, and the skeletal inventory in appendix B.

Preservation of individuals within the mound varied, but tended toward poor to fragmentary. Some individuals were relatively intact, but many consisted of poorly preserved and partial elements. Preservation of skeletal elements is directly related to taphonomic processes, the changes that affect a deposit of buried materials (Miccozi 1991; Reitz and Wing 1999). Among the things that would have affected the preservation of the Palmer burials are the sand matrix of the mound, the groundwater chemicals, human activities, and plant and animal activity. Each is discussed below.

Acidic soils are well known for bone destruction, especially for thinner subadult bones (Gordon and Buikstra 1981; Reitz and Wing 1999:177). As well, percolation of water is an important variable in bone destruction. Soils that retain water can enhance preservation, while those that readily percolate rapidly enable the removal of organic and mineral components of bone. Materials contained with the burials or contained within the soil matrix can also affect bone preservation. Among those materials known to enhance preservation are copper and shell.

Disturbance and destruction of bone is often brought about by plant roots and animals (Miccozi 1991; Reitz and Wing 1999). Plant roots invade skeletal elements, break them apart, and dislodge them from their original locations. Rodents and other animals gnaw on bone to sharpen their teeth and obtain nutrients. Several animals in peninsular Gulf coast Florida burrow in burial mounds, among them rodents and gopher tortoises. They cause either intentional disruption through the movement of skeletal elements into burrows or unintentional movement through their burrowing activities.

Humans often continuously use mortuary spaces for extended periods of time. The maintenance and use of mortuary space often leads to the disruption of previous burials during the act of placing new ones. Skeletal elements can be broken in the process and are often simply placed back in a new location, leading to further erosion. Mortuary practices that result in differential treatment of the dead can also dramatically affect the final burial population. Most important among those burial practices is the differential treatment of age, sex, and status subgroups of the population. For instance, ethnohistoric accounts mention differential treatment of the nobility in charnel structures (Hariot [1590] 1972) and subadult burials are frequently encountered in Mississippian period house floors (e.g., Ledford Island, Tennessee; Sullivan 1995:543).

Analysis of Palmer Population Structure: Age and Sex Estimates

Age estimation for juveniles and subadults is usually performed by using growth and development standards from known reference populations. Among the elements and methods that are commonly used are dental development and eruption (Ubelaker 1989), epiphyseal union of long bones (Krogman and İşcan 1986), and maximum length of cranial elements and long bones (Fazekas and Kósa 1979; Johnston 1961, 1962). There is general agreement that these methods yield relatively accurate age estimates (Fazekas and Kósa 1979; FitzGerald and Rose 2000; Saunders 2000).

Behavioral and biological differences between individuals and populations, as well as between males and females, reduce the ability of osteologists to estimate adult age accurately, particularly beyond the age of 50 years. Often ordinal stages are used rather than precise age estimates, controlling for some of the error in age estimation (Jackes 2000; Milner et al. 2000). For adults, most age estimates are based on the degeneration of the pubic symphyseal face (Brooks and Suchey 1990; Suchey et al. 1988), changes in the auricular surface (Lovejoy et al. 1985a; Bedford et al. 1989), and dental attrition (Lovejoy 1985). Cranial suture closure is also commonly used to estimate adult age (Meindl and Lovejoy 1985).

Of the 429 total burials from Palmer, age estimates were possible for 46 subadults and 346 adults. There were 37 individuals of indeterminate age; based on their robusticity, these were included with the adults for all analyses, resulting in a total adult sample of 383 individuals. Sex estimates were possible for 72 males and 72 females.

Age estimation of the Palmer subadults (table 3.2) was accomplished by examining dental development and eruption ($n = 31$), maximum length of long bones and cranial elements ($n = 2$), epiphyseal closure ($n = 11$), and overall size ($n = 2$). Adult age estimation (table 3.2) was accomplished by dental development, eruption, and wear ($n = 198$), degenerative changes of the auricular surface (sacroiliac joint; $n = 37$), ectocranial suture closure ($n = 48$), epiphyseal union ($n = 41$), overall size ($n = 21$), and dental wear ($n = 1$). When possible more than one method was used (Lovejoy et al. 1985b). If multiple methods were used for age estimation, the method with the most reliable features and smallest standard deviation is the basis for the frequencies presented above.

Osteologists have often restricted their sex estimates to adults because the growth period that results in robusticity differences between males and

Table 3.2. Palmer individuals classified by age and sex

Age[a]	Male	Female	Indeterminate	Total
Fetal			1	1
0–2.9				
3.0–4.9			2	2
5.0–9.9			10	10
10.0–14.9				
15.0–19.9	2	1	7	10
20.0–29.9	2	3		5
30.9–39.9	9	19	2	30
40.0–49.9	15	14	2	31
50.0+	1	3		4
Adult	43	32	200	275
Subadult			24	24
Indeterminate			37	37
Total	72	72	285	429

a. Mean age

females is completed (Krogman and İşcan 1986; St. Hoyme and İşcan 1989; Stewart 1979). Visual estimates of sex that rely on robusticity and skeletal architecture are generally used for the cranium, mandible, and pelvis (Krogman and İşcan 1986; Phenice 1969; Stewart 1979; Ubelaker 1989). Quantitative methods that reduce the error of visual estimates have contributed to correcting problems of accuracy in sex estimation. Those methods focus on the cranium (Giles 1970; Giles and Eliot 1963) and the femur and humerus head (Dittrick and Suchey 1986) and employ discriminant functions to increase the accuracy of sex estimation. Most researchers agree that problems remain in the accurate estimation of sex using skeletons (Konigsberg and Hens 1998; Milner et al. 2000; Weiss 1973).

Sex estimation for the Palmer population was performed for individuals at or greater than the age of fifteen (table 3.2). Sex estimates were made by considering visual cranial and mandibular morphology ($n = 58$), pelvic architecture ($n = 45$), femur head diameter ($n = 33$), humerus head diameter ($n = 6$), and postcranial robusticity ($n = 2$). Robusticity, except in the extreme cases, has substantial overlap for males and females; thus, only in very gracile or very robust cases was robusticity used as a sole criterion for sex estimation. Such a practice results in fewer cases of sex estimation, but those estimates are more reliable.

Analysis of Palmer Population Structure: Demography

Model life tables constructed from living populations are often used for comparison with archaeological skeletal series, both to assess bias in the sample and to make interpretations about past population demography (Coale and Demeny 1966; Meindl and Russell 1998; Milner et al. 2000; Weiss 1973). For this study, one foraging population and one horticultural population were chosen in order to characterize the population structure of two different economic systems, following the strategy of Milner and coworkers (1989) and providing a measure of expected demography against which to measure the Palmer population. The model life tables that most closely approximate the gross reproductive rate (GRR; the total number of female offspring produced, on average, by a female approaching the oldest age) and life expectancy of the Ju/'hoansi and Yanomamo populations were selected from the model West series (Coale and Demeny 1966).

Among the populations of foragers with the most complete ethnographic information are the !Kung (Ju/'hoansi) from south central Africa (Milner et al. 1989). They have a life expectancy of about 32.5 years and gross reproductive rate of about two (Milner et al. 1989). They are not coastal foragers, but there is little ethnographic data regarding coastal foragers (Kelly 1995); they therefore represent the best model available. As well, there is some question whether coastal vs. inland foraging results in significantly different demographic patterns. The Yanomamo are swidden agriculturalists from southern Venezuela and adjacent northern Brazil. The Yanomamo have a higher fertility rate than Ju/'hoansi, with a gross reproductive rate of about 3.5. Their life expectancy rate was set at 20 years by Milner and coworkers (1989) in order to yield a stationary population given their high fertility rate. Their actual life expectancy is considerably higher.

As figures 3.5 and 3.6 illustrate, neither of the living populations approximates the age-at-death profile of the Palmer sample. Per figure 3.5, the percentage of individuals between birth and four years of age is much lower for the Palmer population than for the Yanomamo, as are those dying after 50 years of age. Ages 30–50 are overenumerated at Palmer as compared with the Yanomamo. Figure 3.6 shows that the percentage of individuals between birth and four years of age is much lower for the Palmer population than for the Ju/'hoansi, as are those dying after 50 years of age. Ages 30–50 are overenumerated at Palmer as compared with the Ju/'hoansi.

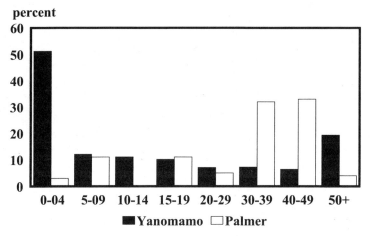

Fig. 3.5. Yanomamo age-at-death compared with Palmer.

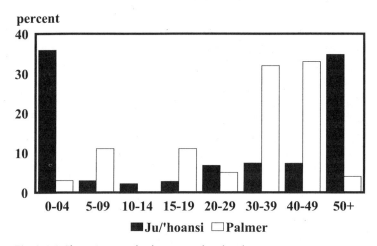

Fig. 3.6. Ju/'hoansi age-at-death compared with Palmer.

Further comparisons also indicate infant underenumeration. The age estimates for the Palmer population (table 3.2) indicate that the sample has severe infant underenumeration. The number of subadults under the age of 5 (n = 3) comprises less than 1% of the total sample. Among the reasons for low frequencies of subadult skeletons in preindustrial mortuary samples are (1) the postmortem deterioration of the smaller and thinner bones of subadults, and (2) differential interments for subadults as compared to adults. Regardless of the reason for a small number of subadults at Palmer, the underenumeration of subadults creates problems for demographic analysis (Angel 1969; Moore et al. 1975; Pfeiffer 1983, 1986; Pfeiffer and Fairgrieve 1994; Saunders 1991, 2000; Saunders et al. 1995; Weiss 1973).

Several modifications of skeletal series with subadult underenumeration have been suggested (e.g., Swedlund 1975). Proportional assignment of all unaged individuals based on the individuals with reliable age estimates has been used (Asch 1976; Larsen 1982; Vradenburg et al. 1997). A second method is to add subadults to match subadult proportions in the burial contexts (i.e., to apportion the unaged subadults; Storey and Hirth 1997). A third method is to recalculate subadult representation based on adjacent, contemporary, larger skeletal series (Storey and Hirth 1997).

Although these methods, especially that of apportioning adults, are commonly used (Milner et al. 1989), they are methods that deflate the interpretive value of the demographic reconstruction. Consequently, they are not used here, although the age and sex data are presented in table 3.2 to enable further demographic estimates by other researchers.

Summary

For more than a century, the prehistoric inhabitants of the Palmer site have intrigued historians and archaeologists. In 1867, John Webb sent collections of human bones, pottery, and tools from the site to the Smithsonian Institution. Between 1959 and 1962, Ripley and Adelaide Bullen excavated the shell middens and burial mound. Later excavations in 1991 produced substantial environmental and subsistence information.

The data derived from the above excavations inform us that the prehistoric Palmer inhabitants focused their subsistence on local coastal resources, with some terrestrial plant use but little use of terrestrial animals. The fish and shellfish were predominantly from near-shore environments, particularly adjacent sea grass beds, and were collected by nets and perhaps by hook and line. Sharks were captured as well, and their skin and teeth used as tools. Scallops, clams, and oysters were collected during all seasons from sea grass beds in Little Sarasota Bay. Plants found in the midden deposits include nuts, fruits, and palms that all indicate plant use during at least two seasons.

The burial mound included the skeletal remains of 429 individuals, several dogs, and an alligator buried with sawfish vertebrae. Artifacts and radiocarbon dates indicate that the mound was used primarily between A.D. 500 and 800. Most burials were flexed interments of a single individual. The age distribution of the 429 individuals analyzed from the

Palmer site is clearly biased toward adults. Comparison with two well-documented living populations, the horticulturalist Yanomamo and the foraging Ju/'hoansi, illustrates this point. Consequently, although age estimates are useful for examining the patterns of pathological lesions, their use for addressing issues of fertility, mortality, and population growth or decline is unwarranted. In chapter 4 I report the method and theory for paleopathological research, and then the results obtained for the Palmer population regarding health and disease. Nutritional quantity and quality are important factors in human health and will be discussed within the context of dental and skeletal pathology in chapter 4 and later chapters.

4

Assessing Health and Disease at Palmer

Bioarchaeologists are interested in the biological aspects of the lives of past humans. They use methods of dietary reconstruction and analysis of pathological lesions to establish the status of nutrition and disease, and then they place those interpretations within a cultural and environmental context in order to make statements about past human biology and behavior.

In this chapter I examine several markers of health, describing briefly how each type of dental or skeletal lesion informs us about health, and then present the data from analysis of the Palmer remains by age and sex subsets. Finally, I summarize the dietary reconstruction that is more thoroughly presented in appendix E by Lynette Norr and in appendix F by Mark Teaford.

General Methods of Pathology Analysis

As explained in chapter 1, pathological lesions are used to estimate the prevalence of a number of health conditions and behaviors that affect the skeleton and dentition. Pathological lesions and hard tissue alterations can be grouped into those that are informative about diet and masticatory behavior (carious lesions, alveolar infection, premortem tooth loss, dental chipping, and dental enamel microwear), metabolic disruption (enamel hypoplasia and porotic hyperostosis), infectious disease (periosteal reactions and osteomyelitis), and lifestyle and activity (osteoarthritis, external auditory exostoses, trauma).

All dental and skeletal elements from Palmer Mound were examined macroscopically for pathological lesions and hard tissue alterations. Some elements required further examination to discern the microscopic character of lesions or to make a differential diagnosis between two or more similar conditions. For those cases, a 5–10X magnifying lens was used and/or radiographs were taken with a Hewlett-Packard cabinet Faxitron. Only elements with a representative portion (those that were not extremely fragmentary) were included as evidence of the absence of pathological changes.

Most pathological lesions discussed in this chapter are recorded by individual. In some cases a comparison by element was conducted when such comparisons facilitated interpretation. Pathological lesion frequencies, when reported in tables, are presented in two subtables: the first presents frequency counts and uses total counts to summarize data, and the second presents percentages and uses the median to summarize data.

All adult skeletal measurements were taken for complete or nearly complete skeletal elements. Formal measurement analysis is not conducted in this study, but the mean measurements are included (appendixes C and D) to facilitate anthropometric studies performed by other researchers. In cases where not all measurements were possible, those that could be taken or estimated were performed. This resulted in the measurement of 18 male and 22 female crania, plus 33 male, 44 female, and 24 indeterminate sex mandibles (appendix C). Postcranial measurements were taken for several individuals, and the measurements by element and sex are presented in appendix D.

Diet and Masticatory Behavior

Carious Lesions

Dental caries is a disease process that causes focal demineralization of the tooth enamel known as carious lesions. The demineralization is caused by organic acids produced during bacterial fermentation of dietary carbohydrates, particularly sugars (Hildebolt et al. 1988, 1989; Hillson 1996; Larsen 1997; Larsen et al. 1991; Milner 1984; Powell 1985). A combination of biological and cultural factors contributes to the cariogenic process, including indigenous oral bacteria (e.g., *Streptococcus mutans* and *Lactobacillus acidophilus*), salivary proteins and inorganic salts, developmental tooth defects, dental attrition, age, heredity, tooth damage, food texture, and diet (Larsen et al. 1991; Leverett 1982; Milner 1984; Newbrun 1978, 1982; Powell 1985; White 1975; Woodward and Walker 1994). Generally, the posterior molars and premolars are more susceptible to caries than the anterior incisors and canines because of their larger size and numerous fissures (fig. 4.1).

All teeth (n = 4,027; table 4.1 and appendix A) were examined for carious lesions; only nine (0.2%) had carious lesions. They were from

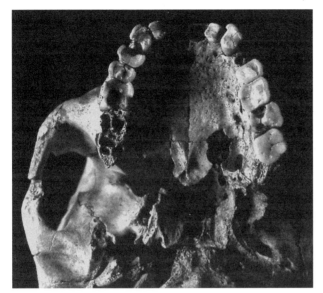

Fig. 4.1. Example of carious lesions of burial 1Z from Baum, North Carolina.

eight adult individuals; thus, eight adult individuals (3%) had carious lesions on at least one tooth (table 4.1). Dental individuals were calculated on the basis of dental remains: 59 males, 54 females, 178 indeterminate sex adults, and 27 subadults. Only one individual had more than one carious tooth. Males (n = 2; 4%) were more often affected compared with females (n = 1; 2%).

Dental Chipping

Dental chipping appears to be common among coastal populations (Costa 1982; Higginbotham 1999; Hutchinson 2002a; Milner and Larsen 1991; Turner and Cadien 1969). Small step fractures originating from the occlusal surface of the tooth are the usual type of damage (fig. 4.2). Fractures of larger portions of the enamel can result in the exposure of the pulp cavity of the tooth and eventual infection of the tooth and surrounding alveolar bone (Hutchinson 1999; fig. 4.2).

Dental chipping results either from dietary inclusions, such as sand, or from the use of teeth as tools. Such tool use has been documented for the anterior teeth of coastal populations in the Virgin Islands (Larsen et al. 1998), and also for interior populations in the western United States (Larsen 1985; Ubelaker et al. 1970). Occlusal and interproximal grooves on the anterior dentition of individuals from populations inhabiting the Georgia coast (Larsen 1985) and British Columbia (Cybulski 1974) may

Table 4.1. Frequency and percentage of individuals affected
by dental pathology by age and sex

Frequency

Age	Male	Female	Indeterminate	Total
Subadult				
Carious lesions	0	0	0	0
Dental chipping	0	0	1	1
Enamel hypoplasia	0	0	6	6
Total[a]	0	0	7	7
Adult				
Carious lesions	2	1	5	8
Dental chipping	14	19	22	55
Enamel hypoplasia	16	17	33	66
Total[a]	32	37	60	129
Total individuals[b]	54	59	178	291

Percentage

Age	Male	Female	Indeterminate	Median
Subadult				
Carious lesions	0	0	0	0
Dental chipping	0	0	4	c
Enamel hypoplasia	0	0	75	75
Adult				
Carious lesions	4	2	3	3
Dental chipping	26	32	12	26
Enamel hypoplasia	80	71	81	80

a. Individuals may be affected by multiple pathological conditions.
b. Number of adult individuals observed for carious lesions and dental chipping,
not enamel hypoplasia.
c. Too few cases to calculate median.

be associated with the production of items such as fish nets, baskets, and
bags. There has been little discussion, however, regarding the relationship
of tooth grooving or dental chipping to later dental infection.

As with carious lesions, all teeth (n = 4,027; table 4.1 and appendix A)
were examined macroscopically for dental chipping and other modifications. One subadult (4%) exhibited chipping on at least one maxillary
tooth. Fifty-five adult individuals (19%) had dental chipping on at least
one tooth (table 4.1). Females (n = 19; 32%) were affected slightly more
often than males (n = 14; 26%). No teeth exhibited occlusal or interproximal grooves associated with the use of the teeth as tools.

Fig. 4.2. Example of dental chipping of right mandibular molar of individual from Useppa Island, Florida.

Alveolar Infection, Premortem Tooth Loss, and Alveolar Resorption

Alveolar infection (periodontal infection) often arises from infection of the teeth that spreads into the surrounding gingival and osseous tissues (Powell 1985). Premortem tooth loss, although a natural event that occurs during the aging process, is also often a result of infection of the teeth (Powell 1985).

All mandibles ($n = 221$) and maxillae ($n = 131$) were examined for alveolar infections and premortem tooth loss (including resorption). As is the case with dental caries, the process often affects the entire dentition; therefore, quantifying the number of individuals affected is more meaningful than quantifying the number of affected teeth or tooth locations. For subadults, 20 mandibles and 10 maxillae were examined for alveolar infection, premortem tooth loss, and resorption. No evidence of any of the conditions was noted.

For adults, 201 mandibles (45 males, 56 females, 100 indeterminate sex) and 121 maxillae (31 males, 39 females, 51 indeterminate sex) were examined for alveolar infection, premortem tooth loss, and resorption. Of the total adults, 96 individuals shared mandibles and maxillae, yielding a

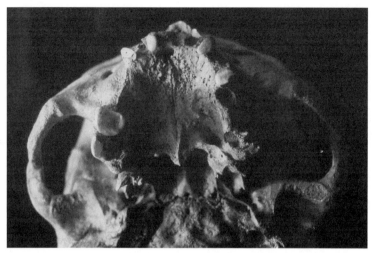

Fig. 4.3. Premortem tooth loss and resorption of the maxilla of individual 223 (FMNH #95489).

Table 4.2. Frequency and percentage of individuals affected by alveolar infection, premortem tooth loss, and alveolar resorption by sex[a]

Frequency

Pathology	Male	Female	Indeterminate	Total
Alveolar infection	7	12	12	31
Premortem tooth loss	15	18	25	58
Resorption	13	17	22	52
Total[b]	35	47	59	141
Total individuals Represented by maxilla/ mandible combinations	51	58	117	226

Percentage[c]

Pathology	Male	Female	Indeterminate	Median
Alveolar infection	14	21	10	14
Premortem tooth loss	29	31	21	29
Resorption	25	29	19	25

a. No subadults exhibited any of the pathological conditions.

b. Total adults; individuals may be affected by multiple pathological conditions.

c. Of the total mandibles and maxillae, 96 of each were shared by single individuals, yielding a total of 226 individuals with mandibles and/or maxillae.

total sample of 226 adult individuals (51 male, 58 female, 117 indeterminate sex) represented by maxillae and/or mandibles.

Alveolar infections were noted for 31 adults, (14%; table 4.2) with females (n = 12; 21%) more affected than males (n = 7; 14%). Premortem tooth loss (fig. 4.3) was noted for 58 adults (26%; table 4.2) with females (n = 18; 31%) more affected than males (n = 15; 29%). Resorption of the alveolar bone following tooth loss was noted for 52 adults (23%; table 4.2) with females (n = 17; 29%) more often affected than males (n = 13; 25%).

Metabolic Disruption

Enamel Hypoplasias

Enamel hypoplasias are circumferential lines or pits caused by a cessation in growth during the formation of the enamel layer of teeth (Larsen 1987: fig. 6.5). Hypoplasias are caused by disruption of the enamel-producing cells by environmental insult (Goodman and Rose 1990, 1991). Many singular factors leading to disruption have been isolated in laboratory studies (Kreshover 1944; Kreshover and Clough 1953a,b; Suckling et al. 1983, 1986), but systemic metabolic stress produced by the interactive effects of malnutrition and disease is often a cause.

Because enamel hypoplasias result from so many individual or combined factors, they are usually interpreted as nonspecific indicators of stress due to an unspecified etiology (Goodman and Rose 1990, 1991; Kreshover 1960; Skinner and Goodman 1992). The utility of enamel hypoplasias as a record of metabolic stress lies in the permanence of their formation. Unlike other parts of the skeleton, which are remodeled throughout an individual's lifetime, dental enamel does not remodel once formed, and only dental attrition is responsible for eliminating the lesions.

Teeth from the Palmer population were examined for enamel hypoplasia if: (1) at least two of the anterior teeth (incisors and canines) were present, (2) not more than half of the tooth crown was worn, and (3) calculus did not obscure observation. Observation was performed using a 5–10X magnifying lens. Hypoplasias were recorded for presence or absence. Of the eight subadult individuals examined for hypoplasias, six (75%) were affected (table 4.1). Eighty-five adult individuals (20 males, 24 females, and 41 indeterminate sex) were examined for hypoplasia, with 66 (78%) exhibiting the defects (fig. 4.4). Females (n = 17; 71%) were less often affected than males (n = 16; 80%).

Fig. 4.4. Enamel hypoplasias of the maxillary dentition of individual 395 (FMNH #97571).

Porotic Hyperostosis

Porotic hyperostosis refers to the porous alterations resulting from the expansion of trabecular bone that is stimulated by the need for increased red blood cell production (Ortner and Putschar 1985; Stuart-Macadam 1985, 1987a,b). It is symptomatic of several conditions that interfere with iron metabolism. The lesions of the eye orbit (*cribra orbitalia*) that are due to the same etiology are included here under the term porotic hyperostosis.

Among the conditions that cause porotic hyperostosis are sickle-cell anemia, thalassemia, G6PD deficiency, iron deficiency anemia, parasitic infections of the gastrointestinal tract, dietary constituents, and cyanotic congenital heart disease (Angel 1964; Cohen and Armelagos 1984; El-Najjar 1977; El-Najjar et al. 1975; Hengen 1961; Layrisse and Roche 1964; Mensforth et al. 1978; Moseley 1965; Reinhard 1996; Steinbock 1976; Stuart-Macadam 1985, 1987a,b).

At one time, anthropologists focused on diet, particularly diets with an emphasis on maize consumption, as a major cause of iron-deficiency anemia in the New World, but further research has revealed a number of other potential causes. Iron withholding by humans and other vertebrates occurs at potential sites of microbial invasion to combat infection, during inflammation, and in the intestinal tract during infectious disease (Kent 1986, 1992; Mensforth et al. 1978; Weinberg 1992). Reinhard (1992) has further suggested that parasite-induced intestinal bleeding accounts for some cases of iron deficiency. Although parasitization is difficult to prove without coprolites containing parasites, evidence such as range of occurrence or analogous contemporary coastal populations that commonly suffer from intestinal parasites obtained from fish and shellfish (e.g., Japan; Desowitz 1981) may be the only sources for interpretation. In a study of nonagricultural coastal California populations, Walker (1986) suggested that the origin of the parasites was contaminated water supplies.

All available subadult and adult crania ($n = 309$) were observed for porotic hyperostosis. Presence or absence of porotic hyperostosis in the Palmer population was assessed using a 5–10X magnifying lens and recorded in the two categories of healing or active lesions. Of the 21 subadult individuals examined for porotic hyperostosis, two (10%) exhibited healing lesions (table 4.3). For adults, 288 individuals (55 males, 64 females, and 169 indeterminate sex) were examined, with 83 (29%) having porotic hyperostosis (figs. 4.5, 4.6). Males were most often affected ($n = 31$; 56%) compared with females ($n = 25$; 39%).

I would issue some caution with regard to interpreting the porotic hyperostosis results, however. Most lesions affected adults and were in the process of healing—in only a few cases were the lesions unremodeled. Furthermore, in a recent study of mission period Florida Atlantic coast populations, Schultz and coworkers (2001) found that microscopic analysis revealed discrepancies in the macroscopic determination of porotic hyperostosis and cribra orbitalia.

Table 4.3. Frequency and percentage of individuals affected by porotic hyperostosis[a] by age category and sex

Frequency

Age	Male	Female	Indeterminate	Total
Subadult healing	0	0	2	2
Adult healing	31	25	27	83
Indeterminate	0	0	0	0
Total	31	25	29	85
Total adults observed	55	64	169	288
Total subadults observed	1	1	19	21

Percentage

Age	Male	Female	Indeterminate	Median
Subadult healing	0	0	10	[b]
Adult healing	56	39	16	39
Indeterminate	0	0	0	0

a. Porotic hyperostosis and cribra orbitalia are combined.

b. Too few cases to calculate median.

Fig. 4.5. Healing porotic hyperostosis of the cranium of individual 364 (FMNH #97539).

Fig. 4.6. Healing cribra orbitalia of the eye orbits of individual 449 (FMNH #97623).

Infectious Disease

Inflammatory and Resorptive Responses (Periosteal Reactions, Osteomyelitis)

A variety of stimuli that include trauma, infection, and injury irritate the periosteum (the outer membrane covering bone), stimulating the formation of woven bone (Ortner and Putschar 1985; Steinbock 1976; Walker et al. 1997). The proliferative bone that grows adjacent to the periosteum is often referred to as a *periosteal reaction*. Osteomyelitis involves infection from a variety of organisms including bacteria, viruses, fungi, or rickettsiae.

Three basic mechanisms allow infection to reach the bone: (1) hematogenous spread via the bloodstream from a remote site of infection, such as the urinary tract, skin, or other organ; (2) tissue invasion from a contiguous source of infection, such as the soft tissues, teeth, or sinuses; and (3) direct infection through a puncture wound or operative procedure (Zimmerman and Kelley 1982). The skeletal changes in osteomyelitis can involve the periosteum as well, and the resulting pathology is termed by some *osteo-periostitis* (Steinbock 1976). Because the primary stimulus for bone proliferation is often unknown, periostitis and osteomyelitis are often interpreted as nonspecific infections (Larsen 1997).

Resorption of the skeleton can occur as part of the normal cycle of skeletal maintenance, such as the reorientation of the bone architecture to meet specific physiological stresses or the remodeling of woven bone into lamellar bone. Resorption is also responsible for the release of calcium into the bloodstream in order to maintain calcium-phosphate homeostasis. Several diseases are responsible for lytic destruction of the skeleton such as tuberculosis, leprosy, and several of the mycotic (fungal) diseases (Ortner and Putschar 1985; Powell 1991b; Steinbock 1976). Proliferative responses are often found in combination with resorptive responses, and the resulting lesions are called *perio-lysis* when confined to the outer cortex and *osteo-perio-lysis* when the inner cortex or medullary cavity is involved.

All cranial elements and long bones from Palmer were examined for proliferative and resorptive lesions. Considering all proliferative and resorptive skeletal lesions together, 24 adults (6%) were affected by these pathological changes (table 4.4; figs. 4.7, 4.8). Females were much more frequently affected (*n* = 10; 14%) than were males (*n* = 6; 8%).

The frequency and percentage of proliferative and resorptive responses by element is presented in table 4.5. Periostitis, osteomyelitis, and resorption are often manifestations of a specific disease process, and patterns in

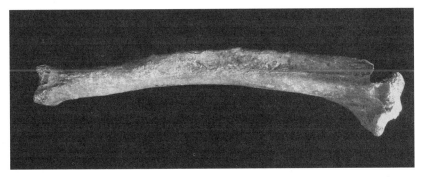

Fig. 4.7. Periostitis of the right tibia of individual 204 (FMNH #95473).

Fig. 4.8. Osteomyelitis due to compound fracture of the left tibia of burial 265, individual 1 (FMNH #95530).

Table 4.4. Frequency and percentage of individuals affected by periostitis, osteomyelitis, and lytic response by sex[a]

Frequency

Element	Male	Female	Indeterminate	Total
Active periostitis	1	0	2	3
Healing periostitis	3	2	2	7
Perio-lysis	0	1	0	1
Osteomyelitis	1	0	1	2
Osteo-periostitis	1	5	3	9
Osteo-perio-lysis	0	2	0	2
Total[b]	6	10	8	24
Total individuals observed[c]	71	71	241	383

Percentage

Element	Male	Female	Indeterminate	Median
Active periostitis	1	0	1	1
Healing periostitis	4	3	1	3
Perio-lysis	0	1	0	d
Osteomyelitis	1	0	0.5	0.75
Osteo-periostitis	1	7	1.5	1.5
Osteo-perio-lysis	0	3	0	d
Individuals affected	8	14	3	8

a. No subadults exhibited any of these pathological conditions.
b. Nine individuals exhibit combinations of these pathological conditions in multiple elements.
c. Adults only.
d. Too few cases to calculate median.

lesion appearance, skeletal element distribution, sex, and age are often crucial for making a diagnosis of specific diseases. The patterns of these lesions and their interpretation are discussed below.

Table 4.5. Frequency and percentage of periostitis, osteomyelitis, and lytic response by element and sex[a]

Frequency

Element	Male	Female	Indeterminate	Total
Active and healed periostitis				
Tibia	3	2	3	8
Fibula	2	0	1	3
Clavicle	1	0	1	2
Humerus	1	0	0	1
Total[b]	7	2	5	14
Perio-lysis				
Tibia	0	2	0	2
Fibula	0	1	0	1
Clavicle	0	1	0	1
Scapula	0	1	0	1
Humerus	0	1	1	1
Ribs	0	1	0	1
Total[b]	0	7	0	7
Osteomyelitis				
Humerus	1	0	0	1
Tibia	0	0	1	1
Total[b]	1	0	1	2
Osteo-periostitis				
Humerus	0	2	0	2
Ulna	1	3	1	5
Radius	0	1	1	2
Femur	0	1	0	1
Tibia	0	7	4	11
Fibula	0	1	2	3
Clavicle	0	1	0	1
Total[b]	1	16	8	25
Osteo-perio-lysis				
Ulna	0	1	0	1
Tibia	0	1	0	1
Fibula	0	1	0	1
Clavicle	0	1	0	1
Total[b]	0	4	0	4

continued

Table 4.5 continued

Percentage

Element	Male	Female	Indeterminate	Median
Active and healed periostitis				
Tibia	6	3	4	4
Fibula	5	0	3	4
Clavicle	3	0	3	3
Humerus	1	0	0	c
Perio-lysis				
Tibia	0	4	0	c
Fibula	0	2	0	c
Clavicle	0	2	0	c
Scapula	0	2	0	c
Humerus	0	1	0	c
Ribs	0	2	0	c
Osteomyelitis				
Humerus	2	0	0	c
Tibia	0	0	1	c
Osteo-periostitis				
Humerus	0	2	0	c
Ulna	1	3	1	1
Radius	0	2	2	2
Femur	0	1	0	c
Tibia	0	9	5	5
Fibula	0	2	6	4
Clavicle	0	2	0	c
Osteo-perio-lysis				
Ulna	0	1	0	c
Tibia	0	1	0	c
Fibula	0	2	0	c
Clavicle	0	2	0	c

a. No subadults exhibited any of these pathological conditions.

b. Nine individuals exhibit multiple affected elements.

c. Too few cases to calculate median.

Specific Infectious Disease

A limited number of diseases affect bone, and they do so only after chronic infection (Ortner and Aufderheide 1991; Ortner and Putschar 1985; Roberts and Manchester 1995; Steinbock 1976; Zimmerman and Kelley 1982). Recognition of specific diseases in the Palmer population was possible either by presence of lesions that occur for a specific disease (i.e., they are *pathognomonic* for that disease) or by the patterning of lesion appearance and skeletal affliction. For individuals not having pathognomonic lesions, systemic infections were delineated on the basis of more than one skeletal element affected by similar pathological lesions.

Fourteen adult individuals (4%) from the Palmer population were classified as having systemic infections. Females were affected (*n* = 6; 8%) slightly more frequently than males (*n* = 5; 7%).

Cranial pathognomonic lesions and postcranial lesion morphology and distribution supported the diagnosis of one specific disease process for many of the individuals with systemic infections: treponemal infection (treponematosis). The four treponemal diseases are pinta, yaws, endemic syphilis, and venereal syphilis; considerable controversy has previously centered on whether these are four different diseases caused by different bacteria of the genus *Treponema,* or whether they are merely clinical manifestations of the same disease caused by one species of bacteria, *Treponema pallidum.* In all four syndromes, there is considerable variation in lesion patterning and form, and distinguishing the diseases based on those indicators is difficult. Recent advances in molecular detection of the diseases, however, has shown DNA differences in the *Treponema pallidum* spirochete (Centurion-Lara et al. 1998; Kolman et al. 1999).

Credit for first diagnosing treponematosis in the Palmer population goes to Adelaide Bullen (1972), who published a seminal article on the presence of the disease process in Florida Native American populations. In that article, Bullen focused much of her discussion on a middle-aged adult female from Palmer, individual 352 (FMNH #97527) with extensive skeletal modification attributed to treponemal infection. Ellis Kerley of the Armed Forces Institute of Pathology also examined the bones and concurred with a diagnosis of treponematosis (Bullen 1972).

Bullen noted that the skull had areas of "inflammatory destruction combined with the formulation of periosteal new bone" (Bullen 1972: 141; fig. 4.9). The frontal bone exhibited several coalescing stellate scars, one of which was an active, unhealed lytic lesion. The left tibia was extensively affected by proliferative periosteal bone (fig. 4.10). Other postcranial elements affected include the left scapula, clavicles, sternum, ribs, right humerus, and left fibula (Bullen 1972). Radiographs of other Palmer long bones were depicted in the article (left tibia, right and left fibulae, right and left humeri; Bullen 1972:fig. 8), but no discussion was presented as to their burial affiliation. My examination of this individual revealed no further pathological lesions.

Bullen (1972:150) states that of the other affected elements "[o]ther

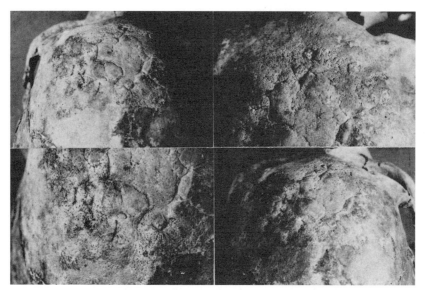

Fig. 4.9. Four views of stellate scars on the cranium of individual 352 (FMNH #97527) (From Bullen 1972:fig. 5. Reproduced with permission of Florida Museum of Natural History.)

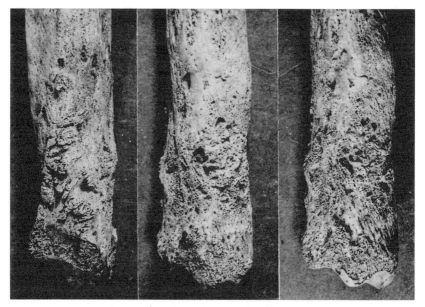

Fig. 4.10. Close-up view of the distal end of the left tibia from individual 352 (FMNH #97527). *Left to right*: lateral view, postero-medial view, medial view. (From Bullen 1972: fig. 7. Reproduced with permission of Florida Museum of Natural History.)

bones of the Palmer series were also diagnosed as syphilitic by Kerley. These will be included in the final report on the Palmer site. It is pertinent here to point out that [FMNH #] 97527—while the most striking case in this series—was not the only person with pathology diagnosed as syphilis."

Unfortunately, the final report was never written. I located excellent photographs of a left humerus and right fibula exhibiting periostitis characteristic of treponemal infection in the photographic archives of the Florida Museum of Natural History for burial 9 (FMNH #97507), but neither element was in the collection when I examined it. I have incorporated both elements into the total element counts used for quantifying periostitis based on the photographs.

In addition to the burials noted by Bullen (1972) in her initial analysis of the Palmer population, several other individuals I examined exhibited pathological modifications indicative of treponemal infection. Including individual 352, six adult individuals exhibited stellate or probable stellate lesions of the cranium (2%; 3 males, 2 females, 1 indeterminate sex). Males were most often affected ($n = 3$; 5%) compared with females ($n = 2$; 3%). One of these, individual 60 (FMNH #95399), exhibited several healed stellate lesions of the frontal (fig. 4.11).

Several long bones were affected by periosteal new bone, resorption, or combinations of those pathological modifications (figs. 4.12, 4.13). One individual, 215B,C (FMNH #95483), exhibited proliferative and resorptive changes in the right clavicle, left radius, right ulna, right femur,

Fig. 4.11. Stellate lesions of the cranium of individual 60 (FMNH #95399).

and right and left tibiae (figs. 4.12, 4.13), and had medullary closure of the right ulna, a classic manifestation of chronic treponemal infection (Hutchinson 1993a; Ortner and Putschar 1985; Steinbock 1976). Another individual (218, FMNH #95486) exhibited extreme proliferative bone in

Fig. 4.12. Periosteal apposition of individual 215 B, C (FMNH #95483). *Top to bottom:* left tibia; right radius (*left*) and right clavicle (*right*); fibula (*left*) and left ulna (*right*); right tibia.

Fig. 4.13. Radiograph of postcranial elements of individual 215 B,C (FMNH #95483). *Right to left diagonally:* radius, ulna, right tibia, left femur, left tibia, fibula (*top*) and right clavicle (*bottom*).

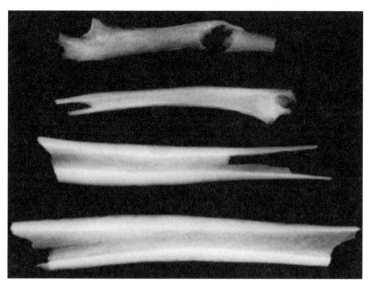

Fig. 4.14. Radiograph of proliferative responses of right ulna, left tibia, and right tibia, individual 218 (FMNH #95486), and fracture of the left ulna of individual 232 (FMNH #95499). *Top to bottom:* left ulna, individual 232 (FMNH #95499); right ulna, left tibia, and right tibia, individual 218 (FMNH #95486).

both tibiae and the right ulna (fig. 4.14). The minimum number of individuals affected by treponemal infection in the Palmer population is estimated to be 13.

Sinus infections were observed for one male and two females, but, as the number of observable maxillary sinuses is difficult to assess, percentages of individuals affected are not available. Although not an infectious disease process, button osteomas were observed on ten crania (3%) of adult individuals. Males (*n* = 5; 9%) were affected equally as often as females (*n* = 5; 8%).

Lifestyle and Activity

Osteoarthritis

Biological anthropologists often use osteoarthritis as a measure of physical activity as it relates to the tasks of food gathering or producing, transportation, construction of houses and adjacent support facilities, and numerous other tasks (Jurmain 1977, 1999). Osteoarthritis results from a combination of predisposing factors that include metabolism, bone density, infection, heredity, sex, and nutrition (Jurmain 1977, 1999; Larsen 1997). It is clear that physical activity and mechanical stress are the primary factors that advance bone tissue degeneration. The destruction of articular cartilage of synovial joints leads to such bone changes as peripheral osteophytes, porosity of the joint surface, and eburnation of the joint (Ortner and Putschar 1985; Rogers and Waldron 1995). Degeneration of the vertebral disks (osteoarthrosis) often results in bony lipping around the margins of the vertebral bodies (Larsen 1997).

All available cranial and postcranial elements were examined on the articular surfaces and margins for osteophytic lipping, degeneration of the vertebral bodies (Schmorl's nodes), resorption and bone loss, and eburna-

Table 4.6. Frequency and percentage of degenerative joint disease by element and sex[a]

Frequency

Element	Male	Female	Indeterminate	Total
Ulna	1	0	0	1
Radius	1	0	1	2
Humerus	3	3	0	6
Hands	1	1	0	2
Patella	1	0	3	4
Feet	2	3	3	8
Vertebrae	11	13	3	27
Scapula	1	1	0	2
Ribs	1	0	0	1
Mandible	0	0	1	1
Total[b]	22	21	11	54
Individuals affected	14	17	10	41

Percentage

Element	Male	Female	Indeterminate	Median
Ulna	2	0	0	c
Radius	0	0	1	c
Humerus	4	3	0	3.5
Hands	3	2	0	2.5
Patella	3	0	7	5
Feet	6	6	6	6
Vertebrae	36	33	8	33
Scapula	2	2	0	2
Ribs	4	0	0	c
Mandible	0	0	2	c
Individuals affected	20	24	4	20

a. No subadults exhibited degenerative joint disease.

b. Total adults; 11 individuals (5 males, 3 females, 3 indeterminate sex) exhibit degenerative joint disease in multiple elements.

c. Too few individuals for median calculation.

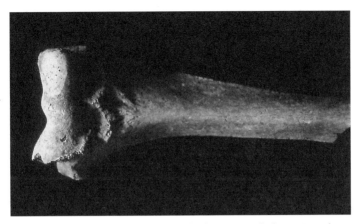

Fig. 4.15. Degenerative joint disease of the humerus with eburnation of individual 225 (FMNH #95492).

tion resulting from bone rubbing on bone. Those observations provide information on mechanical and behavioral stresses. Pathological modifications were noted for 41 adults (11%; 14 males, 17 females, and 10 indeterminate sex; table 4.6; fig. 4.15). The frequency of affected males (n = 14; 20%) was slightly less than that of females (n = 17; 24%). Two males and one indeterminate sex individual were affected by mandibular fossae modifications due to temporal-mandibular joint disease (TMJ).

Trauma

Skeletal trauma is often used for reconstructing behavioral activities and sometimes environmental hazards (Eisenberg and Hutchinson 1996). Weapon wounds are probably the most dramatic traumatic lesions. These include depression fractures of the cranium (Frayer 1997; Lambert 1994, 1997; Martin 1997; Milner et al. 1991; Robb 1997; Walker 1989, 1997; Wilkinson 1997), wounds resulting from weapons that penetrate skeletal elements (often found embedded, such as projectile points) (Lambert 1994, 1997), soft-tissue penetration with limited skeletal involvement (e.g., cut marks from knife wounds), and wounds from slashing metal weapons (Humphreys and Hutchinson 2001; Hutchinson 1996; Merbs 1989; Tucker et al. 2001).

Fourteen adults (4%) exhibited some form of trauma. The frequency and percentage of trauma by element and sex is presented in table 4.7. Males (n = 7; 10%) were affected more often than females (n = 4; 6%). Fractures of the long bones were observed for six adult individuals (table 4.8). The fractures, although healed, were generally extreme and misaligned when healed (figs. 4.14, 4.16–4.19). Most commonly, arm elements were affected, although one tibia exhibited a compound fracture that had resulted in osteomyelitis (fig. 4.17). Descriptions of the individual trauma cases with location, shape, and measurements are presented in table 4.8. Males (n = 3; 4%) were affected more frequently than females (n = 1; 1%) by postcranial trauma, an interpretation that warrants caution given the small number of cases, but that is congruent with the cranial blunt trauma observations.

Cranial blunt trauma, generally healed, was observed for 10 adult individuals (3%; table 4.7). Males (n = 6; 11%) were affected more than twice as often as females (n = 3; 5%). The trauma was usually healed (figs. 4.20–4.23) and singular, although one male (individual 446, FMNH #97620) had three blunt depression fractures. One female (individual 410; FMNH #97586) exhibited a depression fracture in the process of healing (fig. 4.22). The cranial vault was pushed into the cranial cavity (fig. 4.23). Of the ten cases of blunt cranial trauma lesions, six were located on the pari-

Table 4.7. Frequency and percentage of trauma by element and sex[a]

Frequency

Element	Male	Female	Indeterminate	Total
Fracture				
Ulna	2	0	0	2
Radius	1	0	0	1
Tibia	0	0	1	1
Humerus	0	1	1	2
Cranial blunt trauma	6	3	1	10
Total[b]	9	4	3	16
Individuals affected	7	4	3	14

Percentage

Element	Male	Female	Indeterminate	Median
Fracture				
Ulna	3	0	0	c
Radius	2	0	0	c
Tibia	0	0	1	c
Humerus	0	1	1	1
Cranial blunt trauma	11	5	1	5
Individuals affected	10	6	1	6

a. No subadults exhibited any of the pathologies.

b. Two individuals exhibit trauma to the cranium and one postcranial element.

c. Too few elements for median calculation.

Table 4.8. Description of trauma by individual

Individual	Elements affected	Description
25 (FMNH #95390)	Cranium	Blunt trauma, healed (left parietal, oval with pointed ends, 13 x 44 mm)
180, 1 (FMNH #95449)	Left radius	Misaligned fracture
223 (FMNH #95489)	Cranium	Blunt trauma, healed (right parietal, round, 45.6 mm diameter)
232 (FMNH #95499)	Cranium	Blunt trauma, healed (frontal at glabella, oval, 12 x 20 mm)
	Left ulna	Misaligned fracture
265 (FMNH #95530)	Left tibia	Compound fracture with osteomyelitis
298 (FMNH #95559)	Left humerus	Misaligned fracture
370 (FMNH #97545)	Cranium	Blunt trauma, healed (left parietal, oval, 11 x 49 mm)
373 (FMNH #97548)	Cranium	Blunt trauma, healed (right parietal, oval, end pointed, 25 x 10.5 mm)
410 (FMNH #97586)	Cranium	Blunt trauma, unhealed (right parietal/frontal, oval, no measurements possible)
422 (FMNH #97598)	Cranium	Blunt trauma, healed (frontal, oval, no measurements possible)
427 (FMNH #97603)	Cranium	Blunt trauma, healed (left parietal, oval, 20 x 24.5 mm)
433 (FMNH #97609)	Left humerus	Misaligned fracture
446 (FMNH #97620)	Cranium	Blunt trauma, healed, three locations (left parietal, round, 13.5 mm diameter; right parietal, oval, 21.2 x 9.8 mm; frontal right, oval, 32 x 13.8 mm)
	Left ulna	Fracture
456 (FMNH #97630)	Cranium	Blunt trauma, healed (right parietal, oval, 20 x 11 mm)

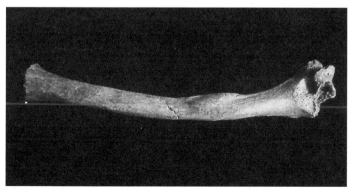

Fig. 4.16. Fracture of left humerus of individual 298 (FMNH #95559).

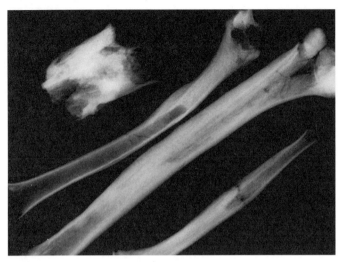

Fig. 4.17. Radiograph of fracture to the left humerus of individual 298 (FMNH #95559).
Top left to bottom right diagonally: left tibia, individual 265 (FMNH #95530); left humerus, individual 298 (FMNH #95559); right tibia, individual 204 (FMNH #95473); left ulna, individual 446 (FMNH #997620).

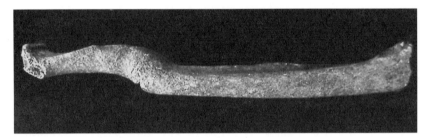

Fig. 4.18. Fracture of the left radius of individual 180 (FMNH #95449).

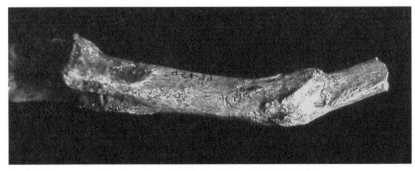

Fig. 4.19. Fracture of the left ulna of individual 232 (FMNH #95499).

etal, three were located on the frontal, and one was on both the parietal and frontal (table 4.8; fig. 4.24). Two individuals exhibited both cranial blunt trauma and misaligned long bone fractures. One male adult (individual 232; FMNH #95499) had a healed blunt trauma cranial lesion and a misaligned fracture of the left ulna (fig. 4.14). A second male adult (individual 446; FMNH #97620) had three healed blunt trauma cranial lesions and a fracture of the left ulna (fig. 4.17).

Fig. 4.20. Blunt trauma of the cranium of individual 25 (FMNH #95390).

Fig. 4.21. Blunt trauma of the cranium of individual 370 (FMNH #97545).

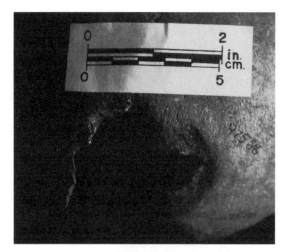

Fig. 4.22. Ectocranial view of blunt trauma of the cranium of individual 410 (FMNH #97586).

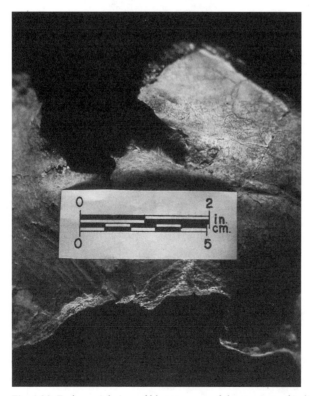

Fig. 4.23. Endocranial view of blunt trauma of the cranium of individual 410 (FMNH #97586).

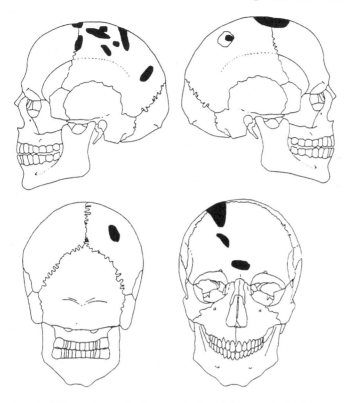

Fig. 4.24. Approximate distribution of all cranial trauma in the Palmer population.

Dietary Reconstruction

Dietary reconstruction using stable isotopes of nitrogen and carbon was performed by Lynette Norr and is reported in detail in appendix E. Dietary reconstruction using dental enamel microwear was performed by Mark Teaford and is reported in detail in appendix F. A summary of their results is reported below.

Stable Isotope Analysis

Stable isotope analysis has dramatically improved our ability to reconstruct the diet of humans by directly accessing chemical information recorded in teeth and bone. In previous studies, the primary evidence used to infer the consumption of horticultural products has been the presence or absence of domesticated plant remains at archaeological sites. Such data, although perhaps indicative of the potential diet of local inhabitants, yield little information regarding dietary focus, quality of diet, and the nutritional results of the diet. Direct measurement of diet is used in this study by examining the stable isotope signatures of dietary items preserved in the human skeleton and by observing the dental enamel microwear that dietary substances leave on the teeth.

Many foods have distinct ratios of the stable isotopes of carbon ($^{13}C/$ ^{12}C) and nitrogen ($^{15}N/^{14}N$). These are incorporated into body tissues when foods are eaten (DeNiro and Epstein 1978, 1981), and the diet can be reconstructed for earlier humans by comparing isotopic values derived from human bones with isotopic values derived from the tissues of plants and animals they have consumed (Ambrose and Norr 1993; Schoeninger and Moore 1992).

Isotopic data from modern plants and animals living in the same climatic zone as the human samples to which they are being compared are often used to establish an interpretive baseline. The selection of modern floral and faunal samples in this study was made by considering archaeological floral and faunal remains (Kozuch 1998; Newsom 1998; Quitmyer 1998; Walker 1992a) as well as ecological diversity.

Isotope ratios are expressed using the delta symbol (δ) as parts per thousand (‰) difference from a reference standard: Pee Dee Belemnite (PDB) for carbon and atmospheric nitrogen (AIR) for nitrogen. The δ values for carbon are generally negative, and those for nitrogen are usually positive. Nitrogen isotopic variation distinguishes between most terrestrial and marine organisms (Schoeninger and DeNiro 1984; Schoeninger et al. 1983). Animals generally exhibit a trophic effect with higher $\delta^{15}N$ values for carnivores than herbivores (Schoeninger and DeNiro 1984; Wada 1980). In most cases where legumes utilize atmospheric nitrogen they show values less than nonlegumes (Shearer and Kohl 1994).

Carbon isotopic variation is used to differentiate C_3, C_4, and CAM (Crassulacean Acid Metabolism) photosynthetic pathway plant foods, animals feeding on those plants, and animals in terrestrial versus marine ecosystems (Bender 1968; DeNiro and Epstein 1978; Schoeninger and DeNiro 1984; Smith and Epstein 1971; Tieszen 1991). C_3 plants have $\delta^{13}C$ values averaging near 26‰ and include most temperate grasses, trees, fruits, and tubers. C_4 plants have less negative $\delta^{13}C$ values averaging near 12‰ and include monocot tropical grasses native to the New World such as corn, and dicot plants such as chenopods, setarias, and some amaranths. CAM plants have $\delta^{13}C$ values that occur across the entire range of C_3 and C_4 plants and include succulents, cacti, and bromeliads (O'Leary, 1988).

Because marine organisms have $\delta^{13}C$ isotope values intermediate between C_3 and C_4 plant values, it is not possible to discriminate between various dietary combinations of marine organisms and C_3 and C_4 plants. Consequently, $\delta^{15}N$ isotope values are used in combination with $\delta^{13}C$ isotope values and are illustrated using bivariate plots with $\delta^{13}C$ values plotted on the X axis and $\delta^{15}N$ values plotted on the Y axis (Schoeninger et al. 1990). The general signatures of some of the foods commonly eaten by humans from the circum-Caribbean region are displayed in figure E.1.

The stable isotope dietary reconstruction for Palmer indicates that marine resources formed the bulk of the diet (appendix E). The subsistence base was focused on marine fish and invertebrates, as well as terrestrial plants such as fruits and tubers. Maize or other C_4 plants and terrestrial fauna appear to have contributed little to the overall diet. Some consumption of C_4 plants, in particular panicoid grasses, likely occurred because they have been found in south Florida archaeological deposits at Horr's Island and Useppa Island (Newsom 1991; Scarry 1999; Scarry and Newsom 1992), but the isotope signatures indicate that they were not a substantial dietary item. There were no significant differences in diet between males and females. The stable isotope results are discussed in much more detail in appendix E.

Dental Microwear

The patterns of enamel wear using scanning electron microscope analyses has contributed enormously to studies of tooth use. It permits more accurate assessment of tooth use than can be made using gross wear, and has been applied during the past two decades to a variety of human (Teaford 1991, 1994, 2002; Teaford and Lytle 1996; Teaford et al. 2001) and nonhuman populations (Teaford 1986; Teaford and Glander 1996; Teaford and Robinson 1989; Teaford and Walker 1984). The great strength of this approach lies in its ability to provide direct evidence of how teeth were used immediately before death. It provides short-term information on tooth use that complements the long-term information provided by stable isotope analyses.

Enamel wear is caused not only by dietary items, but also by other substances included with dietary items, such as grit produced during food preparation, accidental inclusions from dietary items such as shellfish, and abrasive residues present in some plants in the form of silicates. It has also been applied to ascertain the application of teeth as tools (Larsen et al. 1998) and to isolate postmortem tooth damage (Teaford 1988).

Dental microwear patterns of the Palmer population are much like those seen from other coastal sites in Georgia and North Carolina (appendix F; Teaford 2002; Teaford et al. 2001), but with some differences as well. The Palmer population experienced significant pitting of the molar surfaces (appendix F), generally more than occurred on molars from coastal North Carolina populations (Teaford 2002; Teaford et al. 2001). Scratch width was less than on molars from coastal North Carolina populations (Teaford 2002; Teaford et al. 2001). The microwear is in accord with that from the stable isotope data and supports a diet focused on local marine resources.

Summary

Dental and skeletal elements were examined for several indicators that are often used to provide interpretations of health and nutrition. Lesions providing information on diet and masticatory behavior are carious lesions, alveolar infection, premortem tooth loss, and dental chipping. Carious lesions were infrequent in the Palmer population with only eight (3%) adult individuals affected. Furthermore, only one individual exhibited more than one carious tooth. It is probable that the frequency of carious teeth, however, underestimates the severity of dental caries.

Dental chipping was also frequent with one subadult (4%) and 55 adults (19%) having at least one chipped tooth. Alveolar infections, which generally arise from carious lesions, were more frequent, with 31 adults (14%) affected. Premortem tooth loss was also frequent, with 58 adults (26%) affected and 52 adults (23%) exhibiting resorption of the alveolar bone following premortem tooth loss.

Lesions that provide information about metabolic disruption are enamel hypoplasia and porotic hyperostosis. Enamel hypoplasias were present for six subadults (75%) and 66 (78%) of the adults examined. Porotic hyperostosis was present for two subadults (10%) and 83 (29%) adults.

Nonspecific lesions indicating infection are periosteal reactions and osteomyelitis. Their distribution in the skeleton can provide information conducive to differential diagnosis of specific diseases, as can lesions characteristic of specific diseases such as the stellate lesions of treponemal infection. Considering all proliferative lesions together (periosteal reactions and osteomyelitis), 24 adults (6%) were affected. Of the 24 adults with proliferative lesions, 14 had systemic infections; 13 of these probably had treponemal infections. Stellate lesions indicating treponemal infection were present for six adults (2%). Sinus infections were observed for one male and two females. Button osteomas were observed for 10 adults (3%).

Lesions indicating lifestyle and activity include osteoarthritis and trauma. Osteoarthritis was noted for 41 adults (11%). Two males and one female exhibited temporal-mandibular joint disease. Fractures of the long bones, usually extensive and misaligned, were present for six adults (4%). Blunt trauma was present for 10 (3%) adult individuals.

When patterns of pathology were examined by sex, males were affected more frequently by carious lesions, enamel hypoplasias, porotic hyperostosis, trauma, and treponemal infection, while females were affected more frequently by dental chipping, alveolar infections, resorption of the alveolar bone, osteoarthritis, proliferative responses, and systemic infections. Seven pathological indicators (dental chipping, enamel hypoplasia, alveolar infection, porotic hyperostosis, blunt cranial trauma, combined cranial and postcranial trauma, and degenerative joint disease) were examined using chi-square analysis for differences in prevalence by sex. No statistically significant differences were found between males and females for any of the indicators.

The stable isotope analysis shows that the Palmer individuals consumed primarily Gulf of Mexico fish and marine invertebrates with C_3 plants. The dental microwear is indistinguishable from individuals inhabiting the North Carolina outer coast, whose diet was focused on marine fish, shellfish, and C_3 plants. In chapter 5, the Palmer nutrition and disease data are compared with similar data from populations inhabiting adjacent coastal and noncoastal regions in Florida, as well as from populations inhabiting coastal and noncoastal areas in the greater Southeast.

5

Regional Population Comparisons

This chapter focuses on a comparison of nutrition and health among several Florida populations as well as coastal and interior populations in other areas of the Southeast. The Florida populations are organized into those from coastal regions, defined as within 25 km (roughly a day's walk) from the coast, and those from noncoastal regions (map 5.1; table 5.1). Several panregional Southeast populations are included to extend comparisons from both coastal and interior localities. The populations within each geographic division are further subdivided into chronological periods.

Comparative Populations

Comparisons between Palmer and several other populations are made in this chapter. Table 5.1 groups them by regional location, and also lists the number of reported individuals, the chronological period of the sample, and references for further information. Some of these populations are in the immediate vicinity of Palmer and warrant further discussion.

Six large skeletal series were examined from the central peninsular Florida Gulf coast (Perico Island, Manasota Key, Bayshore Homes, Aqui Esta, Safety Harbor, and Tierra Verde). Part of the Perico Island (8MA6) site complex was excavated by M. T. Newman in the winter of 1933–34 (Willey 1949). The site comprised two shell middens, a small shell and sand burial mound, and a cemetery area. Newman excavated all but the larger shell midden. "The burial mound is 60 feet in diameter, dome-shaped, circular, and at its highest point was almost 5 feet above the surrounding flats" (Willey 1949:174). Newman recovered 185 primary, flexed skeletons with few associated artifacts from the burial mound. Among the artifacts were ceramic sherds (Glades plain, Perico plain, Biscayne plain), cut deer bone, polished tortoise shell, a conch shell bowl, and broken flint projectiles (Willey 1949:176–177). Newman also removed 43

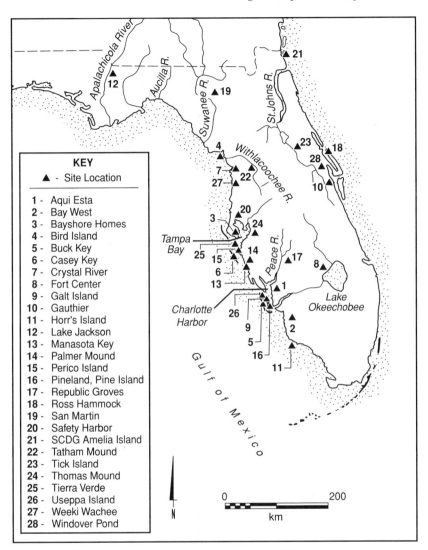

Map 5.1. Archaeological sites of Florida with comparative skeletal series.

skeletons from the cemetery that appear to have been flexed interments buried in groups of three to six individuals. "They had been placed in small pits and the pits had been lined with and covered by shells" (Willey 1949:180). A total of 215 individuals based on crania were examined by Hutchinson (this volume); the postcrania have not yet been systematically examined.

The Manasota Key cemetery (8SO1292) was located during the con-

Table 5.1. Regional populations compared with Florida

Site	N[a]	Period[b]	References
South Gulf coast			
Horr's Island	3	AR	Norr et al. n.d.; Russo et al. 1991
Galt Island	4	E LW	Hutchinson 1990; Marquardt 1992a; Norr et al. n.d.
Buck Key	5	LW	Hutchinson 1992; Marquardt 1992a; Norr et al. n.d.
Useppa Island	6	LW	Hansinger 1992; Hutchinson 1999; Hutchinson et al. 1997; Marquardt 1999; Norr et al. n.d.
Pine Island	1	LW	Hutchinson 2003; Walker and Marquardt 2003
Central Gulf coast			
Palmer	429	E LW	Bullen 1972; Bullen and Bullen 1976; Norr et al. n.d.
Casey Key	43	E LW	Bullen and Bullen 1976
Perico Island	178	E LW	Willey 1949
Manasota Key	120	E LW	Dickel 1991
Bayshore Homes	115	LW	Sears 1960; Snow 1962
Aqui Esta	22	SH	Hutchinson 1991, 2002b; Luer 2002
Safety Harbor	113	SH	Griffin and Bullen 1950; Hutchinson 1991
Tierra Verde	48	SH	Hutchinson 1991, 1993b; Sears 1967
Northern Gulf coast			
Bird Island	36	L AR	Stojanowski 1997
Crystal River	35	MW–LW	Katzmarzyk 1998; Weisman 1995
Weeki Wachee	84	L SH	Hutchinson 1991; Hutchinson and Mitchem 1996
Northern Atlantic coast			
Browne Mound	40	LW	Sears 1959
Holy Spirit	30	LW	Larsen 2001
Santa Catalina de Amelia	122	MISSION	Larsen 2001
Southern noncoastal			
Fort Center	121	MW	Miller-Shaivitz and İşcan 1991
Central and Northern noncoastal			
Republic Groves	37	AR	Saunders 1972
Henderson Mound	35	E LW	Larsen 2001
Lake Jackson	20	MISSIS	Larsen 2001
Tatham Mound Prehistoric	28	L SH	Hutchinson 1991, n.d.; Mitchem 1989
Tatham Mound Protohistoric	339	L SH	Hutchinson 1991, n.d.; Mitchem 1989
San Martin (Fig Springs)	88	MISSION	Hoshower 1992; Larsen 2001

a. Number reported.

b. AR = Archaic; L AR = Late Archaic; MW–LW = Middle Woodland–Late Woodland; E LW = early Late Woodland; LW = Late Woodland; SH = Safety Harbor; L SH = Late Safety Harbor; MISSIS = Mississippian; MISSION = Mission.

struction of a house and excavated in the late 1980s by W. A. Cockrell. There are four radiocarbon dates for the site: 1660 ± 80 and 1630 ± 80 B.P. for shell from the upper midden, 1830 ± 90 B.P. years for shell from the lower midden zone, and 1800 ± 80 B.P. for human bone (Dickel 1991:2). This places the mortuary component at the site at about A.D. 200. A total of 120 individuals were examined by Dickel (1991).

Bayshore Homes (8PI41), located on Boca Ciega Bay, was excavated in 1958 by William Sears. According to Sears (1960:1) "The Bayshore Homes site was one of the major sites of the aboriginally crowded Tampa Bay area in terms of size, midden depth, and number and size of structures." There was an extensive shell midden at the site as well as three mounds. The largest mound was a flat-topped truncated pyramidal mound (mound A) about 150 feet wide by 175 feet long and between 15 and 18 feet high (Sears 1960:13). Mound B was the burial mound, a prominent feature according to Sears (1960:14) and well looted prior to excavation. Based on ceramic series, the Bayshore Homes site dates between A.D. 500 and 1000. A total of 115 individuals were examined by Charles Snow (1962). However, Sears (1960:24) estimates that at least 500 individuals were originally interred in the mound.

Aqui Esta (8CH68) was originally a sand burial mound. It was excavated by amateurs in the 1960s. Three radiocarbon dates have been obtained from shell (A.D. 805 ± 50, A.D. 935 ± 65, and A.D. 1040 ± 60, all uncalibrated; Luer 2002). Approximately 100 burials, most secondary, were removed from the mound. *Busycon* shell cups and typical Safety Harbor period ceramics were recovered from the mound. A total of 22 individuals were examined by Hutchinson (1991, 2002b).

The Safety Harbor (8PI2) site is located near the head of Tampa Bay about 2.4 km north of the modern city of Tampa. The principal mound is a large (21.3 meters) square flat-topped mound approximately 6.1 meters tall (Willey 1949). The burial mound was located west of the principal mound and on the other side of the village area. It is dated between A.D. 900 and 1750 based on ceramics and European artifacts. Matthew Stirling excavated the burial mound in 1930 under the auspices of the Bureau of American Ethnology. He reported that the mound had been disturbed but he nevertheless recovered more than 100 secondary burials from it (Willey 1949:136). Some European artifacts were recovered (clay pipes, iron axes, and a sheet silver tubular bead and ornament), but the majority of the mound appears to be late prehistoric.

John Griffin and Ripley Bullen continued excavations at the Safety Harbor site in 1948, concentrating on the flat-topped mound and the village area in preparation for the park that currently occupies the site (Griffin and Bullen 1950). The burials are curated in a private collection at the National Museum of Natural History. A total of 113 individuals from the two collections were examined by Hutchinson (1991, this volume).

The Tierra Verde Mound (8PI51) is located on Cabbage Key in the Tampa Bay area and was excavated by William Sears of Florida Atlantic University in 1961 (Sears 1967). Based on ceramics, the site dates to A.D. 900–1350. The site had previously been visited by C. B. Moore (1900) on what was then called Pine Key. Although many of the burials that Sears recovered from Tierra Verde were flexed interments, he interpreted them to be secondary burials (Sears 1967:30–31), comparing them with those recovered from Bayshore Homes (Snow 1962), located a few miles to the east. A total of 48 individuals were examined by Hutchinson (1991, 1993b).

Three large coastal series are used for comparison from the northern peninsular Florida Gulf coast (Bird Island, Crystal River, and Weeki Wachee) and one large inland series (Tatham Mound). The Bird Island (8DI52) site was excavated by a series of individuals between the 1960s and the 1990s, with systematic excavations conducted most recently by Doran and Dasovich (Stojanowski 1997). A radiocarbon date of 2620 B.C. has been obtained from human bone (Beta-27221; Stojanowski 1997:8). This places the mortuary component in the Archaic period. A total of 36 individuals were examined by Stojanowski (1997).

Crystal River (8CI1) has been one of the most notable archaeological sites in Florida, with excavations spanning more than a century. C. B. Moore excavated at the site in 1903, 1906, and 1917 (Moore 1903, 1907, 1918). Ripley Bullen excavated there in 1951 and 1960–65 (Weisman 1995). The main burial complex consists of features C–F. Weisman (1995: 52–53) summarizes Moore's (1903) summary of the relationship of the features nicely:

Area C was a circular embankment of sand, 6 feet high and 75 feet wide, that surrounded the burial mound proper; D was "territory on the general level," the ground surface immediately inside the circular embankment; E was an irregularly sloping elevation of sand (what later observers should refer to as the "platform") between area D and the burial mound, and F was the main burial mound, built of sand, with a diameter across the base of approximately 70 feet. The relationship between these features is clearly depicted in Moore (1903:fig. 17) and Bullen's map of his 1960 reconnaissance (Weisman 1995:fig. 7).

The burials span a date of A.D. 1–1200, but most probably date between A.D. 200 and 800 (Milanich 1994; Weisman 1995). A total of 75 individuals were examined by Green (1993) from mounds F and G and the circular embankment. Katzmarzyk (1998) examined 66 individuals from mound G.

The Weeki Wachee Mound (8HE12) was excavated in 1970 by Robert Allen of the Florida Museum of Natural History. The uppermost component of the mound had burials associated with European artifacts (Mitchem et al. 1985). The site is dated to A.D. 900–1550 based on ceramics and European artifacts. The skeletal series was examined by Hutchinson (1991; Hutchinson and Mitchem 1996) and contains 82 individuals.

Tatham Mound (8CI203) was excavated between 1985 and 1987 by Jeffrey Mitchem and Dale Hutchinson, directed by Jerald Milanich. It has an earlier component dating between A.D. 1200 and 1400 and a later component dating between A.D. 1525 and 1550. The date for the later component is based on European artifacts, primarily glass beads, that were associated with several burials. The precontact component of the mound contained 28 individuals and the postcontact component contained 339 individuals. The skeletal series was examined by Hutchinson (1991). Stable isotope dietary reconstruction was performed by Hutchinson and Norr (1994; Hutchinson et al. 1998, 2000).

One inland north Florida site was used for comparative purposes. San Martín de Timucua (also known as Fig Springs; 8CO1) has been the subject of archaeological activity for several decades. Based on European artifacts and documents, it dates to A.D. 1600–1680. Goggin (1953) collected Spanish contact period materials from the spring. In 1986, Ken Johnson located the mission complex (Johnson 1987, 1990). Weisman conducted further auger tests in 1988 and excavated the site over a sixteen-month period following the auger tests (Weisman 1992:36–38). The skeletal series was examined by Hoshower (1992) and further examined by Larsen and coworkers (see various papers in Larsen 2001; Hutchinson et al. 1998, 2000).

Several individuals have been recovered from the southern peninsular Florida Gulf coast, principally from excavations in the Charlotte Harbor region (Galt Island, Buck Key, Useppa Island, and Pine Island) and immediately south of Charlotte Harbor (Horr's Island). Unfortunately, the entire combined sample contains only 19 individuals and the largest single population sample is six individuals (table 5.1). Consequent small sample size has precluded their use as a comparative sample. Hutchinson (1990, 1992, 1999, 2003; Hutchinson et al. 1997) has examined all 19 burials.

One Archaic wet pond site from the south Florida peninsular Gulf coast, however, has more individuals. Bay West (8CR200) was excavated in the early 1980s by Berriault and coworkers (1981). Radiocarbon dates from wooden posts and peat yielded dates of 4900 and 4000 B.C. (Berriault et al. 1981:50). Associated with the burials were leafy mats of wax myrtle and fire-sharpened stakes that suggest the burials were staked down in the water as at Windover. Middle Archaic projectile points, bow drills, and atlatl hooks were recovered. The burials were completely comingled at the time of analysis. Walsh-Haney (1999) estimates that there were at least 50 individuals.

Three large series are used for comparison from the Florida Atlantic coast (Ross Hammock, Windover, and Gauthier). Ross Hammock (8VO13a) was excavated by Ripley and Adelaide Bullen and William Bryant, who removed burials from mound 1 in 1963 (Bullen et al. 1967). Ceramic style and radiocarbon dates indicate that the mound was used primarily between 50 B.C. and A.D. 300 (Bullen et al. 1967:25). The skeletal series was examined by Pober (1996) and contains an estimated 72 individuals.

One of the best known Archaic sites from Florida is Windover Pond (8BR246). It is described in chapter 2, and attention here is focused on the skeletal remains. The burials from Windover appear to have been staked in the wet pond with several artifacts that include seed beads and hods, blankets, baskets, and cordage (Doran et al. 1986). The skeletal sample consists of 168 individuals, of which 40% are subadults (Walsh-Haney 1999). Radiocarbon dates of 6000–4000 B.C. have been obtained for the mortuary component. The skeletal series was examined by Doran (2002) and Walsh-Haney (1999).

Gauthier (8BR193) was excavated in a salvage operation by Calvin Jones and volunteers of the Indian River chapter of the Florida Anthropological Society between 1977 and 1979. Most burials date to the Archaic period (5000–1000 B.C.), but nine were intrusive and of later date (Maples 1987). The skeletal series was examined by Maples (1987), who estimated that 121 individuals are represented. The skeletal remains are currently being reexamined by Heather Walsh-Haney for a dissertation (Walsh-Haney, pers. comm., October 2001).

Two large series are used for comparison from south Florida non-coastal regions (Fort Center and Republic Groves). The oldest is Republic Groves (8HR4), with radiocarbon dates ranging from 3750 to 4530 B.C. (Milanich 1994:82). The site, a pond like Bay West and Windover, was found in 1968. At least 37 people appear to have been staked in the water, as indicated by wooden stakes, cordage, and matting (Milanich 1994:82). Artifacts found with burials included throwing sticks, mammal bone awls, shark teeth, tubular stone beads, antler ornaments, projectile points, and bone pins and knives (Milanich 1994:82; Wharton et al. 1981). The skeletal series was examined by Saunders (1972), who estimated 37 individuals to be represented.

The Fort Center site was excavated between 1966 and 1971 by William Sears (1982). The burials at the site were recovered from a mortuary pond and date between A.D. 200 and 800 (Sears 1982). Sears has constructed the mortuary complex at the site as comprising a pond, a platform with carved wooden animals, and a platform that served as a mortuary preparation area. The mortuary complex dates to A.D. 200–800. The skeletal series was examined by Miller-Shaivitz (1986) and additionally reported by Miller-Shaivitz and İşcan (1991). They (Miller-Shaivitz 1986; Miller-Shaivitz and İşcan 1991) reported a minimum of 121 individuals based on crania.

In sum, there are 19 coastal and 6 noncoastal skeletal series from Florida that are used for comparison with Palmer (table 5.1). They range in date from the Archaic period (8000–1000 B.C.) through the mission period (A.D. 1550–1750). This is the largest synthesis of bioarchaeological data that has been conducted for Florida.

Pathology Comparisons

Pathological lesion and behavioral alteration frequencies are compared in order to make inferences about regional and chronological variation in lifeways, as well as trends in health and disease. The comparisons include lesions and alterations attributed to diet and masticatory behavior (carious lesions, alveolar infections, dental chipping, and dental enamel microwear), metabolic disruption (enamel hypoplasia, porotic hyperostosis), infectious disease (periosteal reactions, osteomyelitis, stellate lesions), and lifestyle (external auditory exostoses, osteoarthritis, trauma).

Dietary reconstructions using dental enamel microwear and stable isotopes are compared with other Florida populations as well. The methods of observation are the same as reported for the Palmer population in the previous chapter. When possible, comparisons between males and females are made for the Florida populations in order to investigate the role of sex in nutrition and health.

Comparisons are made using histograms that categorize the populations into regional categories of coastal and noncoastal populations in Florida, and coastal and noncoastal populations in other Southeast localities. The populations are further subdivided into temporal groups (Archaic, Early/Middle Woodland, Late Woodland/Mississippian, Early Contact (Postcontact Early), and Mission (Postcontact Late). The percentage affected is displayed both in the length of the bar and by a label indicating the percent affected. In many discussions, I refer not only to the percentages for a particular series but also to the midrange (the middle percentage value of the range of percentages) of the percentages for a group of series.

The advantage in displaying the comparisons in histograms is that values are presented for individual populations. However, it is often difficult, in viewing histograms, to appreciate the patterns among and between populations in particular geographic localities or periods by looking at each individual population. For that reason, some comparisons are also displayed using box plots that show the distribution of the midrange values by time period and geographic location. Box plots show robust statistics (median and quartiles) that are resistant to extreme values in the data (Velleman and Hoaglin 1981), rather than the sample mean and standard deviation, which can be affected by extreme values. The boxes show the interquartile range (the middle 50% of the cases); thus the lower end of the box (the lower hinge) occurs at the 25th percentile and the upper end of the box (the upper hinge) occurs at the 75th percentile. The line drawn across the box shows the 50th percentile. The whiskers in box plots extend 1½ times the value of the upper and lower hinges of the box (the interquartile range). Cases outside of that range are outliers and are marked with an asterisk. Extreme outliers (those three times the interquartile range) are marked with circles.

One criticism of box plots is that they can mask gaps in the data since they show only the range of data values, and the whiskers make visual determinations of significant differences difficult. This can be partially overcome by using special intervals located around the median of box plots known as "notches." Notched box plots were also used to assess statistical significance. Notched box plots narrow at the median and return to full width at the upper and lower confidence intervals. When the notches do not overlap, the difference is statistically significant at the 5% ($P \le .05$) level.

Diet and Masticatory Behavior

Carious Lesions

Carious lesions were not common in Florida populations until the mission period (figs. 5.1, 5.2). Prehistoric Florida Gulf coast populations have frequencies at or below 5% teeth and 14% individuals affected prior to missionization. The frequency of individuals affected at Palmer was higher for males (4%) than females (2%). Similarly, males (10%) at Perico Island and at Safety Harbor (22%) were more often affected by carious lesions than females at Perico Island (7%) or at Safety Harbor (12%).

Florida interior populations exhibited similar frequencies of teeth affected by dental caries (up to 5%). The frequency of teeth affected for the postcontact Tatham Mound population was twice as high for females (6%) as for males (3%) (Hutchinson n.d.). Similarly, more female individuals (24%) than male individuals (18%) were affected by carious le-

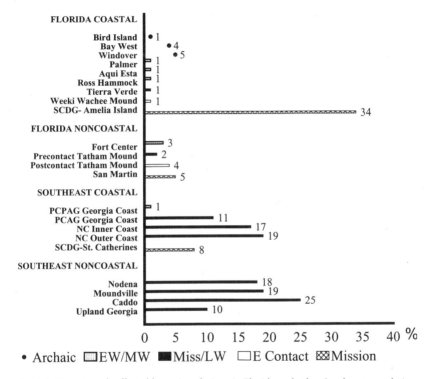

Fig. 5.1. Percent teeth affected by carious lesions in Florida and other Southeast populations. For figs. 5.1–5.4, 5.6, 5.8, 5.12, and 5.13 the approximate chronology is: Archaic = 8000–500 B.C.; Early Woodland/Middle Woodland = 500 B.C.–A.D. 800; Mississippian/Late Woodland = A.D. 800–1500; Early Contact = A.D. 1500–1600; Mission = A.D. 1600–1800.
Sources: Bird Island (Stojanowski 1997), Bay West (Walsh-Haney 1999), Windover (Walsh-Haney 1999), Aqui Esta (Hutchinson 2002b), Ross Hammock (Pober 1996), Tierra Verde (Hutchinson 1993b), Weeki Wachee Mound (Hutchinson and Mitchem 1996), SCDG (Santa Catalina de Guale) Amelia Island (Larsen et al. 1991), Fort Center (Miller-Shaivitz and İşcan 1991), Precontact Tatham Mound (Hutchinson n.d.; Hutchinson and Norr n.d.), Postcontact Tatham Mound (Hutchinson n.d.; Hutchinson and Norr n.d.), San Martin (Hoshower 1992), PCPAG (Precontact Preagricultural) Georgia Coast (Larsen et al. 1991), PCAG (Precontact Agricultural) Georgia Coast (Larsen et al. 1991), N.C. Inner Coast (Hutchinson 2002a), N.C. Outer Coast (Hutchinson 2002a), SCDG (Santa Catalina de Guale) St. Catherines Island (Larsen et al. 1991), Nodena (Powell 1988b), Moundville (Powell 1988a), Caddo (Powell and Rogers 1980), Upland Georgia (Williamson 1998).

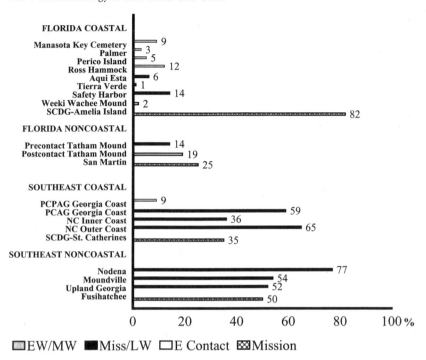

Fig. 5.2. Percent individuals affected by carious lesions in Florida and other Southeast populations. *Sources*: Manasota Key (Dickel 1991), Palmer (this volume), Perico Island (this volume), Ross Hammock (Pober 1996), Aqui Esta (Hutchinson 2002b), Tierra Verde (Hutchinson 1993b), Safety Harbor (this volume), Weeki Wachee Mound (Hutchinson and Mitchem 1996), SCDG (Santa Catalina de Guale) Amelia Island (Larsen et al. 1991), San Martin (Hoshower 1992), PCPAG (Precontact Preagricultural) Georgia Coast (Larsen et al. 1991), PCAG (Precontact Agricultural) Georgia Coast (Larsen et al. 1991), N.C. Inner Coast (Hutchinson 2002a), N.C. Outer Coast (Hutchinson 2002a), SCDG (Santa Catalina de Guale) St. Catherines Island (Larsen et al. 1991), Nodena (Powell 1988b), Moundville (Powell 1988a), Upland Georgia (Williamson 1998), Fusihatchee (Reeves 2000).

sions in the Tatham population (fig. 5.3). In the mission population at San Martin, the frequency of teeth affected by caries is slightly higher for males (6%) as compared with females (5%) (Hoshower 1992).

The Florida Gulf coast carious lesion frequencies are much lower than those exhibited for both coastal and noncoastal precontact agricultural populations in the Southeast. For the interior agricultural populations inhabiting Moundville in Alabama and Nodena in Arkansas, carious lesion frequencies were 18–19% of teeth affected and 54–77% of individuals affected by carious lesions (Powell 1988a,b). Georgia coastal precontact preagricultural population frequency of teeth affected was 1% as compared with 11% for precontact agricultural populations (Larsen et al.

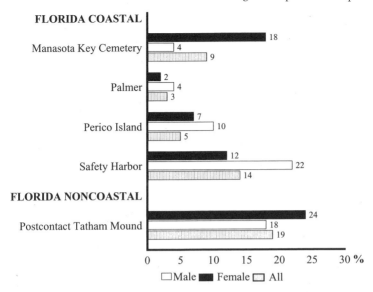

FLORIDA COASTAL

Manasota Key Cemetery

Palmer

Perico Island

Safety Harbor

FLORIDA NONCOASTAL

Postcontact Tatham Mound

0   5   10   15   20   25   30 %

☐ Male ■ Female ▥ All

Fig. 5.3. Percent individuals by sex affected by carious lesions in Florida populations. *Sources*: Manasota Key (Dickel 1991), Palmer (this volume), Perico Island (this volume), Safety Harbor (this volume), Postcontact Tatham Mound (Hutchinson n.d.; Hutchinson and Norr n.d.).

1991). The frequency of Georgia coastal precontact preagricultural individuals affected was 9% as compared with 59% for precontact agricultural individuals (Larsen et al. 1991). Williamson (1998) reported that 52% of upland Georgia individuals experienced carious lesions.

The frequency of individuals and teeth affected by carious lesions tends to increase during the Late Woodland and Mississippian periods throughout much of the Southeast. Larsen and coworkers (1991) have documented high frequencies of carious lesions in many mission populations in Georgia and Florida. Undoubtedly the increased production and consumption of maize during this time contributed to poor dental health, as is evident in the frequent carious lesions for teeth and individuals at Santa Catalina de Amelia Island (figs. 5.1, 5.2). As well, carious lesion frequencies are relatively high (50% of individuals affected) for the interior postcontact population from Fusihatchee in Alabama (Reeves 2000).

In the early mission population from Santa Catalina de Guale on St. Catherines Island, frequencies of carious lesions are actually lower (35% of individuals) than for precontact agricultural populations (59% of individuals). Carious lesion frequencies for the late mission population from San Martin are even lower, 25% of individuals. Nonetheless, our dietary reconstructions (Hutchinson et al. 1998, 2000; Larsen et al. 2001) show that all of these populations consumed maize.

Throughout the Southeast, high frequencies of carious lesions are often associated with frequent maize consumption. Maize consumption undoubtedly contributed toward the frequent cases of dental caries in many of the populations examined from Georgia, Alabama, and Arkansas, where frequencies of teeth affected range 8–25% and the frequencies of individuals affected range 35–77%. The lowest frequencies of carious lesions observed, less than 1% of teeth and 1–14% of individuals affected in the Southeast, were for precontact populations inhabiting the peninsular Florida Gulf coast. More males were affected than females in those populations (fig. 5.3), a trend that is reversed for Florida interior populations, potentially indicating important sex differences in diet, labor, hormones, or other variables linked to cariogenesis (Hutchinson 2002a).

The etiology of dental caries is much more complicated than simply dietary focus on carbohydrates, and the explanation for infrequent cases of dental caries in Florida populations is undoubtedly multifaceted. The low frequency of carious lesions in Florida Gulf coast populations may reflect the infrequent consumption of maize, although nonagricultural outer coastal North Carolina populations experience quite high (Hutchinson 2002a) frequencies of adult teeth (19%) and individuals (65%) affected by carious lesions. I attributed the high frequencies of carious lesions in those populations to dental damage observed in the teeth (Hutchinson 2002a).

In populations with extremely poor dental health, the loss of carious teeth prior to death can result in lower frequencies of observed carious lesions. Lukacs (1995) presented a method for correcting carious lesion frequencies by adding the number of tooth locations with periodontal disease to the carious tooth counts. Although his method is not used here, he articulates the need to consider the influence on premortem tooth loss on carious lesion frequencies.

Alveolar Infections

Periodontal infections were more common for Gulf coast populations before A.D. 800, ranging from a low of 13% for the Bay West population to a high of 50% in the Perico Island population. In the four later populations, there were no cases of periodontal infection in the Aqui Esta and Weeki Wachee populations, 2% affected from Tierra Verde, and 22% from Safety Harbor (fig. 5.4). There are few comparative data for alveolar infection for Southeast populations outside of Florida. Late prehistoric populations located on the North Carolina coast have similar rates of alveolar infection (Hutchinson 2002a), with lower rates for inner coast individuals (20%) than those from the outer coast (32%).

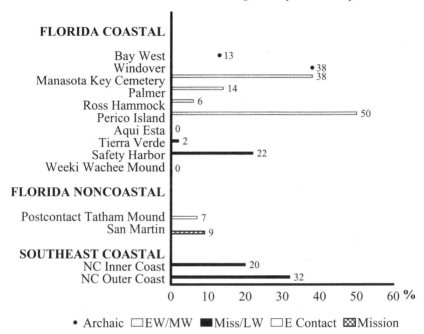

Fig. 5.4. Percent individuals affected by alveolar infection in Florida and other Southeast populations. *Sources*: Bay West (Walsh-Haney 1999), Windover (Walsh-Haney 1999), Manasota Key (Dickel 1991), Palmer (this volume), Ross Hammock (Pober 1996), Perico Island (this volume), Aqui Esta (Hutchinson 2002b), Tierra Verde (Hutchinson 1993b), Safety Harbor (this volume), Weeki Wachee Mound (Hutchinson and Mitchem 1996), Postcontact Tatham Mound (Hutchinson n.d.; Hutchinson and Norr n.d.), San Martin (Hoshower 1992).

There is little chronological trend in periodontal infections. The two Archaic populations (Bay West and Windover) exhibit a range of 13% to 38%, respectively. Only 6% of individuals from Ross Hammock, a little later in date than Windover and a little south on the Atlantic coast, have periodontal infections. Periodontal infections were relatively infrequent for Florida interior populations, with 7% of individuals affected in the postcontact population from Tatham Mound and 9% of individuals affected in the mission population from San Martin. Some of the alveolar infections may have been due to severe damage to the teeth, as seen for a male individual from Useppa Island (figs. 4.2, 5.5). The Useppa Island individual is roughly contemporary with the Palmer population (A.D. 640–770; Beta-35300; Hutchinson 1999:139).

Despite the fact that females (21%) from Palmer and the Manasota Key cemetery (53%) were more often affected than Palmer males (14%) and Manasota Key males (42%), male frequencies for the Tampa Bay popula-

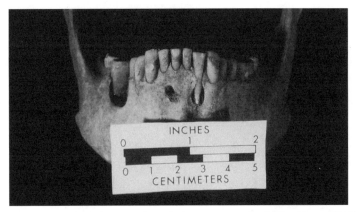

Fig. 5.5. Alveolar infections of a male from Useppa Island (Hutchinson 1999).

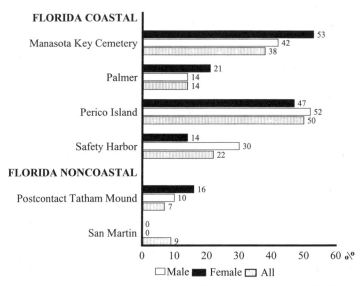

Fig. 5.6. Percent individuals by sex affected by alveolar infection in Florida populations. *Sources:* Manasota Key (Dickel 1991), Palmer (this volume), Perico Island (this volume), Safety Harbor (this volume), Tierra Verde (Hutchinson 1993b), Postcontact Tatham Mound (Hutchinson n.d.; Hutchinson and Norr n.d.), San Martin (Hoshower 1992).

tions of Perico Island (52%) and Safety Harbor (30%) were higher than those for females (47% Perico Island; 14% Safety Harbor; fig. 5.6). For the interior population from postcontact Tatham Mound, female (16%) frequencies were higher than for males (10%). Alveolar infections were more frequent for males (61%) as compared with females (50%) from late prehistoric North Carolina outer coast populations, but more frequent for females (24%) than males (20%) from inner coastal North Carolina (Hutchinson 2002a).

Dental Chipping

Dental damage in the form of chipping was relatively common among adults in the Florida Gulf coast populations (fig. 5.7), ranging from 19% at Palmer to 62% at Perico Island. Unfortunately, there are no dental chipping data for Florida interior populations. However, comparative data are available for North Carolina outer coastal populations, where adults exhibited high chipping frequencies (44% of individuals; Hutchinson 2002a) and male individuals (70%) were far more frequently affected than females (20%).

Dental chipping appears to be more frequent for males in Florida central Gulf coast populations. Males at Perico Island (91%) and Safety Harbor (48%) were more frequently affected than females (60% Perico Island; 30% Safety Harbor). The higher female (32%) frequency at Palmer

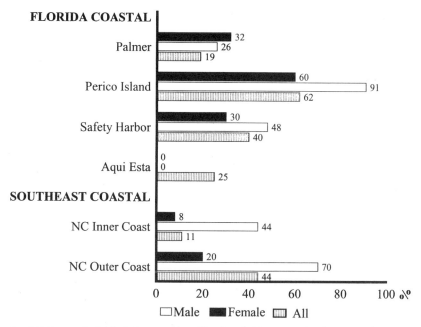

Fig. 5.7. Percent individuals by sex affected by dental chipping in Southeast populations. *Sources*: Palmer (this volume), Perico Island (this volume), Safety Harbor (this volume), Aqui Esta (Hutchinson 2002b), North Carolina (Hutchinson 2002a).

as compared with males (26%) is contrary to that pattern, and could be due to several factors that include differences in diet, tool use of teeth, or food preparation.

Dental Enamel Microwear

Our previous studies (Hutchinson 2002a; Norr 2002; Teaford 2002; Teaford et al. 2001) have shown that localized differences in diet and food processing are apparent for Atlantic coast populations. When compared with a series of estuarine populations from the North Carolina coast, the microwear measurements of the Palmer individuals were similar. The scratch and pit widths of other Atlantic coast populations, however, were quite different and support localized dietary regimes.

Metabolic Disruption

Enamel Hypoplasia

The percentage of individuals affected by at least one enamel hypoplasia in Florida coastal populations is either very low or very high, with the Manasota Key cemetery (8%), Crystal River Mound G (19%), Aqui Esta (23%), and Safety Harbor (35%) populations on the peninsular Gulf coast exhibiting frequencies below 50% of individuals affected. On the Atlantic coast, 29% of individuals from Ross Hammock experienced enamel hypoplasias.

Frequencies of more than 50% of individuals affected by at least one hypoplasia were observed for Perico Island (52%), Santa Catalina de Guale on Amelia Island (67%), Weeki Wachee (75%), and Palmer (78%) (fig. 5.8). Males (80%) from Palmer, Manasota Key cemetery (17%), and Perico Island (65%) were more commonly affected than females (71% Palmer, 12% Manasota Key, 51% Perico Island; fig. 5.9). Males (33%) from Safety Harbor, however, were affected slightly less often than females (36%).

The frequency of individuals affected by hypoplasias for Florida interior populations ranged from 33% in the precontact Tatham mound population to 75% in the mission population at San Martin. Males were more commonly affected in the postcontact Tatham mound population (56%) and the mission San Martin population (74%) than were females (50% Tatham Mound, 65% San Martin).

The high frequency of enamel hypoplasia for Palmer is similar to many populations in the eastern United States (Hutchinson and Larsen 1990, 1996, 2001; Larsen and Hutchinson 1992). In the coastal mission population from Santa Catalina de Guale in Georgia, for instance, 88% of

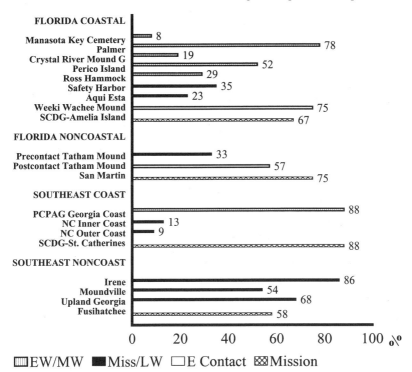

Fig. 5.8. Enamel hypoplasia frequencies by individual in Florida and other Southeast populations. *Sources*: Manasota Key (Dickel 1991), Palmer (this volume), Crystal River Mound G (Katzmarzyk 1998), Perico Island (this volume), Ross Hammock (Pober 1996), Safety Harbor (this volume), Aqui Esta (Hutchinson 2002b), Weeki Wachee Mound (Hutchinson and Mitchem 1996), N.C. Inner Coast (Hutchinson 2002a), N.C. Outer Coast (Hutchinson 2002a), SCDG (Santa Catalina de Guale) Amelia Island (Hutchinson and Larsen 2001), Precontact Tatham Mound (Hutchinson n.d.; Hutchinson and Norr n.d.), Postcontact Tatham Mound (Hutchinson n.d.; Hutchinson and Norr n.d.), San Martin (Hutchinson and Larsen 2001), SCDG (Santa Catalina de Guale) St. Catherines Island (Hutchinson and Larsen 2001), Irene (Hutchinson and Larsen 2001), Moundville (Powell 1988a), Upland Georgia (Williamson 1998), Fusihatchee (Reeves 2000).

individuals were affected by at least one hypoplasia, the same frequency as for precontact preagricultural individuals. Interior populations from Irene in Georgia and Moundville and Fusihatchee in Alabama had frequencies ranging from 54% to 86% (fig. 5.8).

In general, more individuals in the Southeast, including Florida, are affected by hypoplasias following the transition to agriculture and in early contact and mission populations, such as at Santa Catalina de Amelia, Weeki Wachee, San Martin, and Santa Catalina de Guale (fig. 5.8). High frequencies at Palmer, postcontact Tatham Mound, Safety Harbor, and Weeki Wachee cannot be explained by either agriculture or European con-

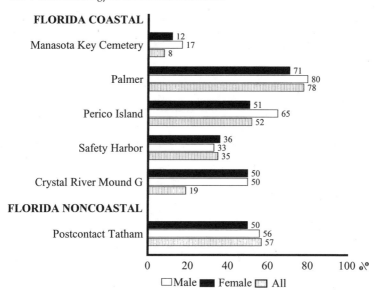

Fig. 5.9. Percent individuals by sex affected by enamel hypoplasias in Florida populations. *Sources*: Manasota Key (Dickel 1991), Palmer (this volume), Perico Island (this volume), Safety Harbor (this volume), Crystal River Mound G (Katzmarzyk 1998), Postcontact Tatham Mound (Hutchinson n.d.; Hutchinson and Norr n.d.).

tact, and may be due to increased settlement density, social ranking, and many other lifestyle changes. The low frequency of enamel hypoplasia for inner coastal North Carolina populations (13%) and outer coastal North Carolina populations (9%) may indicate stable resources or other buffered living conditions.

Porotic Hyperostosis

Florida peninsular Gulf coast populations examined for porotic hyperostosis range in date from A.D. 500 through 1750 and exhibit frequencies ranging between 26% and 44% of individuals affected. Weeki Wachee and Perico Island are clearly the outliers with very low (4%) and very high (44%) frequencies, respectively. The frequency of individuals affected by porotic hyperostosis is nearly identical in seven Florida coastal populations (Manasota Key, Palmer, Crystal River Mound G, Tierra Verde, Safety Harbor, Aqui Esta, Santa Catalina de Guale at Amelia Island; fig. 5.10). Males were more often affected from Palmer (56%), Perico Island (50%), and Safety Harbor (33%) than were females from those populations (39% Palmer, 43% Perico Island, and 27% Safety Harbor; fig. 5.11).

Most of the Florida coastal porotic hyperostosis cases were adults with healing lesions, but there are more serious cases in Florida Gulf coast populations, as one individual from Bishop Harbor illustrates (fig. 5.12).

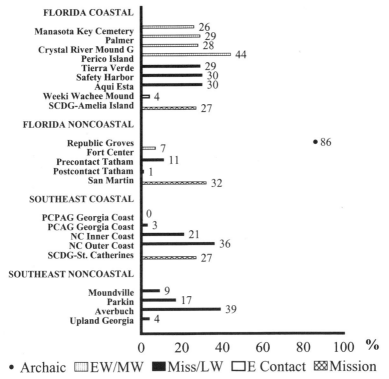

Fig. 5.10. Percent individuals affected by porotic hyperostosis in Florida and other Southeast populations. *Sources*: Manasota Key (Dickel 1991), Palmer (this volume), Crystal River Mound G (Katzmarzyk 1998), Perico Island (this volume), Tierra Verde (Hutchinson 1993b), Safety Harbor (this volume), Aqui Esta (Hutchinson 2002b), Weeki Wachee Mound (Hutchinson and Mitchem 1996), SCDG (Santa Catalina de Guale) Amelia Island (Hutchinson and Larsen 2001), Republic Groves (Saunders 1972), Fort Center (Miller-Shaivitz and İşcan 1991), Precontact Tatham Mound (Hutchinson n.d.; Hutchinson and Norr n.d.), Postcontact Tatham Mound (Hutchinson n.d.; Hutchinson and Norr n.d.), San Martin (Hoshower 1992), PCPAG (Precontact Preagricultural) Georgia Coast (Larsen et al. 1991), PCAG (Precontact Agricultural) Georgia Coast (Larsen et al. 1991), N.C. Inner Coast (Hutchinson 2002a), N.C. Outer Coast (Hutchinson 2002a), SCDG (Santa Catalina de Guale) St. Catherines Island (Hutchinson and Larsen 2001), Moundville (Powell 1988a), Parkin (Murray 1985), Averbuch (Eisenberg 1991), Upland Georgia (Williamson 1998).

This individual experienced a dramatic and proliferative expansion of the red blood cell–producing marrow and did not survive childhood.

Noncoastal Florida populations have much lower frequencies (1–11%), with the exception of San Martin (32%) and Republic Groves (86%). In the San Martin population, males (63%) are much more commonly affected than females (17%) (Hoshower 1992). The frequencies in the other Florida noncoastal populations are too small to permit reliable

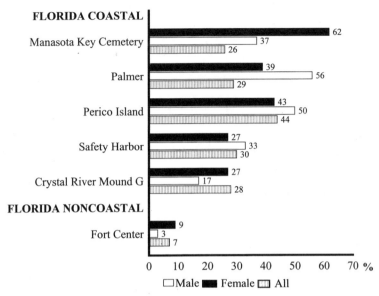

Fig. 5.11. Percent individuals by sex affected by porotic hyperostosis in Florida populations. *Sources*: Manasota Key (Dickel 1991), Palmer (this volume), Perico Island (this volume), Safety Harbor (this volume), Crystal River Mound G (Katzmarzyk 1998), Fort Center (Miller-Shaivitz and İşcan 1991).

Fig. 5.12. Porotic hyperostosis of an individual from Bishop Harbor, Florida.

sex comparisons. However, at Fort Center, females (9%) are more commonly affected than males (3%).

Porotic hyperostosis frequencies for Mississippian and Late Woodland populations in Georgia and Alabama (fig. 5.10) are lower than those for the Florida coast (3–17%), while Mission period populations in Florida and Georgia (27–32%) exhibit similar frequencies to most of the Florida coast populations. For populations north of Florida, it appears that the transition to maize agriculture and the later impact of European mission-ization and colonization resulted in an increase in porotic hyperostosis, undoubtedly through multiple etiologies that include phytate binding of iron, iron sequestration with fever, diarrhea, water contamination, and intestinal bleeding (Cook 1984; Goodman et al. 1984; Hutchinson 2002a; Larsen and Sering 2000; Larsen et al. 1992; Powell 1988a).

Most Florida populations did not adopt maize agriculture until after the arrival of Europeans. Furthermore, unlike either the Florida non-coastal or the panregional Southeast populations, there was no change through time in the percentage of individuals affected by porotic hyper-ostosis in Florida coastal populations. The frequencies exhibited in the Florida coastal populations *may* suggest that similar conditions prevailed from A.D. 500 through 1750 to cause porotic hyperostosis.

Given the apparent continued focus on maritime resources, intestinal parasites ingested with fish and shellfish are one probable source for iron-deficiency anemia. These parasites would cause intestinal bleeding and are a common problem in coastal populations that ingest raw seafood, as in Japan (Desowitz 1981). I have previously speculated (Hutchinson 2002a) that high rates of porotic hyperostosis for individuals inhabiting the inner (21%) and outer (36%) late prehistoric North Carolina coast are due to intestinal parasites. Another potential source of microorganisms is con-taminated freshwater supplies, as has been argued by Walker (1986) for California coastal populations.

Ubelaker (1992) found that porotic hyperostosis was much more fre-quent in coastal populations in Ecuador than in those from the highlands. Population aggregation and poor hygiene are the major causes, Ubelaker contends, for increased rates of helminth infections in late prehistory. Hel-minth disease is a common problem in contemporary coastal Ecuador, and is far less common in less densely populated highland regions.

Infectious Disease

Few specific infectious diseases have been reported for prehistoric or his-toric Florida populations for the reason that many diseases produce no skeletal lesions and those that are produced are usually nonspecific. For instance, proliferative responses (periostitis and osteomyelitis) of crania and long bones can be caused by many stimuli, including trauma, infec-tious diseases, and dietary deficiency. The morphology of proliferative lesions, as well as their occurrence in the skeleton, can provide valuable clues regarding specific infectious diseases.

The number of Florida Gulf coast individuals affected by proliferative responses ranged from 6% to 58% (fig. 5.13). Ross Hammock individuals on the Atlantic coast experienced relatively high frequencies of proliferative responses (32%). Proliferative responses were relatively common for interior precontact (26%) and postcontact (23%) individuals from Tatham Mound and the interior Mission population from San Martin (40%). Thus proliferative responses seem to be more common for interior Florida populations. They are more common for males at Manasota Key (males = 25%; females = 16%; fig. 5.14), but more common for females at Palmer (males = 8%; females = 14%) and Crystal River Mound G (males = 57%; females = 91%).

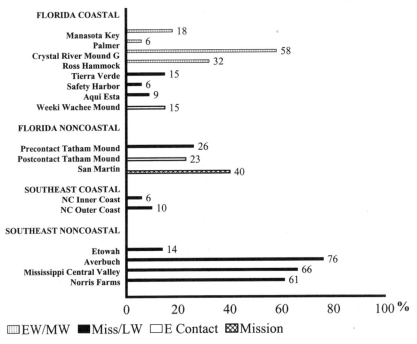

Fig. 5.13. Percentage of individuals affected by proliferative skeletal lesions in Florida and other Southeast populations. *Sources*: Manasota Key (Dickel 1991), Palmer (this volume), Crystal River Mound G (Katzmarzyk 1998), Ross Hammock (Pober 1996), Tierra Verde (Hutchinson 1993b), Safety Harbor (this volume), Aqui Esta (Hutchinson 2002b), Weeki Wachee Mound (Hutchinson and Mitchem 1996), Precontact Tatham Mound (Hutchinson n.d.; Hutchinson and Norr n.d.), Postcontact Tatham Mound (Hutchinson n.d.; Hutchinson and Norr n.d.), San Martin (Hoshower 1992), N.C. Inner Coast (Hutchinson 2002a), N.C. Outer Coast (Hutchinson 2002a), Etowah (Blakely 1977, 1980), Averbuch (Eisenberg 1991), Mississippi Central Valley (Rose et al. 1991), Norris Farms (Milner and Smith 1990; Milner et al. 1991).

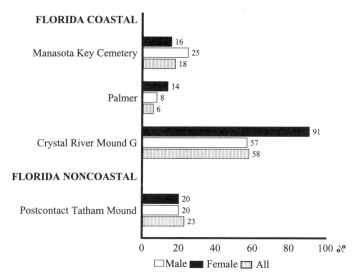

Fig. 5.14. Percent individuals by sex affected by proliferative skeletal lesions in Florida populations. *Sources*: Manasota Key (Dickel 1991), Palmer (this volume), Crystal River Mound G (Katzmarzyk 1998), Postcontact Tatham Mound (Hutchinson n.d.; Hutchinson and Norr n.d.).

Most of the proliferative responses primarily affected the periosteum, although some osteomyelitis was observed. Osteomyelitis in prehistoric Florida populations is often limited to a few individuals and often associated with compound fractures, as in the adult tibia with a compound fracture from Palmer (figs. 4.8, 4.17). Hematogenous osteomyelitis was reported for two Mission period individuals from San Martin (Hoshower 1992) and for at least six individuals in the Safety Harbor population (fig. 5.15).

The frequency of proliferative responses for interior southeastern populations appears to rise dramatically during the Mississippian period. Averbuch (76%), the Central Mississippi Valley (66%), and Norris Farms (61%) all exhibit much higher frequencies than earlier populations. Several researchers have indicated that the high frequencies of proliferative responses that occur in the Mississippian period are linked to the increased consumption of maize (Cohen and Armelagos 1984; Larsen 1995).

It seems likely that the proliferative responses in Florida populations are due to treponemal infections. In a recent study of treponemal infection in prehistoric and protohistoric populations inhabiting Florida and Georgia (Hutchinson et al. 2003a), we found that treponemal infections were present in 10 of 25 populations examined. Cranial stellate lesions (fig. 5.16), although usually found on less than 2% of the population, were

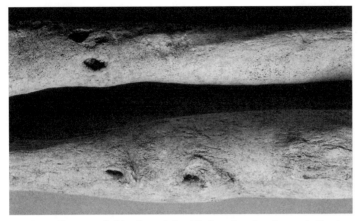

Fig. 5.15. Close-up of tibiae from Safety Harbor showing cloacae indicative of osteomyelitis.

Fig. 5.16. Stellate lesions of frontal of burial 37 from Tierra Verde. (From Hutchinson 1993: fig. 11. Reproduced with permission of John Wiley and Sons.)

observed in that study for individuals from Tatham Mound (Hutchinson 1993a:figs. 3, 4, 8), Weeki Wachee (Hutchinson 1991; Hutchinson and Mitchem 1996), Tierra Verde (Hutchinson 1993a:figs. 10–12), Crystal River (Green 1993; Hutchinson et al. 2003a:fig. 1), Perico Island (Hutchinson, this volume), and Safety Harbor (fig. 5.17).

Postcranial lesions, either associated with cranial stellate scars or singly, are also common in these populations. They range from moderate periosteal reactions (fig. 5.18) to saber tibiae (fig. 5.19; Hutchinson et al. 2003a:fig. 5). Medullary closure is seen in extreme cases (Hutchinson 1993a:figs. 6, 7). Other cases of cranial and postcranial lesions have been

Fig. 5.17. Stellate lesions on adult male cranium 48 from Safety Harbor.

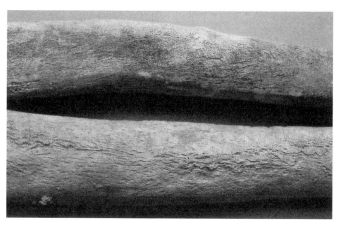

Fig. 5.18. Periosteal apposition of tibiae from Safety Harbor.

reported (table 5.2), indicating not only that the treponemal infections were prevalent in precontact Florida populations, but also that they have considerable antiquity, extending back to 3300 B.C. in peninsular Gulf coast Florida (Bullen 1972).

It does not appear that the skeletal expression of treponemal infection varied in Florida or Georgia during the period between at least A.D. 1 and 1500. The skeletal lesions suggest a disease most like the modern trepone-

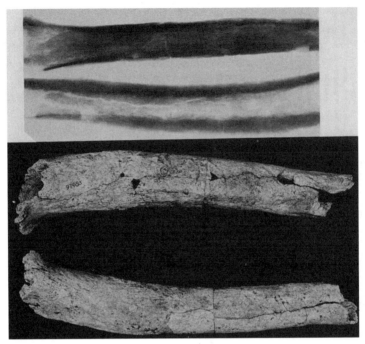

Fig. 5.19. Extreme periostitis of tibiae from Aqui Esta (FMNH #97485). (Adapted from Bullen 1972:fig. 12. Used with permission of the Florida Museum of Natural History.)

mal infections of yaws and endemic syphilis, and the relative frequency of the lesions suggests a continuity in disease pathogens and host populations. The prevalence of treponematosis does seem to increase around A.D. 800, although this may simply be an artifact of increased sample size. If it is a genuine increase in prevalence, then increased population prevalence at mound centers such as Florida Gulf coast Crystal River and Georgia coast Irene suggests that aggregated population centers facilitated transmission of the disease (Hutchinson et al. 2003a).

No lesions suggestive of venereal syphilis such as gummatous cranial lesions (Hackett 1951, 1976) or dental stigmata such as mulberry molars (Cook 1994) were found in any of the Florida Gulf coast populations. One adult individual from Tierra Verde (fig. 5.16) exhibited cranial lesion severity resembling that of venereal syphilis, but in the absence of other evidence it is not a convincing example. It thus appears that an endemic treponemal infection, generally acquired during childhood like the modern treponemal infections of yaws and endemic syphilis, was continuously present in populations inhabiting the Florida Gulf coast since at least the Archaic period.

Table 5.2. Documented cases of treponemal infection in Florida

Skeletal series	Date	N	Reference
Florida coast			
Aqui Esta	Safety Harbor	1	Bullen 1972; Hutchinson 1993a
Tierra Verde	Safety Harbor	3	Bullen 1972; Hutchinson 1993a,b; Sears 1967
Crystal River: main md., circular embankment	Weeden Island	6	Bullen 1972; Green 1993; Moore 1903, 1907
Crystal River: stone md.	Safety Harbor	1	Bullen 1972
Browne Mound	late St. Johns	1	Bullen 1972; Sears 1959
Lighthouse Mound	St. Johns/ Weeden Island	1	Bullen 1972; Bullen and Griffin 1952
Sowell Mound	Weeden Island	1	Bullen 1972; Moore 1902; Willey 1949
Hog Island	Weeden Island	1	Bullen 1972
Palmer Mound	A.D. 500–800	13	Bullen 1972; Bullen and Bullen 1976
Bayshore Homes	A.D. 850–1350	9	Brothwell 1970; Bullen 1972; Snow 1962
Highland Beach	A.D. 600–1200	2	İşcan and Miller-Shaivitz 1985
Horr's Island	Archaic	8	Brothwell 1970
Tidy Island	late prehistoric	1	William Burger, personal communication
Weeki Wachee	early contact	1	Hutchinson 1993a
Perico Island	early LW	2	Hutchinson, this volume
Safety Harbor	Safety Harbor	4	Hutchinson 1993a, this volume
Florida noncoast			
Tick Island	Archaic	1	Bullen 1972
Tick Island	early St. Johns	1	Bullen 1972; Moore 1894
Thursby Mound	early St. Johns	1	Bullen 1972; Moore 1894
Fort Center	A.D. 1–500/1000	1	Miller-Shaivitz and İşcan 1991; W. H. Sears 1982
Margate-Blount	A.D. 750–1200	1	İşcan 1983
Tatham Mound	early contact	4+	Hutchinson 1991, 1993a, n.d.

Lifestyle and Activity

External Auditory Exostoses

Physical anthropologist Aleš Hrdlička conducted one of the earliest systematic studies of external auditory exostoses, and he emphasized that they were probably caused by a combination of heredity and mechanical or chemical stimulation to bone growth (Hrdlička 1935). Since that time, many researchers have emphasized a hereditary origin (e.g., Buikstra and Ubelaker 1994) and few studies have differentiated auditory exostoses due to heredity from those due to other factors (e.g., Hutchinson et al. 1997).

The etiology most often cited for external auditory exostoses that are nonhereditary (pedunculated; Hutchinson et al. 1997) is frequent and prolonged exposure to cold water, and it is based on several sets of observations. First, external auditory exostoses are frequently associated with behaviors such as swimming, surfing, and diving, and thus have often been attributed to cold water exposure (DiBartolomeo 1979; Filipo et al. 1982). Second, experimental studies designed to test the hypothesis of cold-water causation generally support the hypothesis (DiBartolomeo 1979; Fowler and Osmun 1942; Van Gilse 1938). Third, external auditory exostoses are most common in prehistoric coastal populations located between 30° and 45° north and south latitude (Kennedy 1986). Therefore, several researchers have attributed them to cold-water exposure (Ascenzi and Balisteri 1975; Frayer 1988; Lambert 2001; Manzi et al. 1991; Standen et al. 1997; Velasco-Vazquez et al. 2000).

However, Hutchinson and coworkers (1997) contend that cold water is not a sufficient exclusive etiology for external auditory exostoses. Exostosis formation is more likely stimulated by a wide variety of epithelial conditions that reflect hydration, pH imbalance, and other chemical, mechanical, and biological factors. Despite numerous reported instances of external auditory exostoses in archaeologically recovered human remains, there have been only a few systematic studies examining these bony growths across several populations and in multiple climatic zones (Hrdlička 1935; Kennedy 1986).

Regardless of the etiology, the complete absence of external auditory exostoses in many Florida Gulf coast populations (Tierra Verde, Aqui Esta, Weeki Wachee, Galt Island, Palmer, Pine Island, and Buck Key) is contrary to that observed in many other coastal populations. Standen and coworkers (1997) found that 31% of coastal individuals in prehistoric Chilean coastal populations had external auditory exostoses. In the Palmer population, no external auditory exostoses were seen, despite observation of all available crania with temporals as well as disarticulated temporals (n = 165; 12 subadults, 41 adult males, 45 adult females, 67 indeterminate sex adults). Similar results were obtained in the examination of several hundred individuals from the North Carolina coast (Hutchinson 2002a), where only three cases were found.

Located at 20–30° north latitude, the Florida Gulf coast is outside of the cold-water range predicted by Kennedy (1986), but studies of the water temperature in Charlotte Harbor (Estevez et al. 1984) place the January and February temperature within the range of some temperatures

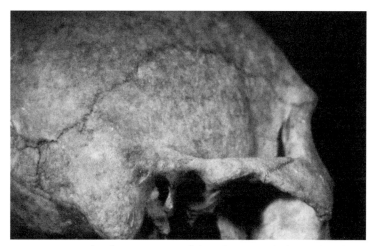

Fig. 5.20. External auditory exostoses of the right temporal of individual from Useppa Island.

used in experimental studies (Fowler and Osmun 1942; Van Gilse 1938). Nonetheless, only one adult male from Useppa Island in Charlotte Harbor exhibited these neoplastic growths. He had multiple exostoses in both ear canals (fig. 5.20).

Exernal auditory exostoses were common, however, in some Tampa Bay populations. Eleven of the adults from Safety Harbor (12%) were affected by external auditory exostoses. Males (18%) were much more commonly affected than females (5%). Perico Island adults (5%) did not exhibit as many exostoses, but males (12%) were again more frequently affected than females (0%).

Interior populations in Florida did not exhibit external auditory exostoses and they are uncommon for interior populations throughout the Southeast. However, Lambert (2001) reports high frequencies of them for piedmont (14%) and mountain (38%) populations in North Carolina and Virginia, hypothesizing that the cold water of high altitude streams was a likely explanation. In coastal North Carolina, external auditory exostoses were uncommon, with frequencies of 1% of individuals affected for inner coastal populations and 2% of individuals affected for outer coastal populations.

My observations of coastal populations inhabiting the Florida Gulf and Atlantic coasts (this volume), as well as the North Carolina coast (Hutchinson 2002a) do not support either coastal habitation or cold water as a sufficient etiology for external auditory exostosis formation. I hypothesize that a combination of behaviors that result in frequent exposure of the auditory canal to water, potentially combined with water temperature, and most importantly resulting in inflammation are the predisposing factors to external auditory exostosis formation. Furthermore, exostosis formation may not be due to univariate causes. The high frequency of exostoses in the Perico Island and Safety Harbor populations may indicate shared behaviors, perhaps the frequent collection of aquatic resources in the more protected Tampa Bay.

Osteoarthritis

Osteoarthritis frequencies were highly variable for Florida populations (fig. 5.21). For instance, Manasota Key individuals had high rates of osteoarthritis (44%), while Tierra Verde individuals experienced very little osteoarthritis (4%). The Palmer population had lower frequencies (11%) than the nearby and roughly contemporary Manasota Key population. The high frequency of osteoarthritis for the Manasota Key cemetery may be due to poor preservation, which inflated the percentage of individuals affected (Dickel 1991:58), both through enhanced bone preservation

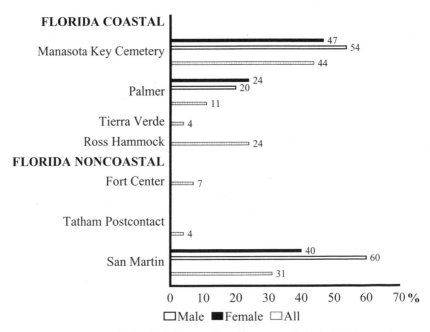

Fig. 5.21. Percentage of individuals by sex affected by osteoarthritis in Florida populations. *Sources*: Ross Hammock (Pober 1996), Manasota Key (Dickel 1991), Palmer (this volume), Tierra Verde (Hutchinson 1993b), Fort Center (Miller-Shaivitz and İşcan 1991), Postcontact Tatham Mound (Hutchinson n.d.; Hutchinson and Norr n.d.), San Martin (Hoshower 1992).

(pathological bone is often denser) and through sample bias. Nonetheless, Snow (1962:19) reports that degenerative joint disease was common in the population from Bayshore Homes. The Ross Hammock population on the Atlantic coast experienced relatively high (24%) rates of osteoarthritis (Pober 1996).

Frequencies of individuals affected by osteoarthritis were generally lower for Florida noncoastal populations, such as those from Fort Center (7%) and postcontact Tatham Mound (4%). However, the interior Mission period population at San Martin had high rates of individuals affected by osteoarthritis (31%), perhaps reflecting the labor demands placed on local indigenous populations by the Spanish (Larsen et al. 1992).

Male and female comparisons are not made in several of the Florida skeletal series because of the inflated percentages that result from small sample size (fig. 5.21). More males (54%) than females (47%) from Manasota Key were affected by osteoarthritis. The trend was reversed in the Palmer population, however, with more females (24%) than males (20%) affected by osteoarthritis. More males (60%) than females (40%) from San Martin were affected by osteoarthritis. Because osteoarthritis frequencies are commonly reported by element rather than by individual, comparisons in the panregional Southeast were not made.

Trauma

Trauma is not particularly frequent in most Florida populations, and cranial trauma is not at all frequent. There were no individuals exhibiting cranial trauma in the Gulf coast populations from Tierra Verde (n = 48; Hutchinson 1993b), Weeki Wachee (n = 84; Hutchinson and Mitchem 1996), or Manasota Key (n = 120) or in the noncoastal postcontact Tatham Mound (n = 339; Hutchinson n.d.). Postcranial trauma was only present in the Gulf coast population from Weeki Wachee (n = 1; 5% of adults) and the interior postcontact Tatham Mound (n = 4; 2% of adults) population. Snow (1962) reports that fractures are rare in the Gulf coast Bayshore Homes population, and are healed with good alignment.

Trauma has been reported in some Florida populations, however. It appears to decline through time from the Archaic period until there is a slight resurgence in frequency following contact with Europeans (fig. 5.22). From the Archaic Atlantic coast Gauthier population, Maples (1987) noted that two females had cranial depression fractures and that "about two dozen individuals" had fractures. Five of these individuals had pseudarthroses (fractures that do not unite properly) of the ulnae. If Maples's fracture and demography figures are correct, then approxi-

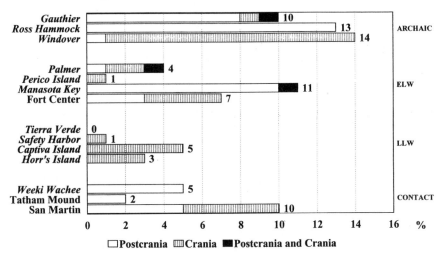

Fig. 5.22. Percentage of adult individuals affected by trauma in Florida populations. Coastal populations are italicized. Only crania were examined for Perico Island, Captiva Island, and Horr's Island. *Sources:* Gauthier (Maples 1987), Ross Hammock (Pober 1996), Windover (Walsh-Haney 1999), Palmer (this volume), Perico Island (this volume), Manasota Key (Dickel 1991), Fort Center (Miller-Shaivitz and İşcan 1991), Tierra Verde (Hutchinson 1993b), Safety Harbor (this volume), Captiva Island (this volume), Horr's Island (this volume), Weeki Wachee Mound (Hutchinson n.d.), Postcontact Tatham Mound (Hutchinson n.d.; Hutchinson and Norr n.d.), San Martin (Hoshower 1992).

mately 20% of the Gauthier population experienced long bone fractures. Individuals in the Archaic Atlantic coast population from Windover Pond frequently experienced trauma; 13% of the individuals interred there exhibited blunt cranial trauma. In the early Late Woodland Gulf coast population from Manasota Key, Dickel (1991) reports that one female (6% of females; 1% of the total population) exhibited blunt trauma to the cranium.

Postcranial trauma in the Manasota Key population was more frequent, with nine individuals (11% of adults; 18% of females and 21% of males) exhibiting fractures. Most of these ($n = 7$) were lower arm fractures. Other Gulf coast trauma cases include one female (0.5% of all adults) from the early Late Woodland population interred at Perico Island ($n = 215$), who exhibited blunt trauma to the cranium, and one male (1% of all adults) from Safety Harbor who had a broken nose. Four adult males (3–5% of all crania) from the interior Florida Fort Center population had cranial depression fractures. Three adults (3%) and one subadult (1%) from Fort Center exhibited postcranial trauma, and 4 adults (4%) exhibited cranial trauma (Miller-Shaivitz and İşcan 1991).

Fourteen adults (4%) from Palmer exhibited some form of trauma. Six of these individuals had fractures of the arms that were healed but misaligned (figs. 4.14, 4.16–4.19), similar to the pseudarthroses reported by Maples (1987) for Gauthier. Ten adults (3%) exhibited blunt cranial trauma (figs. 4.20–4.24). Males (n = 6; 11%) were affected more frequently than females (n = 3; 5%). Two adult individuals exhibited both cranial and postcranial trauma. No cases of embedded stone projectile points or other objects were observed.

Comparison with other southeastern populations with cranial trauma shows that the frequency at Palmer is not particularly high, but is on average with southeastern populations exhibiting numerous trauma cases (fig. 5.23). In Alabama, for instance, 1% of individuals from Moundville and 6% of individuals from Koger's Island had cranial fractures (Bridges et al. 2000). Although cranial fractures were not observed in the western Tennessee valley (Smith 1997), three cases of scalping and one possible case of healed projectile trauma (total of 1%) were observed on crania. More detailed comparison with those populations yields a number of

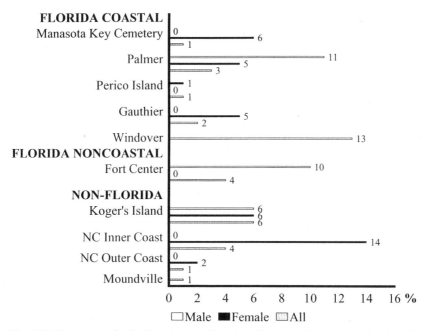

Fig. 5.23. Percentage of individuals by sex affected by blunt cranial trauma in Florida and other Southeast populations. *Sources*: Manasota Key (Dickel 1991), Palmer (this volume), Perico Island (this volume), Gauthier (Maples 1987), Windover (Walsh-Haney 1999), Fort Center (Miller-Shaivitz and İşcan 1991), Koger's Island (Bridges 1996; Bridges et al. 2000), N.C. Inner and Outer Coast (Hutchinson 2002a); Moundville (Powell 1988a).

insights regarding interpretation of the behaviors that resulted in the trauma. Mutilation and dismemberment (trophy-taking) have been observed in populations from Koger's Island in Alabama (Bridges 1996; Bridges et al. 2000) and the western Tennessee valley (Smith 1996, 1997), as well as stab wounds and embedded projectiles (Smith 1997).

None of the Palmer cranial or postcranial elements or those from other Florida Gulf coast populations exhibited mutilation, dismemberment, or stab wounds. DeBry depicted the mutilation of the enemy dead Timucua from north Florida as witnessed by the French between 1561 and 1565 (Lorant 1965:65), but it has not been documented in skeletal materials from Florida. However, projectile points have been found embedded in skeletal elements of individuals interred at McKeithen from the Weeden Island period (A.D. 350–475; Milanich et al. 1984b) and from Windover from the early Archaic period (8000–5000 B.C.; Doran 2002).

The frequency of trauma at Palmer is impressive when compared with Florida coastal and noncoastal populations, as well as with populations from Tennessee and Alabama. More importantly, the higher frequencies of trauma in earlier populations from Gauthier, Manasota Key, Fort Center, and Palmer as compared with later populations may indicate a trend toward less interpersonal violence. Such a trend would support Widmer's (1988) argument that changes in social and political organization after A.D. 800 reduced local disputes and raids brought about by saturated carrying capacity.

All of the cases of trauma from Palmer exhibited some healing; therefore the injuries were not the immediate cause of death. Only one tibia had a cloaca, indicating osteomyelitis. The healed nature of the lesions and the absence of any other trauma, such as cut marks indicating scalping or other mutilation, suggest that the deaths were probably not due to massacre but to more occasional raiding.

Dietary Reconstruction

Stable isotope signatures are available for 18 populations in Florida that lived in diverse ecological zones from the northern peninsula to the southern tip, the Atlantic and Gulf coasts, and the interior (table 5.3). The dietary reconstruction for Palmer indicates that marine resources formed the bulk of the diet (appendixes E and F). There were no statistically significant differences between male and female dietary signatures at Palmer. The isotope signatures from Palmer are very similar for other Gulf coast populations from Tierra Verde, Galt Island, Buck Key, and Useppa Island (Norr et al. n.d.; fig. 5.24). Thus the subsistence base for most of the Gulf coast populations discussed in this study was focused on marine resources and terrestrial fruits and tubers. However, it is possible that there was an increased focus on maritime resources following the Archaic period as indicated by the isotope signatures from the Archaic Gulf coast Horr's Island population, which mark an emphasis on a wider range of terrestrial and marine resources.

With regard to Florida noncoastal populations, the precontact individuals from Tatham ($n = 3$) have isotope values consistent with a diet focused on freshwater lacustrine and riverine fauna, and to a lesser degree on C_3 plants and terrestrial fauna (Hutchinson and Norr 1994). There is no $\delta^{13}C$ signature indicating the consumption of C_4 grasses such as maize. There is a positive shift in the isotope values of the postcontact (A.D. 1525–1550) individuals ($n = 19$). Thus, it is clear that the postcontact population consumed a higher proportion of ^{13}C-rich carbohydrates that may have included limited quantities of maize.

Table 5.3. Dietary reconstruction for Florida and adjacent areas

Series	$\delta^{15}N$	$\delta^{13}Cco$	$\delta^{13}Cca$	Cca-Cco
6000–500 B.C.				
Horr's Island	11.1	-10.2	-6.1	4.4
Bay West	9.9	-11.9	-4.0	7.9
Tick Island	13.2	-11.4		
Windover	11.8	-15.5		
500 B.C.–A.D. 1200				
Coastal Georgia (500 B.C.–A.D. 1000)	12.8	-15.1		
Inland Georgia	11.1	-16.0		
Inland Florida (A.D. 600–1200)	10.3	-15.9		
Palmer	10.9	-9.5	-7.0	2.5
Caloosahatchee Post (A.D. 500)	11.9	-8.1	-5.9	2.3
A.D. 1200–1600				
Georgia coastal	12.6	-13.4		
Georgia inland	10.2	-15.1		
Northern Florida coastal	12.6	-16.1		
Northern Florida inland	10.1	-13.7		
NC LW inner coast[a]	14.0	-14.9	-8.1	6.8
NC LW outer coast[a]	13.9	-11.8	-7.4	4.5
Tierra Verde	12.5	-8.4	-6.0	2.4
Tatham Precontact	10.6	-20.7	-15.4	4.2
Tatham Contact	11.3	-17.3	-11.8	5.7
Post-1600 (Mission)				
Coastal Florida	10.2	-11.8		
Coastal Georgia	9.4	-11.5		
Inland Florida	8.6	-12.4		

a. NC LW = North Carolina Late Woodland.

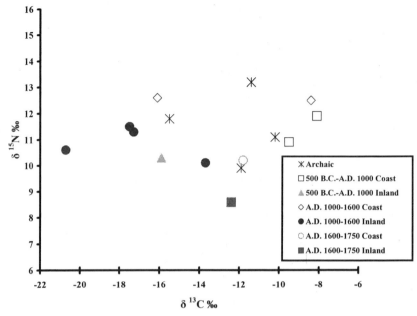

Fig. 5.24. Comparative isotope signatures from Florida.

It is only in the northern peninsular portion of Florida that dietary reconstruction indicates reliance on maize prior to European contact. Archaeological sites in this region show significant architectural and artifactual characteristics of Mississippian groups to the north, and it is therefore not surprising that an emphasis on maize agriculture accompanied those other characteristics (Hutchinson et al. 1998, 2000; Larsen et al. 2001).

Hypothetical Comparisons: Hypotheses 1 through 4

In order to place the comparisons conducted above within a contextual framework, they must be related to the three themes and four hypotheses previously articulated. The three themes are (1) coastal adaptation and a variety of behaviors oriented around coastal foraging and marine foods and food preparation methods, (2) the pervasiveness of the coastal environment for nearly all populations inhabiting Florida, and (3) the early and nearly continuous concentration on maritime resources by Florida populations that began during the Archaic period and persisted until European colonization.

The four hypotheses are (1) that the diet of central peninsular Gulf coast populations after 500 B.C. was focused largely on animals and plants foraged from marine contexts, (2) that central peninsular Gulf coast populations will exhibit differences in pathological lesion frequencies that can be attributed to localized resource exploitation, (3) that interior populations (25 km or more from the coast) had a different dietary focus and different nutritional and disease experiences than central peninsular Gulf coast populations, and (4) that males and females will exhibit differences in dietary focus, health, and behavioral alterations indicating sexual differences in nutrition, disease, and health.

Trends in Diet

Hypothesis 1 is that the diet of central peninsular Gulf coast populations did not include maize, but was focused instead on maritime subsistence resources; further, that the diet was relatively consistent between at least A.D. 500 and 1500. The stable isotope data (table 5.3) demonstrate that marine resources formed the bulk of the diet for Florida peninsular Gulf coast populations from the Archaic through late prehistory (fig. 5.24). Thus, hypothesis 1 is accepted.

Heterogeneity of Peninsular Gulf Coast Florida Populations

Hypothesis 2 states that coastal populations will exhibit considerable differences in pathological lesion frequencies that can be attributed to localized resource exploitation. Pathological lesions reflecting diet (carious lesions and alveolar infection), and behavioral alterations reflecting mastication (dental chipping) tend to support this hypothesis.

The frequency of teeth affected by carious lesions in Florida coastal populations ranges from 1% to 34% with a midrange value of 1% (table 5.4; fig. 5.1). Inland Florida populations, on the other hand, have a much narrower range of teeth affected by carious lesions (2–5%), but a midrange value of 4% (table 5.4; fig. 5.1). The frequency of coastal Florida individuals affected by carious lesions ranges from 1% to 82% with a midrange at 6% (table 5.4; figs. 5.2, 5.3). This is lower than the frequency of interior Florida individuals affected by carious lesions (14–25%; midrange = 19%) (table 5.4).

Alveolar infections show a similar range (0–49% of individuals affected; midrange = 13.5%) (table 5.4; fig. 5.4). Dental chipping is highly variable, with frequencies between 14% and 62% and midrange at 32.5% (table 5.4; fig. 5.7); however, I could not establish any geographic or ecological pattern to the variation. High frequencies of dental chipping and alveolar infection tend to occur for the same populations.

Table 5.4. Comparison of pathological conditions and behavioral alterations in Florida and Southeast populations

	Coastal Florida[a]		Inland Florida[a]			Coastal Southeast[b]		Inland Southeast[b]		
	Range	Mrange	Range	Mrange	Sig	Range	Mrange	Range	Mrange	Sig
Diet and mastication										
Carious lesions: Teeth	1–34	1	2–5	4	n	1–19	11	10–25	18.5	Y
Carious lesions: Individuals	1–82	6	14–25	19	Y	9–65	36	50–77	53	Y
Alveolar infection	0–49	13.5	7–9	8	n	20–32	26	—	—	
Dental chipping	14–62	32.5	—	—		11–44	27.5	—	—	
Metabolic disruption										
Enamel hypoplasia	8–78	35	33–75	57	n	9–88	50.5	54–86	63	n
Porotic hyperostosis	4–44	29	1–86	11	n	0–36	21	4–39	12.5	n
Infectious disease										
Proliferative responses: Individuals	6–58	15	23–40	26	n	6–10	8	14–76	63.5	Y
Lifestyle and activity										
Osteoarthritis: Individuals	4–44	17.5	4–31	7	n	—	—	—	—	
Postcranial trauma: Individuals	0–13	8	1–5	3	n	—	—			
Cranial blunt trauma: Individuals	1–13	2.5	4–5	4.5	n	4–5	4.5	1–6	3.5	n
External auditory exostoses: Individuals	0–12	0	0	0	n	1–2	1.5	14–38[c]	26	n

a. Range = range of percentages affected by condition; mrange = midpoint percentage of range (median); sig = significant difference between Florida coastal and Florida inland: notched box plot.

b. Range = range of percentages affected by condition; mrange = midpoint percentage of range (median); sig = significant difference between Florida coastal and inland, and Southeast coastal and inland: notched box plot.

c. Based entirely on Lambert 2001.

Pathological lesions reflecting metabolic disruption show both extreme variation and remarkable similarity. The percentage of individuals affected by enamel hypoplasias ranges from 8% to 78% with a midrange at 35% (table 5.4; fig. 5.8). The percentage of individuals affected by porotic hyperostosis ranges from 4% to 44% (midrange = 29%), with remarkable similarity for seven of the populations between 26% and 30% (table 5.4; fig. 5.10).

Proliferative responses (periosteal reactions and osteomyelitis) serve as a measure of infectious disease and other insults to the periosteum such as trauma. The percentage of individuals affected by proliferative responses ranged from 6% to 58% (midrange = 15%) in peninsular Florida Gulf coast populations, suggesting differences in disease experience. Hutchinson and coworkers (2003a) examined most of these same populations for lesions suggestive of treponemal infection and found that frequent cases of treponematosis occur in many of those populations with frequent proliferative responses (e.g., Crystal River Mound G).

Pathological lesions and behavioral alterations such as osteoarthritis and external auditory exostoses showed more localized variation. The percentage of individuals affected by osteoarthritis ranged from 4% to 44% (midrange = 17.5%) for peninsular Gulf coast populations. Exostoses were seen in only a few populations (Useppa Island, Perico Island, Safety Harbor) and generally in multiple individuals. They did not exhibit the morphology of hereditarily influenced exostoses (pedunculated), and behavioral similarities probably explain their occurrence in multiple individuals.

All of the populations with exostoses are located on protected areas of Charlotte Harbor and Tampa Bay, suggesting that the behaviors practiced by those populations provided more opportunity for exostosis development. As most current hypotheses of exostosis etiology stress water exposure (but vary on the emphasis of temperature vs. infection), it would seem that the bay-dwelling populations experienced more frequent physical contact of their auditory canals with the water, perhaps in fishing or collecting activities.

Thus, there is supportive data for differences in diet and mastication, metabolic disruption, infectious disease, and lifestyle between peninsular Florida Gulf coast populations. Periodontal infections were frequent for Gulf coast populations, which may be linked in part to dental damage in the form of enamel chipping. Porotic hyperostosis frequencies were remarkably similar between Gulf coast populations and were much more frequent than for interior populations.

I hypothesize that the high frequencies for the coastal populations, at least in part, were caused by intestinal bleeding due to parasites ingested with shellfish and fish. Carious lesions and porotic hyperostosis have often been used to gauge maize consumption by paleopathologists, and we are only now beginning to appreciate that, while high frequencies of those pathological conditions often indicate maize consumption, they cannot be attributed solely to this cause (Hutchinson 2002a).

Comparisons between Coastal and Interior Florida and the Regional Southeast

Hypothesis 3 states that interior populations (those more than 25 km from the coast) have different dietary focus and different nutritional and disease experiences than coastal populations. Futhermore, the patterns of change in pathology frequency will be different between coastal and interior populations, with interior populations exhibiting more change through time than coastal populations. These comparisons are made with other populations inhabiting the southeastern United States as well.

The dietary focus was reconstructed using stable isotopes of carbon and nitrogen. Dental enamel microwear was not compared because it had been applied only to the Palmer population.

Comparison of dietary values between the Florida coastal and noncoastal populations with those from the greater Southeast presents several difficulties (table 5.3; fig. 5.25). First, in this study and in our previous dietary reconstruction for North Carolina coastal populations, we observed significant local variation in dietary focus (and see Hutchinson et al. 1998, 2000; Larsen et al. 2001). Although broad discussions of $\delta^{13}C$ signatures can be made with reference to the potential for maize consumption, more detailed discussions are difficult.

Furthermore, much of our interpretation relies on the difference between the carbon values obtained from apatite and collagen. The calculation of apatite carbon values is a relatively recent procedure, and many earlier dietary reconstructions did not employ it, making comparisons impossible. Consequently, I will limit the Southeast discussion of dietary change through time to Florida and Georgia and to carbon values obtained from collagen.

In our analysis (Hutchinson et al. 1998, 2000; Larsen et al. 2001) of 28 populations inhabiting a range of environments between 400 B.C. and A.D. 1700 in Florida and Georgia, we drew two major conclusions regarding the overall trends in diet. First, although maize became a frequent component of the diet in Georgia following A.D. 1000, it was not a major com-

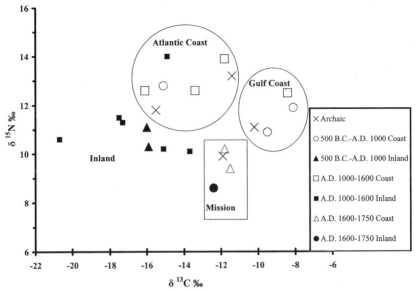

Fig. 5.25. Comparative isotope signatures from Florida, Georgia, and North Carolina. *Sources*: Hutchinson 2002a, this volume; Hutchinson et al. 1998, 2000; Norr 2002; Norr et al. n.d., this volume; Quinn 1999.

ponent of the diet in Florida until after European missionization and colonization. Prior to contact, only those Florida panhandle populations at Lake Jackson and Waddell's Mill Pond had isotope signatures suggesting maize consumption. Both of these populations are located in the northern Florida panhandle and both exhibit Mississippian cultural and settlement characteristics.

Second, prior to European contact, local dietary influences are apparent in both Florida and Georgia, with interior populations having terrestrial resource isotope signatures and those located on the coast having marine resource isotope signatures. Local dietary resources were eaten in Georgia alongside consumption of maize. Following the establishment of Spanish missions and settlements (A.D. 1600–1700), however, all Florida and Georgia populations show a convergence of diet oriented around maize with a major reduction in the contribution of local resources (Hutchinson et al. 1998, 2000; Larsen et al. 2001).

Comparison of the mean isotope signatures from our previous studies (Hutchinson 2002a; Hutchinson et al. 1998, 2000; Larsen et al. 2001; Norr 2002; Norr et al. n.d.) with the data incorporated in this study reveals some interesting trends (fig. 5.25). First, there is very little change in dietary focus between the Archaic peninsular Florida Gulf coast Horr's Island population and those up until A.D. 1400 (Palmer, Galt Island,

Useppa Island, Buck Key, and Tierra Verde), except for the differences noted above for Horr's Island. Second, there is a wide variation in isotope signatures for Archaic populations, with possible contamination of the Bay West samples (see DeLeon 1998 for discussion). Third, there is a definite difference between the Florida Gulf coast populations and those located on the Atlantic coast in Florida, Georgia, and North Carolina, with the Florida Gulf coast populations exhibiting far more positive $\delta^{13}C$ signatures. While these might suggest increased consumption of C_4 plants, the additional analysis of the bone apatite carbonate reveals that there are no C_4 plants in the diet and that the signatures are due to marine resources (appendix E).

Consequently, the data from the Florida peninsular Gulf coast represent a dramatic increase in our knowledge of prehistoric dietary trends through time in the southeastern United States. They demonstrate without doubt that marine resources formed the bulk of the diet for Florida peninsular Gulf coast populations from the Archaic through late prehistory. As well, the data demonstrate that a marine-focused diet was not a phenomenon unique to the Calusa, but was widespread on the Florida Gulf coast. They show as well that there may have been substantial dietary diversity during the Archaic. Such diversity would not be surprising given the tremendous chronological span of the Archaic and the potentially changing environment represented by both temperature and sea level fluctuations.

Pathological lesions that were used to compare diet were carious lesions and alveolar infection. The percentage of teeth affected by carious lesions was slightly higher for interior Florida populations than for those from the coastal (table 5.4; figs. 5.1, 5.26). For instance, six coastal populations exhibited frequencies below or at 1% (midrange = 1%) of teeth affected, while no interior populations had less than 2% (midrange = 4%) of teeth affected. The percentage of individuals affected by carious lesions (table 5.4; figs. 5.2, 5.27) showed more dramatic differences, with only one mission population exceeding 14% (midrange = 6%), while all but one of the inland populations were between 14% and 25% (midrange = 19%). Significant differences were found for carious lesions for individuals between Florida coastal and Florida inland population using notched box plots ($p \leq .05$; table 5.4).

The low frequency of teeth and individuals affected by carious lesions in Florida populations stands in stark contrast to other populations from the Southeast (table 5.4; figs. 5.1–5.3, 5.26, 5.27). With the exception of the preagricultural Georgia coast populations, all coastal and interior Southeast populations had more than 8% of teeth and 35% of individuals affected by carious lesions. In general, more inland teeth (midrange =

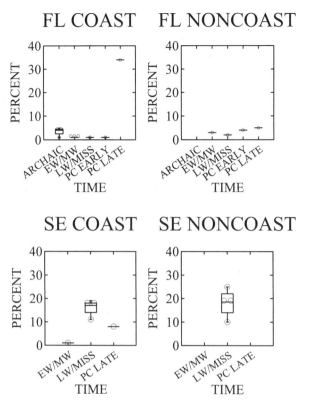

Fig. 5.26. Comparative box plots of carious lesions for teeth in coastal and noncoastal Florida and other Southeast populations.

18.5%) and individuals (midrange = 53%) were affected than coastal teeth (midrange = 11%) and individuals (midrange = 36%). Carious lesions do not increase in frequency in Florida until the Mission period, when the percentage of individuals increases dramatically in the Mission populations from San Martin and Santa Catalina de Guale-Amelia Island. Carious lesion frequencies increase dramatically in the Southeast prior to missionization, especially in Mississippian populations such as Moundville. Statistically significant differences between coastal and inland Florida and Southeast populations for carious lesions for individuals were found using notched box plots ($p \leq .05$; table 5.4).

More coastal Florida individuals were affected by alveolar infections, with many populations having more than 13% (midrange = 13.5%) of the individuals affected (table 5.4; figs. 5.4, 5.28). Inland Florida populations had 7–9% (midrange = 8%) of the individuals affected by alveolar infections. Alveolar infections appear to decrease through time, with the highest frequencies prior to the Mississippian and Late Woodland period.

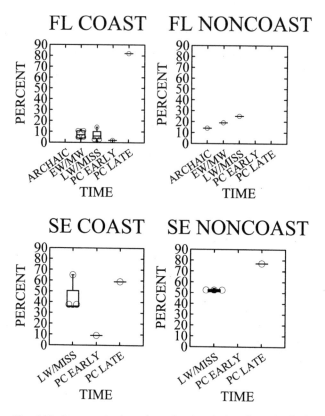

Fig. 5.27. Comparative box plots of carious lesions for individuals in coastal and noncoastal Florida and other Southeast populations.

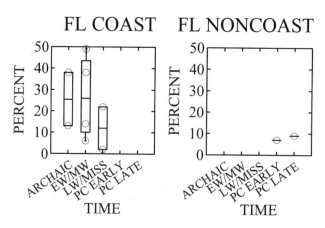

Fig. 5.28. Comparative box plots of alveolar infections for individuals in coastal and noncoastal Florida populations.

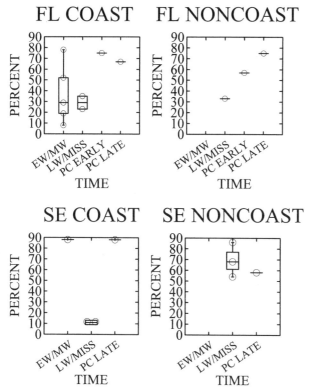

Fig. 5.29. Comparative box plots of enamel hypoplasia for individuals in coastal and noncoastal Florida and other Southeast populations.

Comparative data for other Southeast populations was available only for inner and outer coastal North Carolina, with 20% of the inner and 32% of the outer coastal individuals affected. There were no statistically significant differences for alveolar infection.

Metabolic disruption was measured by enamel hypoplasias and porotic hyperostosis. The Florida coastal populations were bimodal in the percentage of individuals affected by enamel hypoplasia (table 5.4; figs. 5.7, 5.29). Five populations (Manasota Key, Crystal River Mound G, Safety Harbor, Ross Hammock, and Aqui Esta) had less than 50% of individuals affected, while four populations (Palmer, Perico Island, Weeki Wachee, and SCDG-Amelia Island) had more than 50% of individuals affected by enamel hypoplasia (midrange of all populations = 35%). Of the three inland Florida populations, two had frequencies of individuals affected by enamel hypoplasia greater than 50% (midrange = 57%). The percentage of individuals affected by enamel hypoplasia is generally higher for coastal (midrange = 63%) and noncoastal (midrange = 50.5%) Southeast popula-

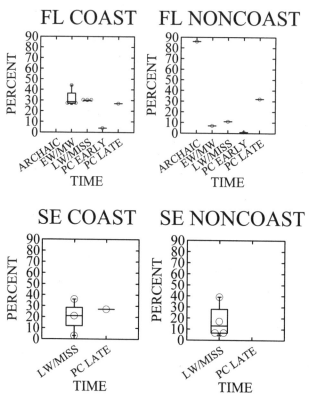

Fig. 5.30. Comparative box plots of porotic hyperostosis for individuals in coastal and noncoastal Florida and other Southeast populations.

tions, with all populations greater than 50% except the North Carolina coastal populations with frequencies between 9% and 13%. There were no clear chronological trends in enamel hypoplasia frequency for either Florida or the greater Southeast. No statistically significant differences were found for enamel hypoplasias.

Porotic hyperostosis was common for coastal Florida populations, with most populations having more than 25% affected (midrange = 29%; table 5.4, figs. 5.10, 5.30). Florida inland populations were less affected by porotic hyperostosis (midrange = 11% of individuals affected). The pattern of populations in the Southeast was remarkably similar, with coastal individuals (midrange = 21%) affected more frequently than interior individuals (midrange = 12.5%). Porotic hyperostosis has no clear chronological trends in Florida coastal populations; however, in noncoastal Florida and the remainder of the Southeast it increases in the Mississippian and later Mission periods for populations from San Martin,

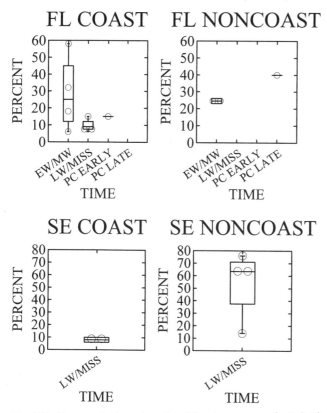

Fig. 5.31. Comparative box plots of proliferative responses for individuals in coastal and noncoastal Florida and other Southeast populations.

Santa Catalina de Guale, and Averbuch. No statistically significant differences were found for porotic hyperostosis.

Proliferative responses (periosteal reactions and osteomyelitis) were used as an indicator of infectious disease. The responses were more frequent for Florida interior individuals (midrange = 26%) than Florida coastal individuals (midrange = 15%; table 5.4; figs. 5.13, 5.31). More coastal individuals (midrange = 63.5%) were affected by proliferative responses throughout the Southeast than those from the interior (midrange = 8%). In general, proliferative responses increased in frequency of individuals affected following the Mississippian period in Florida and greater Southeast populations. No statistically significant differences were found for proliferative responses between Florida coastal and inland populations, but statistically significant differences between Southeast coastal and inland populations were found using notched box plots ($p \leq .05$; table 5.4).

The pathological lesions used to indicate lifestyle were osteoarthritis and trauma. Only Florida populations were considered because the percentage of individuals affected was used as a measure and not the percentage of elements affected. Coastal individuals (midrange = 17.5%) more frequently experienced osteoarthritis as compared with inland individuals (midrange = 7%; table 5.4; fig. 5.21). Postcranial trauma was present for Florida coastal (Weeki Wachee, Manasota Key, Gauthier, Ross Hammock, Windover) and inland (Tatham, Fort Center, San Martin) populations. For both Manasota Key and Ross Hammock, more than 8% of individuals were affected by postcranial trauma. In contrast, San Martin exhibited the highest number of individuals affected (5%) for Florida inland populations.

Cranial blunt trauma was often infrequent for Florida coastal populations, commonly with 1–5% of the individuals affected (midrange = 2.5%; table 5.4; fig. 5.23). Florida inland populations generally had higher frequencies of individuals affected (midrange = 4.5%) by cranial blunt trauma. Similarily, cranial blunt trauma was infrequent for Southeast coastal (midrange = 4.5) and inland (midrange = 3.5) individuals. There are not enough comparative data regarding the percentage of individuals affected by osteoarthritis to discuss temporal trends. Trauma appears to decline in frequency for Florida populations, with high frequencies between the Archaic and Middle Woodland periods and lower frequencies beginning with the Late Woodland and Mississippian periods. There were no statistically significant differences for either osteoarthritis or trauma.

The data support some differences between coastal and inland populations. Florida coastal populations exhibit higher frequencies of alveolar infections, porotic hyperostosis, and osteoarthritis. Florida inland populations exhibit higher frequencies of carious lesions, enamel hypoplasia, proliferative responses, and cranial blunt trauma.

Interestingly, these patterns of inland and coastal differences are virtually the same for other Southeast populations. Often, however, Southeast populations exhibit higher midrange values of individuals affected for most pathological lesions when compared with Florida populations. For instance, midrange values are higher for carious lesions, enamel hypoplasias, and proliferative responses (table 5.4).

Male and Female Comparisons

Hypothesis 4 states that there will be differences between males and females in dietary focus, pathological lesion frequency, and behavioral alteration frequency. Thus, males and females had different experiences that are revealed through stable isotope dietary reconstruction and analysis of pathological lesions and behavioral alterations. There was a minimal difference in the dietary focus of Palmer individuals as revealed through the mean stable isotope signatures of $\delta^{13}C$ between males ($\delta^{13}C = -9.1$) and females ($\delta^{13}C = -10.2$) and the mean stable isotope signatures of $\delta^{15}N$ between males ($\delta^{15}N = 11.2$) and females ($\delta^{15}N = 10.8$). The difference in isotope values of the Palmer population was not statistically significant.

The only other population with a large enough sample size to conduct male and female dietary comparisons is the postcontact Tatham Mound population. In that population, differences in stable isotope signatures of $\delta^{13}C$ between males ($\delta^{13}C = -16.9$) and females ($\delta^{13}C = -16.6$) or the mean stable isotope signatures of $\delta^{15}N$ between males ($\delta^{15}N = 11.8$) and females ($\delta^{15}N = 10.5$) were also not statistically significant, but showed the same elevated values in nitrogen for males as compared with females. These may indicate consumption at the resource extraction and/or preparation site separately between males and females.

Pathological lesions and behavioral alterations informative about diet and mastication showed that in some populations males had higher frequencies while in others females had higher frequencies. No clear pattern for these differences by sex emerged. In three of four Florida peninsular Gulf coast populations (Palmer, Perico Island, and Safety Harbor), male individuals exhibited more carious lesions than female individuals (fig. 5.3). However, the differences were minimal except for the Safety Harbor population (males = 22%; females = 12%). The Manasota Key cemetery population, on the other hand, had far more females (18%) affected by carious lesions than males (4%).

Alveolar infections were higher for females than males in the Manasota Key population (males = 42%; females = 53%), Palmer (males = 14%; females = 21%) and postcontact Tatham Mound (males = 10%; females = 16%) populations (fig. 5.5), but higher for males than females in the Perico Island (males = 52%; females = 47%) and Safety Harbor (males = 30%; females = 14%) populations. Dental chipping also showed mixed results (fig. 5.7), although males in the Perico Island (males = 91%; females = 60%) and Safety Harbor (males = 48%; females = 30%) populations were far more frequently affected than females.

Pathological lesions resulting from metabolic disruption are enamel hypoplasias and porotic hyperostosis. Enamel hypoplasia frequencies (fig. 5.9) were highest for males from Manasota Key (males = 17%; females = 12%), Palmer (males = 80%; females = 71%), Perico Island (males = 65%;

females = 51%), and postcontact Tatham (males = 56%; females = 50%). It was slightly higher for females from Safety Harbor (males = 33%; females = 36%).

Porotic hyperostosis frequencies (fig. 5.11) were higher for females from Manasota Key (males = 37%; females = 62%), Crystal River mound G (males = 17%; females = 27%), and Fort Center (males = 3%; females = 9%). Male frequencies were higher for individuals from the Palmer (males = 56%; females = 39%), Perico Island (males = 50%; females = 43%), and Safety Harbor (males = 33%; females = 27%) populations.

Proliferative responses serve as some indication of infectious disease prevalence. The frequencies of individuals affected by proliferative responses (fig. 5.14) were higher for males from Manasota Key (males = 25%; females = 16%), but higher for females from Palmer (males = 8%; females = 14%) and Crystal River Mound G (males = 57%; females = 91%).

The picture that emerges from these male and female comparisons is complicated. First, there is no clear trend for types of lesions (dietary, metabolic, infection) between males and females. For all individual lesion types some populations have more females affected and some have more males affected. Second, although in general there is no clear trend within particular populations for males or females having higher lesion frequencies, males in the Perico Island and Safety Harbor populations do have higher frequencies of pathological lesions and behavioral alterations. My conclusion, however, is that there are no clear trends in pathological lesion or behavioral alteration frequencies between males and females.

Summary

In this chapter, I have concentrated on comparing pathology frequencies and dietary reconstruction for coastal and noncoastal Florida populations, and on similar comparisons for coastal and noncoastal populations in the panregional Southeast. The goal was to ascertain similarities and differences in the trends for coastal and noncoastal Florida populations as compared with those from the greater Southeast, as well as to delineate change through time in the Southeast region. In tables 5.3–5.5, I compare Palmer with the other regions, dividing each into early (Archaic through early Late Woodland) and late (Late Woodland through Mission) periods.

Carious lesions were infrequent in prehistoric Florida Gulf coast populations, with an average of less than 1% of teeth affected and 6% of individuals affected. Although they were a little more frequent for Florida interior populations, with an average of 3% of teeth affected prior to missionization, carious lesions became much more frequent after the establishment of the Spanish missionaries and their emphasis on maize horticulture.

By comparison, Georgia coastal precontact agricultural populations have rates of 11% teeth and 59% individuals affected. The frequencies of teeth and individuals affected by carious lesions in the precontact interior agricultural populations from Moundville are comparable and they are higher for Nodena. The higher frequencies for populations in Georgia, Alabama, and Arkansas are expected given the maize dietary focus. Our previous dietary reconstructions for Florida document a very late incorporation of maize into the diet (Hutchinson et al. 1998, 2000; Larsen et al. 2001).

The frequency of individuals affected by dental caries is probably underestimated by considering carious teeth. Periodontal infections were common for Florida Gulf coast populations. By contrast, much lower frequencies of periodontal infection were present for interior Florida populations. Although erosive lesions caused by bacterial fermentation may be the origin of many cavities, physical damage to the enamel may also provide a focal point for dental decay.

Dental chipping is common in coastal populations (Hutchinson 2002a), and those from Gulf coast Florida are no exception. Of the four populations examined for dental chipping (Aqui Esta, Palmer, Safety Harbor, Perico Island), the frequencies of affected adult individuals range from 19% for the Palmer population to 62% in the Perico Island population. These frequencies are similar to outer coastal North Carolina adult (44%) individuals. In coastal North Carolina and in most Florida Gulf coast populations, males are much more frequently affected than females, but the reverse was true in the Palmer population.

The number of individuals affected by at least one enamel hypoplasia is variable, but in general it increases through time. The Palmer population has high frequencies (78%) for an early population as compared with Manasota Key (8%) and Crystal River Mound G (19%). Later populations generally have enamel hypoplasia frequencies of individuals affected greater than 50%, undoubtedly due in part to the stresses introduced by dependence on maize and the impact of European colonization. It may be, however, that high frequencies of enamel hypoplasia have as much to do with lifestyle changes that accompany agriculture north of Florida, such as increased settlement density and social ranking, as they do with nutritional deficiencies due to maize consumption. High frequencies at Palmer, postcontact Tatham Mound, Safety Harbor, and Weeki Wachee may therefore be due to increased settlement density and resource inequalities brought about by a more hierarchically structured social system.

The frequency of individuals affected by porotic hyperostosis is remarkably similar for most Florida Gulf coast populations at 26–30%. This is a much higher frequency than for precontact interior Florida populations or for precontact coastal or interior Southeast populations. For populations north of Florida, it appears that dependence on maize and later impact of Europeans result in an increase in porotic hyperostosis. As with enamel hypoplasias, alternative explanations for the high frequencies in the precontact Florida Gulf coast populations need to be presented. I have previously argued (Hutchinson 2002a) that coastal resources, especially fish and shellfish, contain intestinal parasites that can cause intestinal bleeding once ingested. The high frequencies of porotic hyperostosis for Florida Gulf coast populations may be due to anemia caused by parasite-induced intestinal bleeding.

External auditory exostoses are often linked to aquatic activities. Although exostoses are commonly reported for coastal South American populations (Standen et al. 1997), I have observed many coastal populations in the southeastern United States that do not have those proliferative growths. Several individuals from Florida Gulf coast populations (Useppa Island, Perico Island, Safety Harbor) do have exostoses. At Perico Island and Safety Harbor, both on Tampa Bay, males are more often affected than females. It would seem that males are differentially exposed to aquatic activities that lead to the development of external auditory exostoses.

Osteoarthritis may be higher for precontact Florida Gulf coast populations than those from the interior, but the number of populations that can be compared is small. The frequency of osteoarthritis from the interior mission population of San Martin is high, supporting the observations of Larsen and coworkers (2001) that postcontact native populations suffered from work demands of the Spanish. Cranial and postcranial trauma was higher for coastal Florida populations of an earlier date than those inhabiting either coastal or interior localities of later dates. Cranial blunt trauma was especially high in the Palmer population (n = 10 individuals; 3%). One individual from nearby and contemporary Manasota Key exhibited cranial blunt trauma. As well, postcranial fractures were common in both populations, suggesting that interpersonal conflict was common in the region during the time between A.D. 500 and 700.

Proliferative responses ranged between 6% and 58% for precontact Gulf coast Florida populations. They were relatively higher (40%) for the interior Mission population at San Martin, but not as high as the frequencies reported for interior Mississippian maize agriculturalists at Averbuch (76%), the Mississippi Central Valley (66%), or Norris Farms (61%), although Etowah (14%) has relatively low rates. Osteomyelitis was not common in Florida Gulf coast or interior populations except at Safety Harbor and San Martin, where a few cases of hematogenous osteomyelitis were present. Many of the proliferative responses were probably due to treponemal infection, which has been noted for numerous Florida populations between the Archaic and postcontact periods (Hutchinson et al. 2003a). Population prevalence seems to be higher for Gulf coast populations, although exact population prevalence is difficult to estimate because of the difficulty of attributing an etiology to nonspecific infectious lesions.

Finally, hypotheses 1–4 were considered. Hypothesis 1, that central and southern Florida peninsular Gulf coast populations had similar diets between A.D. 500 and 1400 was accepted. There were no statistically significant differences using t-tests. Hypothesis 2, that there were differences in pathological lesion and behavioral alteration frequencies between Florida peninsular Gulf coast populations, was also accepted. I hypothesize that these differences are due to localized resource procurement and living conditions. Hypothesis 3, that there were differences in diet, pathological lesion frequencies, and behavioral alteration frequencies between coastal and interior populations was also accepted. The differences that are seen in Florida populations are mirrored throughout the greater Southeast. Hypothesis 4, that there would be differences in diet, pathology, and behavioral alteration between males and females, was not accepted. There were differences in dental chipping between males and females, but they were not consistent across populations, nor were other pathological lesions or behavioral alterations. As well, there were no clear trends in male and female pathology differences within populations.

6

Gulf Coast Traditions

The peninsular Florida Gulf coast has been one of the least investigated regions in Florida with regard to prehistoric biological adaptation. Although some osteological analyses have been performed, often the small size of the collections investigated has prohibited population-level synthesis. As well, many of the skeletal collections have been from very late prehistoric or protohistoric contexts.

Central to the discussions presented in the previous chapters has been the Palmer population. Together with contemporaneous populations from Perico Island and Manasota Key, these constitute a substantial number of humans who lived during the period between A.D. 500 and 1000, a period that is particularly important for understanding human ecology and adaptation in the Gulf coast region. Below, I consider several aspects of human adaptation along the Florida Gulf coast. I focus first on the four hypotheses discussed throughout the book that address diet, nutrition, and trends in disease. I then discuss the regional dynamics of populations inhabiting the Florida Gulf coast between A.D. 500 and 1750, and their implications for past and future research.

Dietary Focus

Archaeological evidence indicates that maritime subsistence resources were consumed predominantly during the period A.D. 500–1500 throughout most of Florida. Only populations in the northwestern portion of the state appear to have utilized maize in any substantial way prior to the arrival of Europeans (Hutchinson et al. 1998, 2000). The middens formed at residential sites such as Palmer indicate that the majority of the diet was composed of local resources during the period A.D. 1–800. Coastal fish and shellfish predominate in the middens, although wild plant foods and terrestrial mammals are also found.

The targeted species of fish were from sea grass communities adjacent to Palmer, and included pinfish, seatrout, hardhead catfish, scallops, oysters, and sharks. Quitmyer's (1998) seasonality study of scallops, quahog clams, and loons shows that those resources were used throughout the year, and we can assume many other aquatic species were as well. Plant remains from Palmer indicate that local trees were targeted for fuel and that local fruits and nuts were utilized for food (Newsom 1998).

Walker (1992a) reports that maritime aquatic foods represented the majority of faunal remains in the Charlotte Harbor region as well. Furthermore, she finds that the faunal diversity of the assemblages mirrored the contemporary habitats. At Buck Key, for instance, fishes dominate the assemblage at a site closest to an inlet, whereas at Josslyn Island bivalves are rare, as they are in the habitat today (Walker 1992a:293). The focus on locally available species is exactly what we see in the isotope and dental microwear dietary reconstruction.

Dietary reconstruction using human skeletal remains (stable isotopes, appendix E) and dental enamel (microwear, appendix F) from populations inhabiting the central and south Florida Gulf coast between A.D. 500 and 1500 verifies many of the subsistence reconstructions from faunal and botanical remains. The dietary reconstruction indicates that the populations inhabiting the region from Charlotte Harbor to Tampa Bay relied principally on marine fish and shellfish supplemented with C_3 plants, probably terrestrial fruits and tubers (Norr et al. n.d.). There was little change in the diet during this time, with the most visible difference occurring when the earlier and most southern population inhabited Horr's Island. There, the Archaic population (3100 B.C.–A.D. 250) had a diet with a wider range of terrestrial and marine resources, including a variety of C_3 and some CAM or C_4 plants.

By contrast, humans along the Gulf coast centered their subsistence attention on local aquatic resources supplemented by local terrestrial plants and animals. At no point in time was any tropical (C_4) grass such as maize a substantial part of the diet. No maize has been recovered from any archaeological deposits in the region, although charred panicoid grasses have been recovered from south Florida (Norr et al. n.d.).

Likewise, populations located in the interior, such as at Tatham Mound, also focused their attention on local resources, emphasizing those that were aquatic. Little or no maize accompanied those foraged subsistence items until after the arrival of Europeans who promoted the use of maize. In numerous investigations of the stable isotope dietary signatures of prehistoric and early historic populations throughout Florida, we have found that it was only with the advent of missionization that maize was consumed as a dietary staple, except in the very northern panhandle region (Hutchinson n.d.; Hutchinson et al. 1998, 2000; Larsen et al., 1992, 2001; Norr et al. n.d.).

The reasons for the absence of maize are undoubtedly multiple. First, the soils in central and southern Florida are not conducive for maize agriculture (W. Johnson 1990). Second, marine resources were abundant and there was less need for agricultural production. Third, the Mississippian cultural tradition that incorporated maize agriculture in much of the Southeast was not present in central and south Florida.

Dental and skeletal pathology support the dietary reconstruction. Carious lesion frequencies are very low for the populations inhabiting the central and southern Gulf coast, but infections of the mandible and maxilla were more common, probably arising from extensive dental damage due to shell inclusions.

Although anthropologists have thought for some time that maize was of little importance in south Florida, demonstration of its absence in central Florida is recent (Hutchinson and Norr 1994). Furthermore, the role of local subsistence resources in areas without significant trade of foods from other localities is only now appreciated (see, however, Walker 1992a). Hypothesis 1, which states that the diet of central peninsular Gulf coast populations was consistently focused on maritime resources between at least A.D. 500 and 1500, is accepted.

Heterogeneity of Peninsular Gulf Coast Florida Populations

Hypothesis 2 states that coastal populations in central peninsular Gulf coast Florida will exhibit considerable differences in pathological lesion frequencies that can be attributed to localized resource exploitation. Lesions reflecting diet and mastication (carious lesions, alveolar infection, and dental chipping) tend to support this hypothesis. The frequencies of teeth and individuals affected by carious lesions, and individuals affected by alveolar infections have a much larger range in Florida coastal populations than the same lesions do among Florida interior populations. The frequency of individuals affected by dental chipping was also highly variable. Unfortunately, dental chipping data are not often collected in noncoastal populations and therefore it is not possible to compare coastal and interior populations.

The indicators of metabolic disruption (enamel hypoplasia and porotic hyperostosis) are also highly variable. Enamel hypoplasia frequencies are more highly variable for coastal populations than those from interior Florida, but porotic hyperostosis frequencies are less variable for Florida coastal populations. The frequency of individuals affected by proliferative responses, as an indicator of infectious disease, is more highly variable in Florida coastal populations than that from Florida interior populations.

The indicators of lifestyle and activity (osteoarthritis, trauma, and external auditory exostoses) are generally more variable for Florida coastal populations than those from interior Florida. The exception is cranial blunt trauma, which has the same range for Florida coastal and interior populations. External auditory exostoses are much more frequent for populations inhabiting Tampa Bay than for any other population on the Florida Gulf coast. It is still unclear whether the high frequencies exhibited for the populations from Perico Island and Safety Harbor are due to heredity, behavioral exposure to cold water, or ear infections.

Thus, there is a fair amount of supporting data for differences in diet and mastication, metabolic disruption, infectious disease, and lifestyle among peninsular Florida Gulf coast populations. These differences suggest that the biocultural adaptation to restricted coastal and adjacent ecozones is manifested in differing health and disease experiences.

Comparisons between Coastal and Interior Florida and the Regional Southeast

Hypothesis 3 states that interior populations (those more than 25 km from the coast) will have different dietary focus and different nutritional and disease experiences than coastal populations. Furthermore, the patterns of change through time in pathology frequency will be different between coastal and interior populations, with interior populations exhibiting more change than coastal populations because a combination of factors resulted in subsistence and other lifeway changes earlier for interior populations.

The lesions and behavioral alterations examined include those reflecting diet and mastication (carious lesions, alveolar infection, and dental chipping), metabolic disruption (enamel hypoplasias and porotic hyperostosis), infectious disease (proliferative responses), and lifestyle and activity (osteoarthritis, trauma, and external auditory exostoses). These comparisons are made with other populations inhabiting the southeastern United States as well.

The frequency of individuals affected by at least one enamel hypoplasia for Gulf coast populations is highest at Palmer, so high in fact that

Palmer's hypoplasia frequencies are much more similar to later populations than those contemporary with it. For instance, when Palmer is compared with Florida noncoastal populations, the frequency of individuals affected in the Mission population from San Martin is exactly the same. The prevalence of enamel hypoplasias for Palmer indicates that systemic metabolic disruption was commonplace.

Lesions of the cranial vault and frontal orbits termed porotic hyperostosis were much higher in Florida precontact coastal populations than in those from Florida precontact noncoastal populations, or more northern Southeastern coastal or noncoastal populations. Although characteristic of anemia, porotic hyperostosis can be caused by other diseases and by ground erosion, and Schultz and coworkers (2001) urge caution when making interpretations. With frequencies for many Florida Gulf coast populations between 26% and 30% of individuals affected, porotic hyperostosis was as common in nonagricultural coastal populations as it was in maize-dependent populations inhabiting other areas of Florida and the southeastern United States. I hypothesize the anemic conditions were caused by intestinal parasites ingested with marine fish and shellfish. As mentioned in chapter 3, intestinal bleeding due to intestinal parasites is a common problem in populations who consume undercooked seafood, such as in Japan.

Proliferative responses are lower for Florida Gulf coast populations than they are for those from the Florida interior or for southeastern noncoastal populations. One exception is at Crystal River Mound G, where Green (1993) reported that 58% of the individuals were affected. Such a high frequency rivals those from the Southeast interior Mississippian populations at Averbuch in Tennessee (Eisenberg 1986), Mississippi Central Valley (Rose et al. 1991), and Norris Farms in Illinois (Milner and Smith 1990).

Many of the proliferative responses for Florida populations are due to systemic infections, as indicated by multiple elements affected in the same person, and are probably the result of treponemal infections, which were diagnosed for most of the populations examined in this study. Because treponemal infections are common skin infections in contemporary populations where they exist, we can expect that they were common in Florida populations, often affecting adolescent individuals, and for many people constituting a chronic ailment.

The pattern of elements affected by proliferative responses suggests that the specific treponemal infection most closely resembled the modern forms of yaws and endemic syphilis (Hutchinson et al. 2003a). Only two individuals have lesions approaching those of the *caries sicca* of venereal syphilis (an adult of unknown sex from Tierra Verde and an adult female from Palmer) (Hutchinson 1993a,b; Hutchinson et al. 2003a). If the form of treponematosis is yaws or endemic syphilis, then the disease incapacitated some individuals through fever, and aching bones, but most individuals likely suffered from relatively minor symptoms that lasted only a short period of time (Hutchinson et al. 2003a).

Osteoarthritis varied in frequency from population to population. It is especially high in the Florida interior Mission population at San Martin, probably reflecting the use of native labor for transport and other tasks (Larsen 2001). Among the Gulf coast populations, osteoarthritis is especially high in the Manasota Key population (Dickel 1991). The variability in the Florida Gulf coast and interior samples is quite distinct, perhaps reflecting differences in economic task differentiation. As noted for the dietary reconstruction, local foraging appears to be common, and local patterns of bending, lifting, and mobility would be manifested in local patterns of osteoarthritis.

External auditory exostoses were found only in coastal populations in Florida and elsewhere in the Southeast. Lambert (2001), however, found high frequencies of external auditory exostoses in piedmont and mountain populations in North Carolina. It is unclear whether some of those are pedunculated, hereditary forms of exostoses, or whether they would be the result of *otitis externa.*

Trauma appears to be a phenomenon that is far more frequent for early populations than for those from later time periods. High frequencies of postcranial trauma are associated with cases of blunt cranial trauma, such as for populations from Palmer, Manasota Key, Gauthier, and Fort Center. Mutilation or dismemberment is absent. Widmer (1988) postulated that sociopolitical changes following A.D. 800 served to reduce local disputes and raids potentially caused by inundated carrying capacity. The frequent trauma observed in populations dating prior to that time, and the absence of frequent trauma in later populations, supports a proposition of greater intergroup hostility prior to A.D. 800.

The data demonstrate notable differences between coastal and inland populations. Florida coastal populations exhibit higher frequencies of alveolar infections, porotic hyperostosis, and osteoarthritis. Florida inland populations exhibit higher frequencies of carious lesions, enamel hypoplasias, proliferative responses, and cranial blunt trauma. These patterns are virtually the same for coastal and inland comparisons throughout the Southeast for all periods.

Male and Female Comparisons

Hypothesis 4 states that there will be differences between males and females in dietary focus, pathological lesion frequency, and behavioral alteration frequency. Thus, males and females had different experiences, revealed through stable isotope dietary reconstruction and analysis of pathological lesions and behavioral alterations. There was a minimal difference in the stable isotope values between Palmer males and females that was not statistically significant. The postcontact noncoastal Tatham Mound population also showed no statistically significant stable isotope signatures between males and females. However, both populations showed elevated values in nitrogen for males as compared with females.

Carious lesions were more common for males than females in Florida coastal populations. Tatham Mound was the only available Florida inland population for comparison, and males and females were affected nearly equally by carious lesions. Alveolar infection frequencies were varied, with more males affected in the Florida coastal Perico Island and Safety Harbor populations, but with more females affected in the Florida coastal Manasota Key and Palmer populations and the inland postcontact Tatham Mound population.

Dental chipping was much more frequent for males in the central peninsular Gulf coast populations from Safety Harbor and Perico Island. North Carolina outer coastal males also exhibited higher frequencies of dental chipping than females (Hutchinson 2002a). In the central peninsular Gulf coast Florida Palmer population, however, females were more frequently affected. These clear gender differences in dental chipping suggest either differences in mastication or the use of teeth as tools. Most chipping occurred on both anterior and posterior teeth, or on just the posterior, supporting a masticatory origin for the chipping. I attribute dental chipping to inclusions with shellfish (see as well Hutchinson 1996, 2002a), but it may well be that food preparation played a significant role for these populations as well. As well, no anterior or posterior tooth grooving or other alterations resulting from the use of teeth as tools were observed.

The differences in dental chipping frequencies indicate that the masticatory differences between males and females exhibited for Perico Island and Safety Harbor are not present in the Palmer population. It is also true that Palmer had lower frequencies of individuals affected by carious lesions and alveolar infection than either the Perico Island or Safety Harbor populations. Undoubtedly, dental damage and subsequent alveolar infections are linked.

In general, metabolic disruption was more frequent for males than females from Gulf coast Florida. Enamel hypoplasia and porotic hyperostosis frequencies were highest for males from Manasota Key and Palmer. More males were affected by enamel hypoplasia at Perico Island, but fewer males were affected by porotic hyperostosis at Perico Island. Enamel hypoplasias were more frequent for females from the interior postcontact Tatham Mound population.

As measures of infectious disease, proliferative responses show no clear pattern of male and female involvement. More males were affected from the Florida Gulf coast Manasota Key population, but more females were affected from Palmer and Crystal River Mound G.

Male and female comparisons for three types of lesions (dietary, metabolic, infection) showed that the patterns of affliction are complicated at best. There are no clear regional trends between males and females, and for all individual lesion types some populations have more females affected and some have more males affected. My conclusion is that there are no clear trends in pathological lesion or behavioral alteration frequencies between males and females.

Conclusions

The first theme of this book is adaptation, specifically adaptation to the Gulf coastal strand of central Florida. Regional cultures are readily distinguishable in Florida after 500 B.C., differentiated principally on the basis of archaeological assemblages. It has long been noted that they were not isolated, and that they "shared some of their lifeways even while maintaining adaptations well suited to a particular environmental zone" (Milanich 1994:414). However, specific quantitative or qualitative measures of the direct impacts of their lifeways for their health has eluded us until recently.

Populations inhabiting the region, although unified by their emphasis on maritime foraging, differed in the species targeted and perhaps in the methods of acquisition. The prevalence of external auditory exostoses in Tampa Bay populations, for instance, may indicate different methods for the acquisition of aquatic species that exposed those populations to different climatic conditions.

Unlike their more northern neighbors, populations inhabiting peninsular Florida did not turn to maize horticulture but, rather, continued throughout most of prehistory to rely on foraged plants and animals. The diet appears to have been focused on local terrestrial and aquatic plants and animals, and, for coastal populations, heavily concentrated on maritime resources. Although a marine economy has often been stressed for the

Calusa (Goggin and Sturtevant 1964), absence of maize and dependence on marine resources is by no means a characteristic unique to the Calusa.

The exploitation of local habitats and reliance on local foods resulted in some differences in health between coastal and inland dwellers. Most skeletal and dental pathological lesions in Florida Gulf coast populations show little frequency increase until European contact, partially because of the absence of maize horticulture. Inland Florida populations, on the other hand, experienced increased frequencies of several pathological lesions (carious lesions, porotic hyperostosis, proliferative lesions) between the Archaic and Late Mississippian periods.

Conflict is the second theme of this book. The antiquity of and cause for warfare in the region is unclear, and some speculate that it is a phenomenon directly stimulated by the appearance of European wealth (Marquardt 1986, 1987). It may be the case, however, that regional intergroup conflict has considerable antiquity. The expansion of territories and external conflict might be expected when mobile foraging gives way to sedentary, agriculturally based urban centers. Ember and Ember (1997) have shown that warfare is more common for agricultural societies as compared with foraging societies, although "warfare" is a rather unspecified term.

Otterbein (1994) discusses several types of armed conflict, dividing them among four major issues: (1) whether the conflict is external or internal, (2) whether the conflict is premeditated or not, (3) whether the intent of the conflict is to injure or kill, and (4) whether the conflict is mediated or not by elders or political figures such as a chief. Internal conflicts (duels, staff-fights, feuds) are mediated by informal or formal leaders. Kelly (2000) and Otterbein (1994) discuss several smaller foraging societies for whom conflict is rare and disdained among the group. For others, internal conflict appears to be more common. Internal conflicts are generally mediated while external conflicts generally are not mediated. The less serious internal conflicts (duels, staff-fights) are not premeditated or generally lethal, while the more serious internal conflicts (feuds) are premeditated and lethal.

Periodic raids by neighboring populations are common in small societies (Boehm 1984; Gibson 1990; Kelly 2000; Otterbein 1994), and are due to a variety of motivations ranging from prisoner capture to retribution. The goal of the conflict is often to inflict lethal wounds. Kelly (2000) posits a cognitive shift for external conflict from intent to kill a particular person to the intent to kill any members of a group. Even if only an individual is killed in feuds or warfare, *social substitutability* signifies that it is perceived as a killing of the group.

Considering these various types of armed conflict, what can be said of the prehistoric evidence for violence in the Florida Gulf coast region? Evidence of violent death is not common in Florida populations. The antiquity of violent death stretches back into the Archaic period, where a male individual at Windover had a projectile point buried in his pelvis (Doran 2002). Although not excessive compared with other populations in the prehistoric Americas (see various discussions in Martin and Frayer 1997), armed conflict and violence appear to have been a component of the lifestyle of central and south Florida populations between A.D. 500 and 800 as well as earlier, during the Archaic period. When cranial and post-cranial wounds are combined, the frequency for adults ranges between 1% and 14% for all the Florida populations reported here.

Multiple wounds are not common in Florida populations, and all wounds are well healed. The most common locations for wounds are the cranium and the lower arms. Arm wounds are often extreme, with misalignment when healed as a common occurrence. Males are affected more often than females, but females are not unaffected. There are no distinguishable differences between the wounds of men and of women. Wounds of mutilation, such as scalping or dismemberment, are not present.

In later Mississippian societies elsewhere in the Southeast, unhealed trauma and mutilation are common. Mutilation is documented in the late prehistoric for populations in Alabama (Bridges 1996; Jacobi et al. 2000), Tennessee (Smith 1996, 1997), and Illinois (Milner and Smith 1990; Milner et al. 1991). There is no skeletal evidence for mutilation in Florida, although DeBry depicts one scene of mutilation following battle (Lorant 1965:65) and one scene of dismembered limbs hanging from poles while individuals dance around them (Lorant 1965:67). Perhaps his rendition was based more on fearful fantasy than on eyewitness evidence, a possibility also raised by Hann (1996:103). Hann, however, mentions that the caption is from LeMoyne, who apparently witnessed this episode. Embedded projectile points are rare in Florida populations, while in other areas of the Southeast, especially during the Mississippian period, they are common.

All of the above suggests that in central and southern Florida the orientation of the violence was different before A.D. 800 than it was in much of the greater Southeast after A.D. 800. Well-healed wounds and the absence of mutilation suggest that warfare did not occur among Florida Gulf coast populations before A.D. 1000. Rather, the wounds suggest either internal conflicts such as duels or domestic violence, or external conflict in the form of periodic raiding or skirmishes, generally with the goal of injury rather than death. This is supported by absence of other signs of warfare such as palisades (Marquardt 2001). The ethnohistoric accounts for the Timucua support raiding as well. Hann (1996:103) reports that among the Timucua at the time of European contact "intertribal warfare was chronic but episodic. Surprise raids were the standard tactic."

Widmer (1988:273) predicted conflict in south Florida during the period between A.D. 500 and 800 based on the premise that populations living in "limited, highly circumscribed, fixed resource areas" experienced more intergroup conflict as the result of competition. L. H. Larson (1972) had made this argument earlier for Mississippian societies in the Southeast. If the carrying capacity of the Gulf coast region was reached prior to A.D. 800, as Widmer (1988) postulates, then social friction could have resulted from scarce resources.

Widmer (1988) additionally hypothesizes that the reduction in cranial and postcranial trauma following A.D. 800 could be associated with chiefdom political organization. Otterbein (1994) documents that chiefs of the Higi in Nigeria would mediate in feuds, as does Boehm (1984) for other groups. Consequently, the role of chiefs in mediating intergroup violence may have been brought about by shrinking resources and competition between lineages. However, feuds are generally about revenge and not resource stress. It is worth noting that reduction in skeletal trauma through time has also been postulated as a general phenomenon throughout the Southeast. Steinbock (1976) reviewed fracture frequencies in 12 populations ranging in date from 4000 B.C. to A.D. 1700 and found that fracture rates decreased through time.

Evidence for change, the third theme of this book, does occur but it seems to have little impact biologically on the populations examined. The period between A.D. 450 and 750 has been described by some as a period of instability due to increased population and saturated carrying capacity in the Southeast (Anderson and Mainfort 2002; Smith 1986). However, as Smith (1986:50) points out, it can also be viewed as "a period of increasing population pressure and adaptive readjustment that represented an essential preadaptation, a foreshadowing, of the following Mississippian emergence." For most of Florida, however, the Mississippian emergence never occurred.

Along the Florida Gulf coast, population density did increase, as indicated by more and larger sites after A.D. 500. Stable isotope dietary reconstruction for Florida Gulf coast populations indicates the diet remained focused on maritime resources between A.D. 1 and 1400. Studies of plants and animals preserved in the archaeological record have shown few domesticates present, and a predominance of local resources (Kozuch 1998; Newsom 1998; Quitmyer 1998; Scarry and Newsom 1992; Walker 1992a).

Despite continued reliance on foraged resources, however, it seems clear that egalitarian bands gave way to ranked polities sometime after A.D. 500 in some areas of the Florida Gulf coast. Large site complexes appear after A.D. 800 along Tampa Bay, and even earlier (A.D. 200) along Charlotte Harbor. Temples and large mounds are known from several sites, including Ucita on Tampa Bay. The account by the Gentlemen of Elvas clearly describes a temple that rivals descriptions of Carlos's structure: "The town consisted of seven or eight houses. The chief's house stood near the beach on a very high hill which had been artificially built as a fortress. At the otherside of the town was the temple and on top of it a wooden bird with its eyes gilded" (Robertson 1993:57). Our current data indicate that the protected waters of Charlotte Harbor and Tampa Bay provided areas that favored the establishment of larger urban site complexes and dense populations.

Whether or not these ranked societies were associated with external armed conflict is questionable. Although it is often the case that chiefdoms are associated with episodes of territorial expansion and civil conflict, the bioarchaeological data from the Florida Gulf coast do not support an increase in violent conflicts. After A.D. 800, the frequency of trauma decreases dramatically, and there are no late prehistoric cases that support endemic warfare in the region.

Nonetheless, the ethnohistoric records report that warfare was common at the time of European contact. As Widmer (1988:7) states, "Warfare was prevalent, if not a chronic condition, among the Calusa." The accounts of the Calusa, for instance, state that the Tocobaga and Serrope were at war with the Calusa (Hann 1991). The Calusa attempted to have the Spanish help them in their war with the Tocobaga, a common request made by indigenous groups throughout Florida. In northern Florida, Saturiba attempted to enlist the Spanish army in their war with Outina, leader of the Thimagona (Hann 1996:41). In fact, the ethnohistoric accounts state that indigenous populations were constantly allying with Europeans, and generally the most recent arrival was most in favor (Clayton et al. 1993; Hann 1996). The engravings of DeBry depict numerous acts and consequences of war (Lorant 1965).

Hann (1996:41, 103) probably offers a reasonable explanation for this apparent contradiction. He notes that "short surprise raids by relatively small forces seem to have been the standard form of Indian warfare throughout Florida, rather than prolonged campaigns designed to vanquish an enemy completely." As discussed by Otterbein (1994) and Kelly (2000), however, even if these raids are by small forces and episodic, warfare is chronic and designed to inflict lethal wounds.

A variety of reasons have been postulated for the shift from informal raids and skirmishes to formal warfare. Several people emphasize the technological role of the bow and arrow in facilitating new patterns of warfare as early as A.D. 600 (Blitz 1988; Dye 2002; Nassaney and Pyle 1999). It is possible instead that warfare is a relatively recent phenomenon when witnessed by Europeans, perhaps even inaugurated by them through the introduction of new status items and the stimulation of shifting power dynamics. European objects were clearly traded throughout Florida. For instance, a silver celt was recovered from early contact (A.D. 1525–1550) from Tatham Mound (Mitchem 1989; Hutchinson n.d.). It appears to have been fashioned from a silver ingot, a wealth item that the Spaniards were not trading to indigenous people. It was probably recovered from one of the numerous shipwrecks noted in south Florida; Dickinson (1985) among others notes that these wrecks were often scavenged by native people. The recovery of the ingot from Tatham, well inland of the coast, illustrates the trade of items perceived to have been from the coast.

Marquardt (1987) speculates that the appearance of these new wealth items of European derivation were a major impetus for shifting social power dynamics. In fact, he presents the idea that the rising of power of the Calusa was tied to the control of these new wealth items, which appeared predominantly in the shipwrecks off south Florida. Thus, in Marquardt's (1987) opinion, warfare is a social phenomenon that arose after contact with Europeans as a result of the control of scarce resources.

Regardless of the changes that took place for populations inhabiting the Florida Gulf coast region, they do not appear to have suffered many of the changes in nutritional quality or impacts on health associated with the period following A.D. 800 for societies located farther north in the Southeast. Undoubtedly their unique health profile is due to their unique ecological circumstances and lack of maize diet.

Perhaps the most pervasive information presented in this study involves the complexity of human ecology in Florida. The Florida peninsula is unlike most of the Southeast in topographic, climatic, or cultural context. The examination of human biological adaptation that is made in this volume indicates that populations inhabiting Florida should be approached with those differences in mind.

At no prior time has it been more fruitful to practice archaeology in Florida and the greater Southeast, and the combined efforts of anthropologists, botanists, zoologists, geologists, and historians ensure that the quantity and quality of data used to reconstruct prehistoric lifeways will provide interpretations hitherto impossible to achieve. Unfortunately, the destruction of archaeological sites, especially along the Florida Gulf coast, has also accelerated to an unprecedented level. I hope that this volume contributes to the ongoing efforts of those interested in our pre-Columbian history to recapture at least part of the story.

Appendix A. Frequency of subadult and adult teeth by sex[a]

Tooth	Male	Female	Indeterminate	Total
Maxillary permanent				
First incisor	31	51	116	198
Second incisor	30	53	89	172
Canine	68	59	163	290
First premolar	54	66	125	245
Second premolar	56	71	118	245
First molar	56	77	179	312
Second molar	49	70	142	261
Third molar	57	57	155	269
Maxillary deciduous				
First incisor	0	0	1	1
Second incisor	0	0	3	3
Canine	0	0	5	5
First molar	1	1	11	13
Second molar	0	0	8	8
Mandibular permanent				
First incisor	26	27	80	133
Second incisor	41	41	96	178
Canine	42	51	114	207
First premolar	56	67	135	258
Second premolar	55	65	145	265
First molar	67	77	203	347
Second molar	61	71	195	327
Third molar	56	65	137	258
Mandibular deciduous				
First incisor	0	0	1	1
Second incisor	0	0	1	1
Canine	0	0	2	2
First molar	0	1	17	18
Second molar	1	1	8	10
Total	807	971	2,249	4,027

a. Right, left, and indeterminate side combined.

Appendix B. Frequency of subadult and adult cranial and postcranial skeletal elements by element and sex[a]

Element	Male	Female	Indeterminate	Total
Adult				
Cranium	55	64	169	288
Mandible	45	56	100	201
Vertebrae[b]	31	39	39	109
Ribs[b]	25	41	26	92
Innominate	37	65	10	112
Sacrum	6	12	2	20
Scapula	49	52	30	131
Clavicle	39	62	36	137
Sternum	4	2	0	6
Humerus	69	95	120	284
Ulna	68	87	68	223
Radius	49	65	48	162
Hands[b]	36	48	68	152
Patella	39	43	42	124
Femur	87	97	123	307
Tibia	53	75	77	205
Fibula	41	59	37	137
Feet[b]	35	47	51	133
Total	768	1,009	1,046	2,823
Subadult				
Cranium	1	1	19	21
Mandible	0	1	20	21
Vertebrae[b]	0	0	11	11
Ribs[b]	1	0	7	8
Innominate	2	2	5	9
Sacrum	0	1	0	1
Scapula	1	1	6	8
Clavicle	1	1	6	8

continued

Element	Male	Female	Indeterminate	Total
Sternum	0	0	0	0
Humerus	2	2	21	25
Ulna	2	1	11	14
Radius	2	0	9	11
Hands[b]	0	0	8	8
Femur	1	2	25	28
Patella	0	0	2	2
Tibia	2	1	13	16
Fibula	0	2	6	8
Feet[b]	0	1	9	10
Total	15	16	178	209

a. Right, left, and indeterminate side combined.

b. Separate elements treated collectively.

Appendix C. Adult cranial and mandibular measurements by sex (in mm)

Measurement[a]	Male	Female	Indeterminate
Min/max no. individuals	1/18	1/22	0/0
Maximum length	180.3	175.3	
Maximum breadth	136.9	131.8	
Bizygomatic breadth	139.0	126.0	
Cranial height	144.0	135.0	
Cranial base length	104.0	99.8	
Basion-Prosthion	100.5	95.7	
Maximum palate breadth	63.4	61.0	
Miminum palate breadth	39.5	38.1	
Minimum palate length	34.8	31.8	
Maximum palate length	53.9	51.7	
Biauricular breadth	123.8	114.2	
Upper facial height	66.6	60.6	
Minimum frontal breadth	97.0	94.1	
Upper facial breadth	102.8	103.0	
Mastoid length	29.1	22.4	
Nasal height	52.5	51.2	
Nasal breadth	25.4	24.6	
Orbital breadth	41.1	35.6	
Orbital height	35.0	35.6	
Biorbital breadth	105.1	99.5	
Frontal chord	117.2	112.4	
Parietal chord	112.1	108.6	
Occipital chord	99.0	98.9	
Foramen-magnum length	40.0	37.3	
Lambda-Inion chord	82.8	87.0	
Inion-Opisthion chord	53.2	49.1	
Biasterionic chord	124.7	111.0	
Prosthion-Opisthion	179.3	168.6	
Opisthion-Nasospinale	177.3	168.8	

continued

Measurement[a]	Male	Female	Indeterminate
Bregma-Inion	156.1	149.7	
Bregma-Opistion	148.7	142.5	
Lambda-Basion	122.6	114.7	
Nasion-Opisthion	168.8	164.1	
Nasion-Lambda	177.1	171.0	
Basion-Nasospinale	99.3	94.3	
Mandible	5/33	5/42	2/24
Symphysis height	33.3	32.5	32.1
Symphysis breadth	18.0	16.0	16.7
Condylar breadth	21.8	20.2	23.2
Bigonial breadth	108.8	100.7	108.6
Bicondylar breadth	128.6	122.3	—
Ascending Ramus height coronoid	68.1	62.7	66.2
Ascending Ramus height condyle	65.2	58.0	63.3
Ascending Ramus minimum breadth	39.0	35.7	38.3
Mandible length	109.5	103.3	111.5

a. References for measurements include Hrdlička 1939, Larsen 1982.

Appendix D. Adult postcranial measurements by sex (in mm)

Measurement[a,c]	Male	Female	Indeterminate
Ulna n =[b]	8/31	16/36	0/20
Maximum length	265.4	244.3	—
Maximum dia. midshaft	18.1	16.5	16.7
Humerus n =[b]	9/39	15/48	1/40
Maximum length	318.8	297.6	308
Epicondylar breadth	61.8	56.0	55.0
Maximum diameter head	44.7	40.8	41.1
Maximum dia. midshaft	25.1	21.5	22.9
Minimum dia. midshaft	19.1	16.0	17.2
Biepicondylar breadth	44.7	42.0	43.0
Circumference midshaft	76.3	64.6	69.0
Radius n =[b]	6/25	13/35	1/11
Maximum length	243.7	222.4	224.0
Maximum diameter head	22.5	19.8	21.0
Interosseous crest Max.	18.0	16.0	16.6
Interosseous crest Min.	12.9	11.5	12.0
Clavicle n =[b]	2/19	8/33	0/11
Maximum length	155.0	139.0	—
Maximum dia. midshaft	14.1	11.6	13.5
Femur n =[b]	7/39	12/47	1/49
Maximum length	441.3	419.7	430.0
Bicondylar width	68.2	64.1	66.5
Epicondylar breadth	79.9	73.1	74.3
Maximum diameter head	45.4	41.9	41.6
A-P subtro. dia.	28.6	25.7	25.4
Trans. subtro. dia.	32.7	31.3	31.0
A-P diameter midshaft	31.4	28.6	29.1

continued

Measurement[a,c]	Male	Female	Indeterminate
Trans. dia. midshaft	27.4	25.8	26.0
Circumference midshaft	93.9	87.3	87.9
Vertical diameter neck	30.6	27.5	26.8
Trans. diameter neck	27.2	28.8	25.7
Tibia n =[b]	6/27	10/38	0/28
Maximum length	376.5	353.8	—
A-P diameter midshaft	32.5	28.6	30.7
Trans. dia. midshaft	21.4	19.2	20.5
Circumference midshaft	88.3	77.9	84.0
Fibula n =[b]	0/23	3/27	0/10
Maximum length	—	336.0	—
Maximum dia. midshaft	17.8	15.8	17.8

a. References for measurements include Hrdlička 1939, Larsen 1982.

b. Minimum/maximum number of individuals observed. A zero indicates no values recorded for a measurement for at least one individual.

c. A-P = anterior-posterior; subtro. = subtrochanteric; trans. = transverse; dia. = diameter.

Appendix E. Stable Isotope Analysis and Dietary Inference

Lynette Norr

Stable carbon and nitrogen isotope analysis of archaeological human skeletal remains and modern and archaeological food resources is now a well established analytical technique (DeNiro 1987; Norr 1995; Schoeninger et al. 1983; van der Merwe 1982) for the reconstruction of patterns of prehistoric subsistence. This method relies upon natural variation in the global abundance of stable isotopes in different biological systems (fig. E.1) and has the potential to identify the degree to which a population's subsistence strategy relied on agricultural maize and/or marine vs. terrestrial protein resources. Marine vertebrates and maize are usually isotopically distinct from most other plant and terrestrial animal resources. Because the isotopic composition of food resources is incorporated into body tissues, the presence and relative proportions of certain food types in the diet can be identified through the analysis of bone collagen and bone apatite carbonate. The assessment of relative proportions of dietary resources consumed by humans is dependent upon accurate and detailed knowledge of the isotopic composition of local food resources.

Recent advances in the interpretation of isotope ratio data from bone have come from laboratory experiments using animals fed isotopically controlled diets and the subsequent analysis of body tissues (Ambrose and Norr 1993). Accurate interpretation of human bone isotope data will identify changes in human dietary patterns over time as well as intrasite variations in individual diet that can be correlated with age, sex, stature, social status, burial treatment, and patterns of disease.

The analysis of stable carbon ($^{13}C/^{12}C$) and nitrogen ($^{15}N/^{14}N$) isotopic ratios in organic and carbonate fractions of prehistoric human bone was used to identify differences in diet and resource use among prehistoric and protohistoric Amerindian populations in central and southern Gulf coast

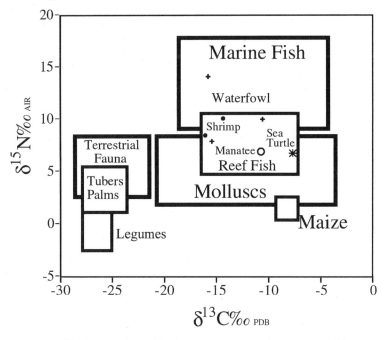

Fig. E.1. Stable isotope values of modern resources from the circum-Caribbean.

Florida. These are reported as delta (δ) values in parts per mil (‰), relative to known standards.

In the case of coastal, estuarine, and riverine populations of the southeastern United States, diets were likely derived from a number of isotopically varied resources, which can make paleodietary interpretations challenging (Hutchinson and Norr 1994, 1999; Hutchinson et al. 1998; Norr and Hutchinson 1998). Three direct isotopic indicators of diet and one indirect isotopic evaluation strengthen the interpretation of bone stable carbon and stable nitrogen isotope values. Nitrogen isotopes in bone collagen were originally intended to identify protein source: terrestrial, marine, or some combination of the two, but actually distinguished between terrestrial and aquatic protein sources, since the freshwater and marine fish had similar nitrogen values. Carbon isotopes in bone collagen were interpreted following the model that carbon in collagen is derived mostly from dietary protein, and carbon isotopes in bone apatite carbonate are derived proportionately from carbon sources in the whole diet. The relationship between the carbon isotope values of the bone collagen and the bone apatite carbonate indicates either a monoisotopic diet or the relative isotopic compositions of the protein and carbohydrate portions of the diet (Ambrose and Norr 1993; Norr 1995).

Methods and Materials

Approximately 5 g of clean, dry bone were sampled from each individual from the early Late Woodland Palmer population ($n = 28$). Although cortical bone is preferred, this bone was often taken from a mandible or pelvis, from which other biological information could be obtained. The bone was sonicated in distilled water, rinsed, and freeze-dried before crushing by hand in a porcelain mortar and pestle. Crushed bone was sieved to <0.25 mm and 0.25–0.50 mm. The larger fraction was used for collagen extraction and the finer fraction was used to prepare the bone apatite.

Bone crushed and sieved to 0.25–0.50 mm was demineralized in 0.2 molar HCl in a glass, fritted disk funnel fitted with a Teflon stopcock. The demineralized residue was soaked in 0.125 molar NaOH to remove humic acid contamination before solubilizing in 10^{-3} molar HCl at 95°C. Percent carbon and nitrogen by weight (%C/wt and %N/wt) in collagen was determined with a Carlo Erba elemental CHN analyzer. The carbon to nitrogen ratio (C/N) was calculated by dividing the %C/wt by the %N/wt. The resulting value was multiplied by 1.16667 to obtain an atomic C/N ratio as reported by DeNiro (1985) and Ambrose (1990). One to three mg of filtered and freeze-dried collagen was converted to CO_2 and N_2 in a Carlo Erba, and isotope ratios were determined on a VG IsoGas Prism II Series mass spectrometer.

Bone crushed and sieved to <0.25 mm was prepared in 14 cc centrifuge tubes with a 50% chlorine bleach solution to break down organic contents, followed by 1 molar acetic acid to remove environmental and non-structural biological carbonates. Percent carbon and nitrogen by weight (%C/wt and %N/wt) in apatite was determined with the same Carlo Erba elemental CHN analyzer. The carbon to nitrogen ratio (C/N) was again calculated by dividing the %C/wt by the %N/wt and the resulting value multiplied by 1.16667 to obtain an atomic C/N ratio as reported by DeNiro (1985) and Ambrose (1990). Apatite was converted to CO_2 in an automated multiprep inlet system, and isotope ratios were determined on the same VG Prism Series II mass spectrometer.

Modern food resources and other local plants and animals were rinsed in distilled water and freeze dried before being ground in a Wiley Mill and sieved to <0.25 mm.

Sample Quality

An assessment of sample quality is necessary before dietary interpretations can be made from the isotopic values of the bone fractions. Percent yield from bone, %C and %N by weight, and C/N ratios were all used to evaluate sample quality (Ambrose 1990; DeNiro 1985; Norr 1995), and are presented in table E.1. Unacceptably poor quality samples are indicated in italics and are not included in the mean calculations.

Table E.1. Percent yield and percent carbon and nitrogen from Palmer site[a]

Burial number	DH lab number	Percent yield coll.	%N/ wt coll.	%C/ wt coll.	C/N	Percent yield apat.	%N/ wt apat.	%C/ wt apat.	C/N
149	243	8.6	10.4	29.8	3.3	45.5	0.48	3.50	8.5
155	244	5.8	8.5	23.8	3.3	52.2	0.05	1.37	32.0
204	245	3.0	5.8	15.5	3.1	79.8	0.07	1.35	22.5
216	246	5.5	9.1	25.6	3.3	54.6	0.28	2.30	9.6
218	247	7.4	9.9	28.2	3.3	59.7	0.62	3.10	5.8
221	248	9.9	14.1	40.3	3.3	45.2	1.00	4.71	5.5
245	249	7.3	11.7	33.7	3.4	26.1	0.27	2.24	9.7
254	250	5.7	11.4	32.2	3.3	68.9	0.49	2.57	6.1
257	251	9.9	12.7	35.9	3.3	53.0	1.13	4.83	5.0
294	252	9.2	12.4	35.5	3.3	42.9	0.95	4.71	5.8
425	254	10.4	12.7	36.1	3.3	51.7	1.12	4.75	4.9
339	53	4.1	14.7	39.7	3.2	—	0.04	1.27	37.0
428	256	6.1	9.1	25.7	3.3	49.0	0.37	2.77	8.7
436	258	5.8	10.3	29.4	3.3	56.7	0.41	2.55	7.3
437	259	8.1	11.6	33.0	3.3	54.3	0.74	3.42	5.4
444	260	5.1	7.9	22.3	3.3	58.8	0.27	2.12	9.2
446	261	3.8	8.6	24.4	3.3	77.1	0.22	1.88	10.0
447	262	2.0	5.5	14.9	3.2	50.6	0.13	1.79	16.1
449	263	3.3	7.4	20.8	3.3	66.7	0.11	1.70	18.0
217	272	7.1	13.0	37.0	3.3	41.2	0.19	1.82	11.2
448	292	6.3	10.8	30.8	3.3	63.6	0.19	1.67	10.3
429	298	2.8	10.5	28.9	3.2	65.3	0.04	1.42	41.4
448	299	5.0	11.4	32.1	3.3	64.9	0.14	1.54	12.8
401	25	7.1	14.8	39.7	3.1	—	0.05	1.34	31.3
432	300	7.8	11.7	33.3	3.3	—	0.04	1.17	34.1
Mean		6.3	10.6	29.9	3.3	55.8	0.4	2.5	14.7
s.d.		2.3	2.5	7.0	0.1	12.3	0.4	1.2	11.4
97528	*253*	*2.0*	*0.3*	*0.0*	*0.0*	*77.7*	*0.05*	*1.56*	*36.4*
97603	*255*	*1.0*	*0.4*	*0.0*	*0.0*	*84.2*	*0.05*	*1.72*	*40.1*
97520	*297*	*0.6*	*0.6*	*0.0*	*0.0*	*65.4*	*0.04*	*1.44*	*42.0*

a. Unacceptably poor quality samples are indicated in italics.

Stable Isotope Results

The results of the stable carbon and nitrogen isotopic determinations on human bone and potential food resources are presented in tables E.2–E.10.

Internal laboratory and international standards for the stable isotopes of carbon and nitrogen were run along with the archaeological human bone samples and the modern food samples. These standards are for the assessment of intralab precision and interlab comparability. The results of our standard runs are presented in table E.11.

Table E.2. Stable carbon and nitrogen isotope results from collagen and stable carbon isotope results from apatite carbonate from central Gulf coast Florida, early Late Woodland site, Palmer 8SO2

	Lab #	$\delta^{15}N\text{‰}$	$\delta^{13}Cco\text{‰}$	$\delta^{13}Cca\text{‰}$	$\delta^{13}Cca\text{-}co$
Bur 149 95420	DH243	11.3	-16.0	-11.3	4.7
Bur 155 95426	DH244	11.1	-11.9	-9.0	2.9
Bur 204 95473	DH245	10.2	-9.1	-6.7	2.4
Bur 216 95484	DH246	11.3	-8.2	-7.3	0.9
Bur 218 95486	DH247	10.7	-9.6	-7.8	1.8
Bur 221 95488	DH248	11.0	-10.2	-8.3	1.9
Bur 245 95511	DH249	11.0	-9.1	-5.8	3.3
Bur 254 95520	DH250	11.3	-8.8	-6.5	2.3
Bur 257 95523	DH251	10.7	-8.6	-6.5	2.1
Bur 294 95555	DH252	12.0	-8.0	-6.0	2.0
Bur 425 97601	DH254	10.6	-9.1	-7.1	2.0
Bur 339 97514	DH53	11.8	-8.8	-6.4	2.4
Bur 428 97604	DH256	10.7	-9.1	-6.7	2.4
Bur 436 97612	DH258	10.8	-9.8	-6.4	3.4
Bur 437 97613	DH259	10.7	-9.7	-6.6	3.1
Bur 444 97618	DH260	10.9	-8.3	-6.3	2.0
Bur 446 97620	DH261	11.1	-8.7	-6.6	2.1
Bur 447 97621	DH262	9.8	-9.3	-5.9	3.4
Bur 449 97623	DH263	10.8	-8.9	-6.7	2.2
Bur 217 95485	DH272	10.5	-9.2	-6.4	2.8
Bur 448 97622	DH292	9.7	-9.9	-7.7	2.2
Bur 429 97605	DH298	11.4	-8.6	-6.5	2.1
Bur 448 97622	DH299	11.0	-8.4	-6.7	1.7
Bur 401	DH25	12.1	-9.3	-6.8	2.5
Bur 432 97608	DH257/300	10.6	-10.8	-7.6	3.2
Mean		10.9	-9.5	-7.0	2.5
s.d.		0.6	1.6	1.2	0.8

Table E.3. Archaeological animal bone collagen results from south Gulf coast Florida, with conversions of the delta values to edible portions equivalents

	Lab number	%Yld Coll	%N/wt Coll	%C/wt Coll	C/N	$\delta^{15}N\%$	Coll $\delta^{13}C\%$	Edible $\delta^{15}N\%$	Edible $\delta^{13}C\%$
Pinfish	137	3.9	8.8	25.7	3.4	5.7	-4.4	7.4	-8.1
Mullet	138	4.8	10.0	29.3	3.4	5.6	-8.9	7.3	-12.6
Sea catfish	139	4.3	8.0	23.3	3.4	6.8	-7.8	8.5	-11.5
Sheepshead	140	6.9	7.7	23.4	3.5	7.4	-6.8	9.1	-10.5
Spot' seatrout[a]	141	4.3	9.2	27.1	3.4	7.7	-4.0	9.4	-7.7
B'nose shark[a]	142	6.4	9.6	29.1	3.0	9.6	-9.1	11.3	-12.8
W'tail deer[a]	143	6.5	8.1	24.3	3.4	6.2	-19.6	7.9	-23.3
Duck	144	8.2	10.4	31.4	3.5	8.5	-19.8	10.2	-23.5
Sea turtle	145	1.4	4.0	11.4	3.3	7.2	-7.4	8.9	-11.1

a. Spot' seatrout = spotted seatrout; b'nose shark = blacknose shark; w'tail deer = whitetail deer.

Table E.4. Modern marine fish delta values from southern and central Gulf coast Florida, with adjustments to estimated values prior to the modern industrial enrichment of ^{12}C

	Lab number	Modern $\delta^{15}N\permil$	Modern $\delta^{13}C\permil$	Adjusted $\delta^{13}C\permil$
Atlantic croaker	DH35	10.9	-23.7	-22.2
Nurse shark	DH33	9.6	-11.3	-9.8
Pompano	DH326	9.8	-19.4	-17.9
Sheepshead	DH327	9.2	-14.7	-13.2
Striped mullet #2	DH72	13.5	-22.8	-21.3
Striped mullet #3	DH73	7.1	-12.4	-10.9
Striped mullet #1	DH64	7.3	-17.8	-16.3
Herring	DH37/38	9.2	-16.6	-15.1
Pinfish	DH61	8.2	-17.2	-15.7
Spotted seatrout	DH62	10.4	-10.8	-9.3
Hardhead catfish	DH65	9.4	-16.4	-14.9
Barred grunt	DH80	9.8	-23.3	-21.8

Table E.5. Modern freshwater fish delta values from central Gulf coast Florida, with adjustments to estimated values prior to the modern industrial enrichment of ^{12}C[a]

	Lab number	Modern $\delta^{15}N‰$	Modern $\delta^{13}C‰$	Adjusted $\delta^{13}C‰$
Bluegill #1	DH105	9.4	-25.2	-23.7
Spotted sunfish #1A	DH106	9.8	-24.4	-22.9
Bluegill #4	DH107	8.3	-26.1	-24.6
Spotted sunfish #3	DH108	8.6	-25.9	-24.4
Warmouth perch	DH109	10.5	-26.2	-24.7
Bluegill #3	DH100	8.7	-25.5	-24.0
Spotted sunfish	DH101	13.1	-26.8	-25.3
Flier	DH102	10.6	-25.5	-24.0

a. Citrus County near Inverness.

Table E.6. Modern invertebrate delta values from southern and central Gulf coast Florida, with adjustments to estimated values prior to the modern industrial enrichment of ^{12}C

	Lab number	Modern $\delta^{15}N‰$	Modern $\delta^{13}C‰$	Adjusted $\delta^{13}C‰$
Lightning whelk #1	DH60	5.8	-14.9	-13.4
Lightning whelk #2	DH74	6.3	-14.2	-12.7
Lightning whelk #3	DH66	6.2	-15.2	-13.7
Crown conch	DH68	8.3	-13.6	-12.1
Royal conch	DH34	10.5	-21.1	-19.6
Oyster #1	DH69	7.0	-17.5	-16.0
Oyster #2	DH70	9.8	-17.0	-15.5
Oyster	DH31	8.3	-22.1	-20.6
Oyster	DH32	4.0	-23.1	-21.6
Quahog clam	DH71	6.9	-15.2	-13.7
Spotted mud crab	DH63	10.8	-17.0	-15.5
Ghost crab	DH328	8.9	-16.2	-14.7
Burgers fiddler crab	DH325	5.5	-15.5	-14.0
Gray marsh crab	DH335	4.0	-22.2	-20.7
Shellfish	DH336	4.6	-18.8	-17.3
Coffee bean snail	DH329	3.6	-22.4	-20.9
Squid	DH315	11.8	-19.5	-18.0
American pink shrimp	DH67	10.1	-15.9	-14.4
Rock shrimp	DH59	8.5	-17.8	-16.3

Table E.7. Modern reptile delta values from central Gulf coast Florida, with adjustments to estimated values prior to the modern industrial enrichment of ^{12}C

	Lab number	Modern $\delta^{15}N‰$	Modern $\delta^{13}C‰$	Adjusted $\delta^{13}C‰$
Alligator[a]	DH339	6.9	-22.6	-21.1
Coral snake[a]	DH348	7.5	-23.8	-22.3
Cottonmouth[a]	DH349	6.2	-21.6	-20.1
Coach whip[b]	DH350	4.8	-22.2	-20.7
Eastern diamondback[a]	DH104	7.8	-23.6	-22.1

a. Citrus County near Inverness.

b. Marion County.

Table E.8. Modern bird delta values from central Gulf coast Florida, with adjustments to estimated values prior to the modern industrial enrichment of ^{12}C[a]

	Lab number	Modern $\delta^{15}N‰$	Modern $\delta^{13}C‰$	Adjusted $\delta^{13}C‰$
Wild turkey	DH345	5.7	-19.2	-17.7
Pileated woodpecker	DH341	3.1	-23.4	-21.9

a. Citrus County near Inverness.

Table E.9. Modern mammal delta values from central Gulf coast Florida, with adjustments to estimated values prior to the modern industrial enrichment of ^{12}C[a]

	Lab number	Modern $\delta^{15}N‰$	Modern $\delta^{13}C‰$	Adjusted $\delta^{13}C‰$
Bobcat	DH347	8.7	-23.1	-21.6
Whitetail deer	DH343	4.3	-25.1	-23.6
Gray fox	DH346	5.0	-17.5	-16.0
Fox squirrel	DH342	3.2	-22.9	-21.4
Gray squirrel	DH344	2.5	-24.9	-23.4
Opossum	DH338	7.1	-19.8	-18.3
Rat	DH340	5.9	-22.6	-21.1

a. Citrus County near Inverness.

Table E.10. Modern plant delta values from southern and central Gulf coast Florida, with adjustments to estimated values prior to the modern industrial enrichment of ^{12}C

	Lab number	Modern $\delta^{15}N‰$	Modern $\delta^{13}C‰$	Adjusted $\delta^{13}C‰$
Slender blue flag[a]	DH113	2.8	-30.1	-28.6
Alligator weed[a]	DH111	3.5	-29.2	-27.7
Arrowhead #2[a]	DH114	2.1	-27.9	-26.4
Bermuda grass	DH311	-1.0	-13.8	-12.3
Cabbage palm berries	DH267	1.3	-28.8	-27.3
Cattail[a]	DH117	0.6	-26.6	-25.1
Cattail head	DH313	2.5	-28.5	-27.0
Cattail tuber	DH314	—	-28.0	-26.5
Cattail tuber	DH331	—	-29.6	-28.1
Cucurbita pepo	DH98	3.7	-23.4	-21.9
Cucurbita texana	DH99	2.7	-23.1	-21.6
Forked sea	DH318	5.0	-17.7	-16.2
Forked sea	DH323	4.4	-17.2	-15.7
Grass #1	DH334	—	-12.0	-10.5
Hooked weed	DH321	4.9	-14.7	-13.2
Manatee grass	DH337	0.8	-6.7	-5.2
Mastic fruit	DH269	2.6	-28.5	-27.0
Palmetto berries	DH330	—	-27.7	-26.2
Panicoid grass #1	DH84	7.8	-12.2	-10.7
Panicoid grass #2	DH85	4.3	-12.5	-11.0
Aquatic grass	DH121	9.9	-33.5	-32.0
Freshwater[a] plant	DH88	3.5	-27.5	-26.0
Poss arrowhead #3	DH116	2.3	-27.6	-26.1
Prickly pear fruit	DH316	3.0	-12.6	-11.1
Prickly pear fruit	DH271	4.1	-11.9	-10.4
Prickly pear seeds	DH97	5.2	-12.4	-10.9
Rush #1[a]	DH123	2.9	-29.8	-28.3
Saltwort	DH324	7.7	-29.6	-28.1
Saltwort	DH333	3.8	-26.9	-25.4
Saw palmetto	DH309	—	-30.6	-29.1
Sea grape fruit	DH270	2.3	-29.7	-28.2
Sea grape	DH319	1.1	-26.8	-25.3
Sea lettuce	DH317	4.2	-20.2	-18.7
Sea oats	DH308	4.3	-13.5	-12.0
Seaside purslane	DH322	1.1	-27.7	-26.2
Sedge, Cyperaceae	DH86	4.7	-10.9	-9.4
Shoal grass	DH312	-1.6	-12.3	-10.8
Smilax 1[a]	DH112	1.3	-27.8	-26.3

continued

Table E.10 continued

	Lab number	Modern $\delta^{15}N‰$	Modern $\delta^{13}C‰$	Adjusted $\delta^{13}C‰$
Smilax 2 juvenile[a]	DH122	0.1	-27.8	-26.3
Smilax	DH78	2.8	-24.8	-23.3
Spanish moss	DH120	-1.1	-16.5	-15.0
Turtle grass	DH310	-0.4	-10.5	-9.0
Turtle grass	DH320	-1.2	-9.3	-7.8
Turtle grass	DH332	-0.4	-10.6	-9.1
Water tuber 1[a]	DH119	0.3	-29.9	-28.4
Water tuber 2[a]	DH115	3.0	-28.4	-26.9
Waterlily[a]	DH110	12.3	-29.3	-27.8
Yaupon[a]	DH118	0.4	-28.3	-26.8
Zamia tuber	DH268	-2.2	-28.1	-26.6

a. Citrus County near Inverness.

Table E.11. Number analyzed, means, and standard deviations (per mil) of internal and international standards run with the archaeological and modern samples reported here

Thiourea $\delta^{13}C$ org	NBS-22 $\delta^{13}C$ org	Thiourea $\delta^{15}N$	Peptone $\delta^{15}N$	NBS-19 $\delta^{13}C$ inorg	CM-UF $\delta^{13}C$ inorg	BYM $\delta^{13}C$ inorg
N = 35	N = 80	N = 32	N = 70	N = 22	N = 8	N = 22
-23.88	-29.75	-0.73	6.99	1.93	2.15	-2.27
±0.11	±0.11	±0.17	±0.13	±0.07	±0.08	±0.08

Interpretation

Bone stable isotopes reflect the natural variation in carbon and nitrogen isotope composition of the foods eaten. Because of this variation in food resources and in the ways carbon isotopes of different food components (e.g., proteins vs. carbohydrates) are incorporated into bone tissues, bone stable isotopes can provide several different kinds of dietary information for each individual. The $\delta^{15}N$ in bone collagen generally distinguishes between terrestrial and marine protein, although both environments can be highly variable. The $\delta^{13}C$ in collagen predominantly reflects dietary protein sources, and can distinguish between terrestrial and marine dietary protein, or between proteins in C_3 or C_4 photosynthetic pathway food chains. The $\delta^{13}C$ in apatite carbonate reflects the isotopic composition of the whole diet, both carbohydrates and proteins, in the proportions they are consumed (Ambrose and Norr 1993; Norr 1995).

The distribution of carbon isotopes in dietary protein and carbohydrates is particularly important for paleodietary reconstruction when the protein and carbohydrate portions of the diet had dramatically different stable carbon isotope compositions (Ambrose and Norr 1993; Klepinger and Mintel 1986; Norr 1995). The difference between $\delta^{13}C$ apatite carbonate and collagen ($\Delta^{13}Cca$-co) in an individual indicates the isotopic relationship of dietary protein compared with other dietary components in that person's diet. The regularities, or patterns, observed in these isotope data in controlled diet studies (Ambrose and Norr 1993) can be applied to paleodietary reconstruction in the coastal areas of the Americas (Norr 1995).

If the difference between the $\delta^{13}C$ of the apatite carbonate and the collagen is small, a marine protein and nonmaize C_3 carbohydrate diet is indicated. If this difference is large, a terrestrial protein and C_4 maize diet is indicated. If the difference is intermediate between those two extremes, then the overall isotopic values for the proteins and carbohydrates in the diet are similar, and the diet could be all C3-like, all C4-like, or a mixture of C_3 and C_4 carbohydrates and terrestrial and marine protein.

The results of the isotopic analyses of the Palmer population, and comparisons of the mean human dietary values with potential food resources are presented in table E.2 and figures E.2–E.5. When viewing the individual graphs, remember that collagen nitrogen data always reflect dietary protein, while the collagen carbon data tend to reflect the carbon isotope composition of the dietary protein, but are a mixture of carbon sources that also include some dietary carbohydrate and fats. The bone apatite carbonate graphs indicate carbon isotope ratios derived from whole diet. Those data, combined with close examination of the $\Delta^{13}Cca$-co, indicate patterns of food resources consumption.

The isotopic composition of human diet was estimated by subtracting 2.5‰ from the bone collagen stable nitrogen value, and by subtracting 9.5‰ from the bone apatite carbonate stable carbon value, since the carbonate represents whole diet far more accurately than does collagen (Ambrose and Norr 1993; Norr 1995). Archaeological animal bone samples were converted to edible portions by adding 1.7‰ to the collagen stable nitrogen value, and by subtracting 3.7‰ from the collagen stable carbon value (Keegan and DeNiro 1988; Norr 1990, 1995). The modern plants and animal flesh that were collected as potential food resources were adjusted for modern industrial production of ^{12}C by adding 1.5‰ to each modern stable carbon isotope value (see tables E.2–E.9). Comparison of the isotopic composition of the mean human diet for each site with the isotopic composition of the preindustrial isotopic composition of the potential food resources allows for an assessment of marine vs. freshwater vs. terrestrial protein sources and C_3 vs. C_4 and CAM plants in the diet.

The collagen and carbonate isotope compositions (figs. E.2, E.3) indicate the consumption of marine fish. The $\delta^{15}N$ is lower than it is for many

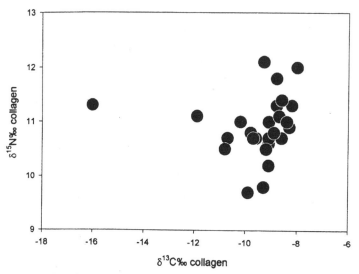

Fig. E.2. Plot of collagen data from Palmer.

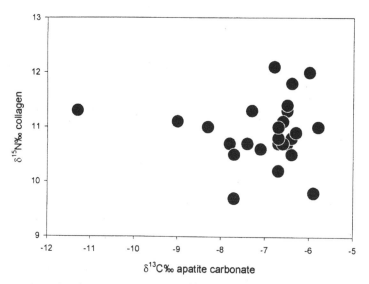

Fig. E.3. Plot of apatite carbonate data from Palmer.

coastal populations, which might suggest either a more terrestrial diet or selective fishing for species that have lower $\delta^{15}N$ values. By comparison with the modern plants and animals from the region, it is apparent that the lower $\partial^{15}N$ values for the Palmer individuals are due to the lower $\delta^{15}N$ values of the marine fish from that region, which are similar to many of the marine invertebrates from the Gulf coast of Florida (tables E.2–E.9).

The $\Delta^{13}Cca$-co indicates, as explained, the protein vs. carbohydrate mix of carbon isotope ratios in the diet. The $\Delta^{13}Cca$-co from the Palmer individuals is the smallest spacing of all coastal populations we have examined from Florida and North Carolina (Norr 2002; Norr et al. n.d.), and fully supports a marine-based dietary protein and a C3-based dietary carbohydrate source (fig. E.4). A comparison of the human diet with that of the potential food resources (fig. E.5) also indicates a mixed diet, but from the $\Delta^{13}Cca$-co, we can say that carbohydrate sources rich in ^{13}C, such as maize, other C_4 plants, or CAM plants, contributed little or nothing to the diet.

Comparison with other central and southern Gulf coast sites yields further information on regional and chronological dietary strategies. One other central Gulf coast population (Tierra Verde) and four southern Gulf coast populations (Useppa Island, Galt Island, Buck Key, and Horr's Island) were compared with Palmer in another study (Norr et al. n.d.; map

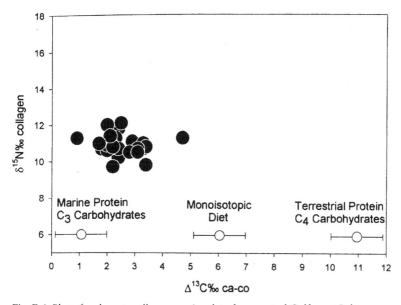

Fig. E.4. Plot of carbonate collagen spacing data from central Gulf coast Palmer.

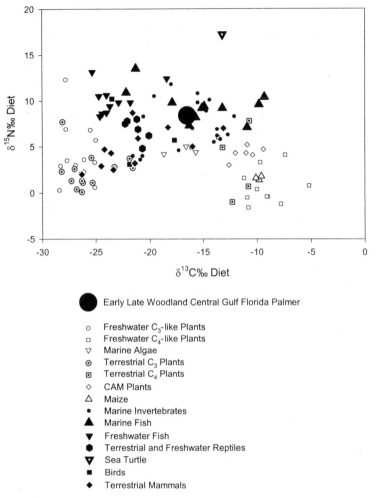

Fig. E.5. Comparison of the isotopic composition of the mean human diet for Palmer with the isotopic composition of potential food resources.

5.1; table 5.3). The $\delta^{13}C$, $\delta^{15}N$, and $\Delta^{13}C$ca-co all indicate similar diets for the individuals from Palmer, Tierra Verde, Useppa Island, Galt Island, and Buck Key. The earlier and more southern population from Horr's Island, however, shows a $\Delta^{13}C$ca-co that is more intermediate, likely a result of a wider range of terrestrial and marine resources, including a variety of C_3 and some CAM or C_4 plants. The $\delta^{13}C$ values from the collagen also indicate a more terrestrial protein source than that of the later and more northern Gulf coast populations.

Conclusions

The analysis of the stable isotopes of human bone collagen and apatite carbonate and of the local food resources from the Gulf coast of Florida has resulted in an interpretable database indicative of paleodiet. Comparisons of recognizable dietary patterns with studies of the botanical and faunal remains at sites from these regions, and comparisons with studies of the human demographic and health status, strengthen our biocultural and ecological interpretations of human coastal adaptations.

Acknowledgments

I would like to acknowledge the assistance of Theresa M. Schober, who worked as a graduate research assistant and processed nearly all of the samples reported here. Her experience and efficiency in the bone chemistry laboratory meant that we processed a large number of samples in a small amount of time, a task that otherwise could not have been accomplished. I also want to acknowledge the assistance and expertise of Jason Curtis of the department of geology, University of Florida, who also dedicated considerable time and energy to running and sometimes rerunning on the mass spectrometer and the Carlo Erba CHN analyzer the samples reported here.

References Cited

Ambrose, S. H.
1990   Preparation and Characterization of Bone and Tooth Collagen for Isotopic Analysis. *Journal of Archaeological Science* 17:431–451.
Ambrose, S. H., and L. Norr
1993   Experimental Evidence for the Relationship of the Carbon Isotope Ratios of Whole Diet and Dietary Protein to Those of Bone Collagen and Carbonate. In *Prehistoric Human Bone: Archaeology at the Molecular Level*, edited by J. Lambert and G. Grupe, 1–37. Berlin: Springer-Verlag.
DeNiro, M. J.
1985   Postmortem Preservation and Alteration of In Vivo Bone Collagen Isotope Ratios in Relation to Paleodietary Reconstruction. *Nature* 317:806–809.
1987   Stable Isotopy and Archaeology. *American Scientist* 75:182–191.
Hutchinson, D. L., and L. Norr
1994   Late Prehistoric and Early Historic Diet in Gulf Coast Florida. In *In the Wake of Contact: Biological Responses to Conquest*, edited by C. S. Larsen and G. Milner, 9–20. New York: Wiley-Liss.
1999   Maize, Midden, and Mollusc. Paper presented at the 1999 Annual Meeting of the American Association of Physical Anthropologists, Columbus, Ohio.

Hutchinson, D. L., C. S. Larsen, M. J. Schoeninger, and L. Norr
1998 Regional Variation in the Pattern of Maize Adoption and Use in Florida and Georgia. *American Antiquity* 63:397–416.

Keegan, W., and M. J. DeNiro
1988 Stable Carbon- and Nitrogen-Isotope Ratios of Bone Collagen Used to Study Coral-Reef and Terrestrial Components of Prehistoric Bahamian Diet. *American Antiquity* 53:320–336.

Klepinger, L. L., and R. Mintel
1986 Metabolic Considerations in Reconstructing Past Diet from Stable Carbon Isotope Ratios of Bone Collagen. In *Proceedings of the 24th Archaeometry Symposium,* edited by J. S. Olin and M. J. Blackman, 43–48. Washington, D.C.: Smithsonian Institution Press.

Norr, L.
1990 Nutritional Consequences of Prehistoric Subsistence Strategies in Lower Central America. Ph.D. diss., University of Illinois, Urbana-Champaign.
1995 Interpreting Dietary Maize from Bone Stable Isotopes in the American Tropics: The State of the Art. In *Archaeology in the American Tropics: Current Analytical Methods and Applications,* edited by P. W. Stahl, 198–223. Cambridge: Cambridge University Press.

Norr, L., and D. L. Hutchinson
1998 Reconstructing Prehistoric Subsistence in South Florida. Paper presented at the annual meeting of the Florida Anthropological Society, Gainesville.

Norr, L., D. L. Hutchinson, W. H. Marquardt, K. J. Walker, and L. A. Newsom
n.d. Calusa Subsistence in Southwest Florida. Manuscript in possession of the authors.

Schoeninger, M. J., M. J. DeNiro, and H. Tauber
1983 Stable Nitrogen Isotope Ratios of Bone Collagen Reflect Marine and Terrestrial Components of Prehistoric Human Diet. *Science* 220:1381–1383.

van der Merwe, N. J.
1982 Carbon Isotopes, Photosynthesis, and Archaeology. *American Scientist* 70: 596–606.

Appendix F. Dental Microwear Analysis

Mark Teaford

Experimental research on animals has shown that certain diets and food processing techniques can leave distinctive microwear patterns. Animals that incorporate more hard objects in their diets tend to have more and larger pits on their molars (Teaford and Runestad 1992; Teaford and Walker 1998). Animals with fibrous diets have polished enamel surfaces, and those with fine inclusions (such as phytoliths) have scratches on their molars. The multitude of food preparation techniques of humans, however, complicates the use of microwear as a technique for determining diet.

Previous examinations of populations inhabiting Florida, Georgia, and North Carolina (Teaford 1991, 2002; Teaford et al. 2001) have presented a unique opportunity to examine differences in diet using several categorical distinctions that include environment (coastal vs. inland), time period (prehistoric vs. historic), and geography (states). In this section, the microwear of the Palmer population is compared with several other populations inhabiting the eastern United States.

Materials and Methods

Molars from 9 Palmer individuals were initially examined. Teeth included a mixture of molars (M1, M2, or M3, and upper or lower), but each tooth was from a different individual. As teeth must be exceptionally clean for dental microwear analyses, a large amount of time was first spent in cleaning the teeth. Cotton swabs and acetone were used to remove any dirt, grease, or preservative on the teeth. Once the cleaning process was completed, high resolution casts of the teeth were prepared for scanning electron microscopy.

Impressions were taken with Coltene-Whaledent's President Jet Regular polysiloxane impression material, as described elsewhere (Teaford and Oyen 1989; Teaford et al. 1996). The impressions were then poured with

Ciba-Geigy's Araldite epoxy (956 hardener, 506 resin). After curing for 24 hours at room temperature, the epoxy casts were glued onto aluminum pin-type mounts; after another 12 hours, a dab of silver paint was applied to the junction of the cast, glue, and stub, and after 8–10 hours the stubbed casts were removed from their molds. Each cast was then left in an airtight box for at least two weeks to fully cure at room temperature. All casts were then sputter-coated with 200A of gold-palladium and examined in an Amray 1810 scanning electron microscope in secondary emissions mode. As a result of the initial SEM work, a number of teeth had to be removed from the analyses because they had significant amounts of post-mortem wear (Teaford, 1988). This was probably due, in large part, to acids percolating through groundwater at the sites while the teeth were still *in situ* (see fig. F.1).

Whenever possible, two micrographs were taken of each tooth. In some cases, only one micrograph could be taken because of the fragile nature of the specimen. Each micrograph was taken at a magnification of 500X and a working distance of 12 mm, with only enough tilt to ensure good contrast in the image (Pastor 1993). All micrographs were taken of either (1) the basin side of the protocone or hypocone (for the upper molars), or (2) the basin side of the protoconid or hypoconid (for the lower molars). The images were recorded on Polaroid 55 film and then scanned onto disk for analyses using the Microware 3.0 program developed by Peter Ungar at the University of Arkansas. The program uses a 4:1 ratio of length:width

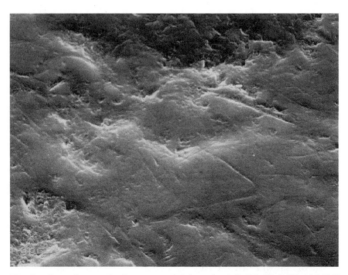

Fig. F.1. Dental enamel microwear of Palmer burial 428 (FMNH #97604), maxillary right second molar. Photo by Mark Teaford.

of each feature as the cutoff for determining which features are pits and scratches. For each micrograph, four attributes were analyzed: measures of average pit and scratch width (in μm), percentage of pits, number of microwear features, and homogeneity of scratch orientation. The last measure reflects merely whether scratch orientation is homogeneous or heterogeneous. Thus, the measurement is not dependent on tooth or micrograph orientation.

The dental microwear of the Palmer population was significant (fig. F.1). Comparisons were run between Palmer and a series of other coastal populations from Florida, Georgia, and North Carolina. In all comparisons, Lilliefors test was run to check for normal distributions (Zar 1984). When necessary, the microwear data were either rank- or log-transformed to meet the assumptions of parametric statistics (Conover and Iman 1976; Zar 1984). The two-sample t-test was run for the simple two-part comparisons (i.e., inner vs. outer estuarine), while single-factor ANOVA, followed by Tukey's HSD test, was used for multiple comparisons of microwear measurements; e.g., between individual sites. To determine an effect of location, a three–factor ANOVA was used for comparisons between sites in Florida (Hutchinson et al. n.d.), Georgia (Teaford et al. 2001), and North Carolina (Teaford 2002), with time period (Prehistoric & Mission), state (North Carolina, Georgia, Florida), and habitat (inland vs. coastal) as factors.

Results

Simple single factor ANOVAs revealed no significant differences between the inner and outer estuarine populations in North Carolina or Palmer (table F.1). Palmer was statistically indistinguishable from the North Carolina inner and outer coastal populations. Analyses for the combination of sites from Florida, Georgia, and North Carolina proceeded in roughly the same fashion. Thus, single factor ANOVAs or t-tests were run separately for each of the factors (state, time period, and habitat), followed by multifactor ANOVA. Results of the single factor ANOVA for the three states indicated that teeth from the sites in North Carolina showed significantly more microwear than those from Florida, but the teeth from North Carolina also had significantly narrower scratches and pits than those from the sites in Georgia (table F.2).

Analyses by time period (Prehistoric & Mission) showed that teeth from the Prehistoric sites had more microwear, but narrower scratches than those from the Mission sites (table F.3). The orientation of scratches was also almost significantly different between the sites from different

Table F.1. Molar microwear among Palmer and inner and outer estuarine populations in North Carolina

	Number of features per micrograph	Average pit width (microns)	Average scratch width (microns)	Scratch orientation homogeneity	Average percent pits
Inner (n = 12)	311 ± 27	2.21 ± .10	.90 ± .03	.440 ± .05	45.8 ± 4
Outer (n = 27)	359 ± 28	2.05 ± .09	.86 ± .02	.520 ± .03	50.1 ± 3
Palmer (n = 9)	361 ± 45	2.17 ± .14	.87 ± .02	.530 ± .04	55.4 ± 3

Note: All measurements are means ± standard error; no significant differences between sites.

Table F.2. Molar microwear among sites in North Carolina, Georgia, and Florida

	Number of features per micrograph	Average pit width (microns)	Average scratch width (microns)	Scratch orientation homogeneity	Average percent pits
N. Carolina (n = 39)	344 ± 21[a]	2.1 ± .07[b]	.87 ± .02[c]	.494 ± .02	48.8 ± 2
Georgia (n = 27)	291 ± 31	2.5 ± .16[b]	.99 ± .05[c]	.580 ± .02	45.3 ± 2
Florida (n = 74)	280 ± 13[a]	2.3 ± .07	.91 ± .02	.485 ± .02	48.0 ± 1

Notes: All measurements are means ± standard error.
a. Significantly different ($p \leq .028$).
b. Significantly different ($p \leq .010$).
c. Significantly different ($p \leq .034$).

Table F.3. Molar microwear in prehistoric and mission sites

	Number of features per micrograph	Average pit width (microns)	Average scratch width (microns)	Scratch orientation homogeneity	Average percent pits
Prehistoric (n = 100)	327 ± 15[a]	2.28 ± .07	.870 ± .015	.523 ± .02	48.9 ± 1
Mission (n = 40)	261 ± 14[a]	2.30 ± .07	.975 ± .03[b]	.473 ± .02[c]	46.0 ± 1

Note: All measurements are means ± standard error.
a. Significantly different ($p \leq .002$).
b. Significantly different ($p \leq .002$).
c. Almost significantly different ($p \leq .052$).

time periods ($p < .052$). Finally, when all sites were grouped into either inland or coastal sites, results indicated that the teeth from the inland sites had significantly more microwear than those from the coastal sites. However, those from the coastal sites had significantly wider pits and scratches than those from the inland sites (table F.4).

Table F.4. Molar microwear in coastal and inland sites in Georgia, Florida, and North Carolina

	Number of features per micrograph	Average pit width (microns)	Average scratch width (microns)	Scratch orientation homogeneity	Average percent pits
Coastal (n = 100)	279 ± 13[a]	2.4 ± .06[b]	.94 ± .02[c]	.500 ± .015	48.4 ± 1
Inland (n = 40)	352 ± 20[a]	2.0 ± .07[b]	.86 ± .03[c]	.509 ± .030	45.9 ± 1

Note: All measurements are means ± standard error.
a. significantly different ($p \leq .002$).
b. significantly different ($p \leq .002$).
c. almost significantly different ($p \leq .026$).

Table F.5. Results of three-factor ANOVA of molar microwear measurements from populations in different time periods, habitats, and states

	Number of features per micrograph	Average pit width (microns)	Average scratch width (microns)	Scratch orientation homogeneity	Average percent pits
Time period	insig	insig	$p \leq .003$	$p \leq 0.47$	insig
Habitat	$p \leq .051$	$p \leq .002$	insig	insig	insig
State	insig	insig	insig	insig	insig
Time/habitat interaction	insig	insig	insig	$p \leq .03$	insig
Time/state interaction	insig	insig	$p \leq .01$	insig	insig
Time/habitat /state interaction	$p \leq .007$	$p \leq .001$	insig	$p \leq .028$	insig

Single factor comparisons neglect the possibility of variation attributable to other overriding factors and their interactions. For instance, grouping sites from different states as "coastal" sites might mask the effect of particular location on the coast; the patterns documented for coastal sites in one state may not be the same as those patterns from coastal sites in another state. To avoid this possibility, as noted above, a three–factor ANOVA of molar microwear measurements was run incorporating the factors of time period, habitat, and state. Results, for the most part, echoed those from the single factor ANOVAs, but for certain microwear measurements there were significant interactions between factors (table F.5). Teeth from the coastal sites in North Carolina had a relatively large amount of microwear, whereas those from the coastal sites in Georgia had much less microwear (table F.6).

Table F.6. Molar microwear measurements of populations in North Carolina, Georgia, and Florida

	Number of features per micrograph	Average pit width (microns)	Average scratch width (microns)	Scratch orientation homogeneity	Average percent pits
Time period comparisons					
N. Carolina prehistoric (*n* = 39)	344 ± 21	2.10 ± .07	.87 ± .02	.494 ± .02	48.8 ± 2
Georgia prehistoric (*n* = 19)	331 ± 39	2.27 ± .18	.89 ± .05	.597 ± .03	46.9 ± 2
Georgia mission (*n* = 8)	158 ± 20	3.17 ± .19	1.22 ± .08	.481 ± .06	41.4 ± 4
Florida prehistoric (*n* = 24)	285 ± 25	2.59 ± .19	.87 ± .02	.513 ± .03	50.6 ± 2
Florida mission (*n* = 50)	277 ± 15	2.16 ± .06	.94 ± .03	.472 ± .02	46.7 ± 1
Habitat comparisons					
North Carolina coastal (*n* = 39)	344 ± 21	2.10 ± .07	.87 ± .02	.494 ± .02	48.8 ± 2
Georgia inland (*n* = 14)	402 ± 41	1.99 ± .13	.84 ± .06	.605 ± .04	47.0 ± 3
Georgia coastal (*n* = 13)	170 ± 14	3.13 ± .20	1.15 ± .06	.517 ± .04	43.4 ± 3
Florida inland (*n* = 26)	325 ± 20	2.07 ± .08	.87 ± .03	.458 ± .03	45.2 ± 1
Florida coastal (*n* = 48)	255 ± 16	2.42 ± .09	.94 ± .03	.500 ± .03	49.4 ± 2

Discussion

Comparisons between sites in Florida, Georgia, and North Carolina also pointed to localized differences in molar microwear. Single factor ANOVAs gave hints of interesting possibilities. For instance, comparisons of inland and coastal sites indicated that the teeth from the coastal sites showed larger microwear features than those from the inland sites; however, those from the inland sites showed more microwear than those from the coastal sites. This reaffirms what was found in analyses of a much smaller subset of these samples (i.e., those from southeastern Georgia) (Teaford, 1991), and may reflect the incorporation of more large-grained abrasives such as sand into the foods of the coastal people. The three–factor ANOVA indicated significant interaction effects of time, habitat, and state for three of the variables, indicating that patterns documented for a particular habitat and time period in one of the three states were significantly different than those from another habitat and time in a different state.

References Cited

Conover, W. J., and R. L. Inman
1981   Rank Transformation as a Bridge Between Parametric and Nonparametric Statistics. *American Statistician* 35:124–129.
Teaford, M. F.
1988   Scanning Electron Microscope Diagnosis of Wear Patterns versus Artifacts on Fossil Teeth. *Scanning Microscopy* 2:1167–1175.
1991   Dental Microwear: What Can It Tell Us about Diet and Dental Function? In *Advances in Dental Anthropology*, edited by M. A. Kelley and C. S. Larsen, 341–356. New York: Wiley-Liss.
Teaford, M. F., and O. J. Oyen
1989   Live Primates and Dental Replication: New Problems and New Techniques. *American Journal of Physical Anthropology* 62:255–1175.
Teaford, M. F., M. C. Maas, and E. L. Simons
1996   Dental Microwear and Microstructure in Early Oligocene Fayum Primates: Implications for Diet. *American Journal of Physical Anthropology* 101:527–543.
Teaford, M. F., C. S. Larsen, R. F. Pastor, and V. E. Noble
2001   Pits and Scratches: Microscopic Evidence of Tooth Use and Masticatory Behavior in La Florida. In *Bioarchaeology of Spanish Florida: The Impact of Colonialism,* edited by C. S. Larsen, 82–112. Gainesville: University Press of Florida.
Zar, J. H.
1984   *Biostatistical Analysis.* 2d ed. Englewood Cliffs, N.J.: Prentice-Hall.

References Cited

Almy, M. M., and G. M. Luer
1993   *Guide to the Prehistory of Historic Spanish Point.* Osprey, Fla.: Historic Spanish Point.

Ambrose, S. H., and L. Norr
1993   Experimental Evidence for the Relationship of the Carbon Isotope Ratios of Whole Diet and Dietary Protein to those of Bone Collagen and Carbonate. In *Prehistoric Human Bone: Archaeology at the Molecular Level,* edited by J. Lambert and G. Grupe, 1–37. Berlin: Springer-Verlag.

Anderson, D. G.
1994   *The Savannah River Chiefdoms: Political Change in the Late Prehistoric Southeast.* Tuscaloosa: University of Alabama Press.

Anderson, D. G., and R. C. Mainfort
2002   An Introduction to the Woodland Archaeology in the Southeast. In *The Woodland Southeast,* edited by D. G. Anderson and R. C. Mainfort, 1–19. Tuscaloosa: University of Alabama Press.

Andrews, R., J. Adovasio, and D. Harding
1988   Textile and Related Perishable Remains from the Windover Site (8BR246). Paper presented at the 53rd annual meeting of the Society for American Archaeology, Phoenix.

Angel, J. L.
1964   Osteoporosis: Thalassemia? *American Journal of Physical Anthropology* 22:369–374.
1966   Porotic Hyperostosis, Anemias, Malarias and Marshes in the Prehistoric Eastern Mediterranean. *Science* 153:760–763.
1969   The Basis of Paleodemography. *American Journal of Physical Anthropology* 30:427–438.

Ascenzi, A., and P. Balisteri
1975   Aural Exostoses in a Roman Skull Excavated at the "Baths of the Swimmer" in the Ancient Town of Ostia. *Journal of Human Evolution* 4:579–584.

Asch, D. L.
1976   *The Middle Woodland Population of the Lower Illinois Valley: A Study in Paleodemographic Methods.* Northwestern University Archaeological Program Scientific Papers no. 1. Evanston: Northwestern University.

Austin, R. J.
1987   An Archaeological Site Inventory and Zone Management Plan for Lee County, Florida. Performed for the Lee County Department of Community Development, Division of Planning.
Austin, R. J., and M. Russo
1989   *Limited Excavations at the Catfish Creek Site (8SO608), Sarasota County, Florida.* Piper Archaeological Research, St. Petersburg.
Bass, W. M.
1996   *Human Osteology: A Laboratory and Field Manual,* 4th ed. Columbia: Missouri Archaeological Society.
Bedford, M. E., K. F. Russell, and C. O. Lovejoy
1989   The Utility of the Auricular Surface Aging Technique. *American Journal of Physical Anthropology* 78:190–191.
Bender, M. M.
1968   Mass Spectrometric Studies of Carbon-13 in Corn and Other Grasses. *Radiocarbon* 10:468–172.
Bender, M. M., D. A. Baerreis, and R. L. Steventon
1981   Further Light on Carbon Isotopes and Hopewell Agriculture. *American Antiquity* 46:346–353.
Bennett, C. E. (translator)
2001   *Three Voyages* by René Laudonnière. First published 1975. Tuscaloosa: University of Alabama Press.
Bense, J. A.
1994   *Archaeology of the Southeastern United States: Paleoindian to World War I.* New York: Academic Press.
Bernard, H. R.
2002   *Research Methods in Anthropology: Qualitative and Quantitative Approaches,* 3rd ed. Walnut Creek, Calif.: Altamira.
Berriault, J., R. Carr, J. Stipp, R. Johnson, and J. Meeder
1981   The Archeological Salvage of the Bay West Site, Collier County, Florida. *Florida Anthropologist* 34:39–58.
Black, G. A.
1967   *The Angel Site.* Indianapolis: Indiana Historical Society.
Blake, L. W., and H. C. Cutler
1979   Plant Remains from the Upper Nodena Site. *Arkansas Archeologist* 20: 53–58.
Blitz, J. H.
1988   Adoption of the Bow in Prehistoric North America. *North American Archaeologist* 9:123–145.
Boehm, C.
1984   *Blood Revenge: The Anthropology of Feuding in Montenegro and Other Tribal Societies.* Lawrence: University Press of Kansas.
Borremans, N. T.
1993a   The Paleoindian Period. In *Florida's Cultural Heritage: A View of the*

Past, edited by C. Payne and J. T. Milanich. Tallahassee: Florida Division of Historical Resources. (www.dos.state.fl.us/dhr/bar/hist_contexts)

1993b   North Peninsular Gulf Coast, 500 B.C.–A.D. 1600. In *Florida's Cultural Heritage: A View of the Past*, edited by C. Payne and J. T. Milanich. Tallahassee: Florida Division of Historical Resources. (www.dos.state.fl. us/dhr/bar/hist_contexts)

Bridges, P. S.
1996   Warfare and Mortality at Koger's Island, Alabama. *International Journal of Osteoarchaeology* 6:66–75.

Bridges, P. S., K. P. Jacobi, and M. L. Powell
2000   Warfare-Related Trauma in the Late Prehistory of Alabama. In *Bioarchaeological Studies of Life in the Age of Agriculture: A View from the Southeast*, edited by P. M. Lambert, 35–62. Tuscaloosa: University of Alabama Press.

Brooks, S. T., and J. M. Suchey
1990   Skeletal Age Determination Based on the Os Pubis: A Comparison of the Acsadi-Nemeskeri and Suchey-Brooks Methods. *Human Evolution* 5: 227–238.

Brothwell, Don R.
1970   Real History of Syphilis. *Science Journal* 6: 27–33.

Buikstra, J. E., and D. H. Ubelaker (editors)
1994   *Standards for Data Collection from Human Skeletal Remains*. Arkansas Archeological Survey Research Series 44.

Bullen, A. K.
1972   Paleoepidemiology and Distribution of Prehistoric Trepanemiasis (Syphilis) in Florida. *Florida Anthropologist* 25:133–174.

Bullen, R. P.
1950   Tests at the Whitaker Site, Sarasota, Florida. *Florida Anthropologist* 3: 21–30.
1951   *The Terra Ceia Site, Manatee County, Florida*. Florida Anthropological Publications no. 3.
1952   *Eleven Archaeological Sites in Hillsborough County, Florida*. Report of Investigations no. 8. Tallahassee: Florida Geological Survey.
1955   Archaeology of the Tampa Bay Area. *Florida Historical Quarterly* 34: 51–63.
1962   Indian Burials at Tick Island. *American Philosophical Society Yearbook 1961*, 477–480.
1971   The Sarasota County Mound, Englewood, Florida. *Florida Anthropologist* 24:1–30.

Bullen, R. P., and A. K. Bullen
1953   The Battery Point Site, Bayport, Hernando County, Florida. *Florida Anthropologist* 6:85–92.
1956   *Excavations at Cape Haze Peninsula, Florida*. Contributions of the Florida State Museum, Social Sciences No. 1.

1963   The Wash Island Site, Crystal River, Florida. *Florida Anthropologist* 16: 81–92.

1976   The Palmer Site. *Florida Anthropologist* 29:1–55.

Bullen, R. P., and J. W. Griffin

1952   An Archaeological Survey of Amelia Island, Florida. *Florida Anthropologist* 5:37–62.

Bullen, R. P., A. K. Bullen, and W. J. Bryant

1967   *Archaeological Investigations at the Ross Hammock Site, Florida.* Orlando: William L. Bryant Foundation, Report no. 7.

Bullen, R. P., W. L. Partridge, and D. A. Harris

1970   The Safford Burial Mound, Tarpon Springs, Florida. *Florida Anthropologist* 23:81–118.

Bullen, R. P., W. Askew, L. M. Feder, and R. McDonnell

1978   *The Canton Street Site, St. Petersburg, Florida.* Gainesville: Florida Anthropological Society Publication no. 9.

Bullen, R. P., G. R. Reeder, B. Bell, and B. Whisenant

1952   The Harbor Key Site, Manatee County, Florida. *Florida Anthropologist* 5:21–23.

Burger, B. William

1982   Cultural Resource Management in Manatee County, Florida: The Prehistoric Resources Base. Master's thesis, New College of the University of South Florida, Tampa.

Bushnell, D. I.

1926   Investigation of Shell and Sand Mounds on Pinellas Peninsula, Florida. *Explorations and Fieldwork of the Smithsonian Institution in 1925,* 125–132.

Cabanilla, R. Quinn

1999   Evidence for Diet and Climate in Archaic Florida: Analyses of the Tick Island Human and Faunal Skeletal Samples. Master's thesis, University of Florida.

Centurion-Lara, A., C. Castro, R. Castillo, J. M. Shaffer, W. C. Van Voorhis, and S. A. Lukehart

1998   The Flanking Sequences of the 15–kDA Lipoprotein Gene Differentiate Pathogenic Treponemes. *Journal of Infectious Diseases* 177:1036–1040.

Chapman, J., and A. B. Shea

1981   The Archaeobotanical Record: Early Archaic Period to Contact in the Lower Little Tennessee River Valley. *Tennessee Anthropologist* 6:61–84.

Clausen, C. J., A. D. Cohen, C. Emiliani, J. A. Holman, and J. J. Stipp

1979   Little Salt Spring, Florida: A Unique Underwater Site. *Science* 203:609–614.

Clayton, L. A., V. J. Knight, and E. C. Moore (editors)

1993   *The De Soto Chronicles: The Expedition of Hernando de Soto to North America in 1539–1543,* vols. 1–2. Tuscaloosa: University of Alabama Press.

Coale, A. J.
1972   *The Growth and Structure of Human Populations: A Mathematical Investigation.* Princeton: Princeton University Press.
1974   The History of Human Populations. *Scientific American* 231:41–51.

Coale, A. J., and P. Demeny
1966   *Regional Model Life Tables and Stable Populations.* Princeton: Princeton University Press.

Cockrell, W. A., and L. Murphy
1978   Pleistocene Man in Florida. *Archaeology of Eastern North America* 6:1–13.

Cohen, M. N., and G. J. Armelagos (editors)
1984   *Paleopathology at the Origins of Agriculture.* Orlando: Academic Press.

Collins, H. B.
1929   The "Lost" Calusa Indians of Florida. *Explorations and Fieldwork of the Smithsonian Institution in 1928*, 151–156.

Cook, D. C.
1984   Subsistence and Health in the Lower Illinois Valley: Osteological Evidence. In *Paleopathology at the Origins of Agriculture,* edited by M. N. Cohen and G. J. Armelagos, 235–269. Orlando: Academic Press.
1994   Dental Evidence for Congenital Syphilis (and Its Absence) Before and After the Conquest of the New World. In *L'Origine de la Syphilis en Europe: Avant ou Après 1493?* edited by O. Dutour, G. Pálfi, J. Berato, and J.-P. Brun, 169–175. Paris: Editions Errance.

Cook, D. C., and K. D. Hunt
1998   Sex Differences in Trace Elements: Status or Self-Selection. In *Sex and Gender in Paleopathological Perspective,* edited by A. L. Grauer and P. Stuart-Macadam, 64–78. Cambridge: Cambridge University Press.

Costa, R. L.
1982   Periodontal Disease in the Prehistoric Ipiutak and Tigaraa Skeletal Remains from Point Hope, Alaska. *American Journal of Physical Anthropology* 59:97–110.

Curren, C., C. Claassen, L. A. Newsom, and M. Russo
1987   Archaeology at Bluewater Bay (8OK102), a Late Archaic Period Site in Northwest Florida. University of West Florida Office of Cultural and Archaeological Research Report of Investigations no. 9.

Cushing, F. H.
1896   Explorations of Ancient Key Dwellers' Remains on the Gulf Coast of Florida. *Proceedings of the American Philosophical Society* 35:329–448.

Cybulski, J. S.
1974   Tooth Wear and Material Culture: Precontact Patterns in the Tsimshian Area, British Columbia. *Syesis* 7:31–35.

Daniel, R. I.
1987   *Harney Flats: A Florida Paleo-Indian Site.* Farmingdale, N.Y.: Baywood Publishing.

DeLeon, V. B.
1998   Stable Isotope Analysis and Paleodiet at the Bay West Site, Collier County, Florida. Master's thesis, University of Florida.

DeNiro, M. J., and S. Epstein
1978   Influence of Diet on the Distribution of Carbon Isotopes in Animals. *Geochimica et Colmochimica Acta* 42:495–506.
1981   Influence of Diet on the Distribution of Nitrogen Isotopes in Animals. *Geochimica et Colmochimica Acta* 45:341–351.

DePratter, C. B., and J. D. Howard
1981   Evidence of Sea Level Lowstand Between 4500 and 2500 years B.P. on the Southeast Coast of the United States. *Journal of Sedimentary Petrology* 51:1287–1295.
1983   Evidence of Sea Level Lowstand Between 4500 and 2500 years B.P. on the Southeast Coast of the United States: A Discussion. *Journal of Sedimentary Petrology* 53:682–685.

Desowitz, R. S.
1981   *New Guinea Tapeworms and Jewish Grandmothers: Tales of Parasites and People*. New York: W.W. Norton.

DiBartolomeo, J.
1979   Exostoses of the External Auditory Canal. *Annals of Otolaryngology, Rhinology, and Laryngology,* supp. 61, 88:1–17.

Dickel, D.
1991   *Descriptive Analysis of the Skeletal Collection from the Prehistoric Manasota Key Cemetery, Sarasota County, Florida (8SO1292)*. Tallahassee: Florida Archaeological Reports no. 22.

Dickinson, J.
1985   *Jonathan Dickinson's Journal, or God's Protecting Providence, Being the Narrative of a Journey from Port Royal in Jamaica to Philadelphia, August 23, 1696 to April 1st, 1697*. Port Salerno: Florida Classics Library.

Dittrick, J., and J. M. Suchey
1986   Sex Determination of Prehistoric Central California Skeletal Remains Using Discriminant Analysis of the Femur and Humerus. *American Journal of Physical Anthropology* 70:3–9.

Doran, G. H. (editor)
2002   *Windover: Multidisciplinary Investigations of an Early Archaic Florida Cemetery*. Gainesville: University Press of Florida.

Doran, G. H., and D. N. Dickel
1988   Multidisciplinary Investigations at the Windover Site. In *Wet Site Archaeology*, edited by B. Purdy, 263–289. Caldwell, N.J.: Telford Press.

Doran, G. H., D. N. Dickel, W. E. Ballinger, Jr., O. F. Agee, P. J. Lapis, and W. W. Hauswirth
1986   Anatomical, Cellular, and Molecular Analysis of 8,000-Year-Old Human

Brain Tissue from the Windover Archaeological Site. *Nature* 323:803–806.

Doran, G. H., D. N. Dickel, and L. Newsom
1990   A 7,200-Year-Old Bottle Gourd from the Windover Site. *American Antiquity* 55:354–360.

Dunbar, J. S., S. D. Webb, and D. Cring
1989   Culturally and Naturally Modified Bones from a Paleoindian Site in the Aucilla River, North Florida. In *First International Bone Modification Conference,* edited by R. Bonnichsen, 473–497. Orono: Center for the Study of the First Americans, University of Maine.

Dunn, M. E.
1981   Botanical Remains from the Cemochechobee Site. In *Cemochechobee: Archaeology of a Mississippian Ceremonial Complex on the Chattahoochee River,* by F. T. Schnell, V. J. Knight, Jr., and G. S. Schnell, 252–255. Gainesville: University of Florida Press.

Dye, D. H.
2002   Warfare in the Protohistoric Southeast, 1500–1700. In *Between Contacts and Colonies: Archaeological Perspectives on the Protohistoric Southeast,* edited by C. B. Wesson and M. A. Rees, 126–141. Tuscaloosa: University of Alabama Press.

Eisenberg, L. E.
1986   Adaptation in a "Marginal" Mississippian Population from Middle Tennessee: Biocultural Insights from Paleopathology. Ph.D. diss., New York University.
1991   Mississippian Cultural Terminations in Middle Tennessee: What the Bioarchaeological Evidence Can Tell Us. In *What Mean These Bones? Studies in Southeastern Bioarchaeology,* edited by M. L. Powell, P. S. Bridges, and A.M.W. Mires, 70–88. Tuscaloosa: University of Alabama Press.

Eisenberg, L. E., and D. L. Hutchinson
1996   Introduction: Special Issue on Trauma. *International Journal of Osteoarchaeology* 6:1.

El-Najjar, M. Y.
1977   Maize, Malaria and the Anemias in the Pre-Columbian New World. *Yearbook of Physical Anthropology* 20:329–337.

El-Najjar, M. Y., B. Lozoff, and D. J. Ryan
1975   The Paleoepidemiology of Porotic Hyperostosis in the American Southwest: Radiological and Ecological Considerations. *American Journal of Roentgenology and Radiation Therapy* 125:918–924.

Ember, C. R., and M. Ember
1997   Violence in the Ethnographic Record: Results of Cross-Cultural Research on War and Aggression. In *Troubled Times: Violence and Warfare in the Past,* edited by D. L. Martin and D. W. Frayer, 1–20. Amsterdam: Gordon and Breach.

Estevez, E. D., J. Miller, and J. Morris
1984   Charlotte Harbor Estuarine Ecosystem Complex and the Peace River: A
        Review of Scientific Information. Mote Marine Laboratory, Sarasota.
        Submitted to the Southwest Florida Regional Planning Council.
Fazekas, I.G.Y., and F. Kósa
1979   *Forensic Fetal Osteology.* Budapest: Akademiai Kiado.
Fernald, E. A.
1981   *Atlas of Florida.* Tallahassee: Florida State University Foundation.
Fewkes, J. W.
1924   *Preliminary Archaeological Explorations at Weeden Island, Florida.*
        Washington, D.C.: Smithsonian Miscellaneous Collections 76.
Filipo, R., M. Fabiani, and M. Barbara
1982   External Ear Canal Exostosis: A Physiopathological Lesion in Aquatic
        Sports. *Journal of Sports Medicine and Physical Fitness* 22:329–339.
Fitzgerald, C.
1987   Analysis of the Faunal Remains at the Bayonet Field Site (8CI197), Citrus
        County, Florida. Manuscript on file, Florida Museum of Natural History.
Fitzgerald, C. M., and J. C. Rose
2000   Reading Between the Lines: Dental Development and Subadult Age As-
        sessment Using the Microstructural Growth Markers of Teeth. In *Biologi-
        cal Anthropology of the Human Skeleton,* edited by M. A. Katzenberg
        and S. R. Saunders, 163–186. New York: Wiley-Liss.
Florida Anthropological Society
2000   *Florida Archaeology: An Overview.* Tallahassee: Florida Anthropological
        Society.
Fontaneda, Do. D'Escalante
1944   *Memoir of Do. D'Escalante Fontaneda Respecting Florida. Written in
        Spain About the Year of 1575.* Translated by Buckingham Smith. Anno-
        tated by David O. True. Coral Gables, Fla.: Glades House.
Fowler, E., Jr., and P. Osmun
1942   New Bone Growth Due to Cold Water in the Ear. *Archives of Otolayng-
        ology* 36:455–466.
Fradkin, A.
1976   The Wightman Site: A Study of Prehistoric Culture and the Environ-
        ment on Sanibel Island, Lee County, Florida. Master's thesis, University
        of Florida.
Frayer, D. W.
1988   Auditory Exostoses and Evidence for Fishing at Vlasic. *Current Anthro-
        pology* 29:346–349.
1997   Ofnet: Evidence for a Mesolithic Massacre. In *Troubled Times: Violence
        and Warfare in the Past,* edited by D. L. Martin and D. W. Frayer, 181–
        216. Amsterdam: Gordon and Breach.
Fried, M., M. Harris, and R. Murphy
1968   *War: The Anthropology of Armed Conflict and Aggression.* Garden City,
        N.Y.: Natural History Press.

Gallagher, J. C., and L. O. Warren
1975   The Bay Pines Site, Pinellas County, Florida. *Florida Anthropologist* 28: 96–116.

Gibson, T.
1990   Raiding, Trading and Tribal Autonomy in Insular Southeast Asia. In *The Anthropology of War*, edited by J. Haas, 125–145. Cambridge: Cambridge University Press.

Giles, E.
1970   Discriminant Function Sexing of the Human Skeleton. In *Personal Identification in Mass Disasters*, edited by T. D. Stewart, 99–109. Washington, D.C.: Smithsonian Institution.

Giles, E., and O. Elliot
1963   Sex Determination by Discriminant Function Analysis of Crania. *American Journal of Physical Anthropology* 21:53–68.

Gilliland, M. S.
1975   *The Material Culture of Key Marco, Florida*. Gainesville: University Presses of Florida.

1988   *Key Marco's Buried Treasure: Archaeology and Adventure in the Nineteenth Century*. Gainesville: University Presses of Florida.

Girons, I. S., S. J. Norris, and U. Göbel
1992   Genome Structure of Spirochetes. *Research in Microbiology* 143:615–622.

Goggin, J. M.
1953   An Introductory Outline of Timucua Archaeology. *Southeastern Archaeological Conference Newsletter* 3:4–17.

Goggin, J. M., and W. C. Sturtevant
1964   The Calusa: A Stratified Nonagricultural Society with Notes on Sibling Marriage. In *Explorations in Cultural Anthropology*, edited by W. Goodenough, 179–219. New York: McGraw-Hill.

Goodman, A. H., and J. C. Rose
1990   Assessment of Systemic Physiological Perturbations from Dental Enamel Hypoplasias and Associated Histological Structures. *Yearbook of Physical Anthropology* 33:59–110.

1991   Dental Enamel Hypoplasias as Indicators of Nutritional Status. In *Advances in Dental Anthropology*, edited by M. A. Kelley and C. S. Larsen, 279–293. New York: Wiley-Liss.

Goodman, A. H., J. Lallo, G. J. Armelagos, and J. C. Rose
1984   Health Changes at Dickson Mounds, Illinois (A.D. 950–1300). In *Paleopathology at the Origins of Agriculture*, edited by M. N. Cohen and G. J. Armelagos, 271–305. Orlando: Academic Press.

Gordon, C. C., and J. E. Buikstra
1981   Soil pH, Bone Preservation, and Sampling Bias at Mortuary Sites. *American Antiquity* 48:566–571.

Grauer, A. L., and P. Stuart-Macadam (editors)
1998   *Sex and Gender in Paleopathological Perspective*. Cambridge: Cambridge University Press.

Grauer, A. L., E. M. McNamara, and D. V. Houdek
1998   A History of Their Own: Patterns of Death in a Nineteenth-Century Poor-house. In *Sex and Gender in Paleopathological Perspective,* edited by A. L. Grauer and P. Stuart-Macadam, 149–164. Cambridge: Cambridge University Press.

Green, V. D.
1993   Endemic Syphilis: A Prehistoric Controversy at Crystal River, Florida. B.A. thesis, Hampshire College, Amherst, Mass.

Gremillion, K.
1996   Early Agricultural Diet in Eastern North America: Evidence from Two Kentucky Rockshelters. *American Antiquity* 61:520–536.

Griffin, J. W.
1949   Notes on the Archaeology of Useppa Island. *Florida Anthropologist* 2: 92–93.
1951   Madira Bickel Mound State Monument. *Florida Highways* 19:10–11.
1988   The Archeology of Everglades National Park: A Synthesis. Tallahassee: Southeast Archeological Center, National Park Service, contract CX5000-5-0049.

Griffin, J. W., and R. P. Bullen
1950   *The Safety Harbor Site, Pinellas County, Florida.* Gainesville: Florida Anthropological Society Publication no. 2.

Grismer, K.
1946   *The Story of Sarasota: The History of the City and County of Sarasota, Florida.* Sarasota: M. E. Russell.

Hackett, C. J.
1951   *Bone Lesions of Yaws in Uganda.* Oxford: Blackwell Scientific Publications.
1976   *Diagnostic Criteria of Syphilis, Yaws, and Treponarid (Treponematoses) and of Some Other Diseases in Dry Bone.* New York: Springer-Verlag.

Hale, S.
1984   Environmental Exploitation around Lake Okeechobee. *Southeastern Archaeology* 3:173–187.

Hann, J. H. (editor and translator)
1991   *Missions to the Calusa.* Gainesville: University of Florida Press.
1996   *A History of the Timucua Indians and Missions.* Gainesville: University Press of Florida.

Hansinger, M. J.
1992   Skeletal and Dental Analysis of Burials from the Collier Inn Site, Useppa Island. In *Culture and Environment in the Domain of the Calusa,* edited by W. H. Marquardt, 403–409. Gainesville: University of Florida, Institute of Archaeology and Paleoenvironmental Studies, Monograph 1.

Hariot, T.
[1590] 1972   *A Briefe and True Report of the New Found Land of Virginia.* Reprint. New York: Dover Publications.

Hauswirth, W. W., C. D. Dickel, G. H. Doran, P. J. Laipis, and D. N. Dickel
1988   8,000-Year-Old Brain Tissue from the Windover Site: Anatomical, Cellular, and Molecular Analysis. In *Human Paleopathology: Current Syntheses and Future Options*, edited by D. J. Ortner and A. C. Aufderheide, 60–72. Washington, D.C.: Smithsonian Institution Press.

Hengen, O. P.
1961   Cribra Orbitalia: Pathogenesis and Probable Etiology. *Homo* 22:57–75.

Higginbotham, L. C.
1999   Gender-Specific Dental Health Patterns in Late Prehistoric Populations from the Southeastern Coast. Master's thesis, East Carolina University, Greenville.

Hildebolt, C. F., S. Molnar, M. Elvin-Lewis, and J. K. McKee
1988   The Effect of Geochemical Factors on Prevalences of Dental Diseases for Prehistoric Inhabitants of the State of Missouri. *American Journal of Physical Anthropology* 75:1–14.

Hildebolt, C. F., M. Elvin-Lewis, S. Molnar, J. K. McKee, M. D. Perkins, and K. L. Young
1989   Caries Prevalences among Geochemical Regions of Missouri. *American Journal of Physical Anthropology* 78:79–92.

Hillson, S.
1996   *Dental Anthropology*. Cambridge: Cambridge University Press.

Hoshower, L. M.
1992   Bioanthropological Analysis of a Seventeenth-Century Native American Spanish Mission Population: Biocultural Impacts on the Northern Utina. Ph.D. diss., University of Florida.

Hrdlička, A.
1907   *Skeletal Remains Suggesting or Attributed to Early Man in North America*. Washington, D.C.: Bureau of American Ethnology Bulletin 33.
1922   *The Anthropology of Florida*. DeLand: Florida Historical Society.
1935   *Ear Exostoses*. Smithsonian Miscellaneous Collections 93:1–100.
1940   Catalog of Human Crania in the United States National Museum Collections: Indians of the Gulf States. Washington, D.C.: *Proceedings of the United States National Museum* 87:315–464.

Humphreys, J., and D. L. Hutchinson
2001   Macroscopic Observations of Hacking Trauma. *Journal of Forensic Sciences* 46:228–233.

Hutchinson, D. L.
1990   Human Skeletal Remains from Galt Island. Report on file at the Florida Museum of Natural History, Gainesville.
1991   Postcontact Native American Health and Adaptation: Assessing the Impact of Introduced Diseases in Sixteenth-Century Gulf Coast Florida. Ph.D. diss., University of Illinois, Urbana-Champaign.
1992   Prehistoric Human Burials from Buck Key. In *Culture and Environment in the Domain of the Calusa*, edited by W. H. Marquardt, 411–422.

Gainesville: University of Florida, Institute of Archaeology and Paleo-environmental Studies, Monograph 1.

1993a   Treponematosis in Regional and Chronological Perspective from Central Gulf Coast Florida. *American Journal of Physical Anthropology* 92:249–261.

1993b   Analysis of Skeletal Remains from the Tierra Verde Site, Pinellas County, West-Central Florida. *Florida Anthropologist* 46:263–276.

1996   Brief Encounters: Tatham Mound and the Evidence for Spanish and Native American Confrontation. *International Journal of Osteoarchaeology* 6:51–65.

1999   Prehistoric Human Skeletal Remains from Useppa Island, Florida 8LL51. In *The Archaeology of Useppa Island,* edited by W. H. Marquardt, 139–147. Gainesville: University of Florida, Institute of Archaeology and Paleoenvironmental Studies, Monograph 3.

2002a   *Foraging, Farming, and Coastal Biocultural Adaptation in Late Prehistoric North Carolina.* Gainesville: University Press of Florida.

2002b   Osteological Analysis of the Aqui Esta Mound Population. In *Archaeology of Upper Charlotte Harbor, Florida,* edited by George M. Luer, 183–193. Florida Anthropological Society Publication no. 15.

2003   Prehistoric Human Skeletal Remains from Pine Island. In *The Archaeology of Pineland: A Coastal Southwest Florida Village Complex, ca.* A.D. *100–600,* edited by K. J. Walker and W. H. Marquardt. Gainesville: University of Florida, Institute of Archaeology and Paleoenvironmental Studies, Monograph 4.

n.d.   *Tatham Mound and the Bioarchaeology of Spanish Contact in West Central Florida.* Gainesville: University Press of Florida.

Hutchinson, D. L., and L. V. Aragon

2002   Collective Burials and Community Memories: Interpreting the Placement of the Dead in the Southeastern and Mid-Atlantic United States with Reference to Ethnographic Cases from Indonesia. In *The Space and Place of Death,* edited by H. Silverman and D. B. Small, 27–54. Washington, D.C.: Archeological Papers of the American Anthropological Association no. 11.

Hutchinson, D. L., and C. S. Larsen

1988   Determination of Stress Episode Duration from Linear Enamel Hypoplasias: A Case Study from St. Catherines Island, Georgia. *Human Biology* 601: 93–110.

1990   Stress and Lifeway Change on the Georgia Coast: The Evidence from Enamel Hypoplasia. In *The Archaeology of Mission Santa Catalina de Guale: Biocultural Interpretations of a Population in Transition,* edited by C. S. Larsen, 50–65. Anthropological Paper 68. New York: American Museum of Natural History.

1996   Brief Encounters: Tatham Mound and the Evidence for Spanish and Native American Confrontation. *International Journal of Osteoarchaeology* 6:51–65.

2001   Enamel hypoplasia and stress in North Florida. In *Bioarchaeology of Spanish Florida: The Impact of Colonialism,* edited by C. S. Larsen, 181–206. Gainesville: University Press of Florida.

Hutchinson, D. L., and J. M. Mitchem

1996   The Weeki Wachee Mound, an Early Contact Mortuary Locality in Hernando County, West-Central Florida. *Southeastern Archaeology* 15:47–65.

2001   Correlates of Contact: Epidemic Disease in Archaeological Context. *Historical Archaeology* 35:58–72.

Hutchinson, D. L., and L. Norr

1994   Late Prehistoric and Early Historic Diet in Gulf Coast Florida. In *In the Wake of Contact: Biological Responses to Conquest,* edited by C. S. Larsen and G. R. Milner, 9–20. New York: Wiley-Liss.

n.d.   Nutrition and Health on the Eve of European Contact in Late Prehistoric Central Gulf Coast Florida. Manuscript in possession of authors.

Hutchinson, D. L., and D. S. Weaver

1998   Two Cases of Facial Involvement in Probable Treponemal Infection from Late Prehistoric North Carolina. *International Journal of Osteoarchaeology* 8:444–453.

Hutchinson, D. L., L. Norr, and M. Teaford

n.d.   Coastal Adaptation along the Central Florida Gulf Coast. In *Beyond Midden and Maize,* edited by D. L. Hutchinson. In preparation.

Hutchinson, D. L., C. B. Denise, H. J. Daniel, and G. Kalmus

1997   A Reevaluation of the Cold Water Etiology of External Auditory Exostoses. *American Journal of Physical Anthropology* 103:417–422.

Hutchinson, D. L., C. S. Larsen, L. Norr, and M. J. Schoeninger

2000   Agricultural Melodies and Alternative Harmonies in Florida and Georgia. In *Bioarchaeological Studies of Life in the Age of Agriculture: A View from the Southeast,* edited by P. M. Lambert, 96–115. Tuscaloosa: University of Alabama Press.

Hutchinson, D. L., C. S. Larsen, M. J. Schoeninger, and L. Norr

1998   Regional Variation in the Pattern of Maize Adoption and Use in Florida and Georgia. *American Antiquity* 63:397–416.

Hutchinson, D. L., C. S. Larsen, M. A. Williamson, V. D. Green Clow, and M. L. Powell

2003   Temporal and Spatial Variation in the Pattern of Treponematosis in Georgia and Florida. In *The Natural History of Syphilis in North America,* edited by M. L. Powell and D. C. Cook. Gainesville: University Press of Florida.

Hyams, V. J., G. J. Batsakis, and L. Michaels

1988   Tumors of the Upper Respiratory Tract and Ear. *Armed Forces Institute of Pathology,* 2d ser., fascicle 25, Washington, D.C.

İşcan, M. Y., and P. Miller-Shaivitz

1983   A Review of Physical Anthropology in *The Florida Anthropologist. Florida Anthropologist* 36:114–123.

Jackes, M.
2000   Building the Bases for Paleodemographic Analysis: Adult Age Determination. In *Biological Anthropology of the Human Skeleton,* edited by M. A. Katzenberg and S. R. Saunders, 417–466. New York: Wiley-Liss.
Jeffries, R. W., E. Breitburg, J. Flood, and C. M. Scarry
1996   Mississippian Adaptation on the Northern Periphery: Settlement, Subsistence and Interaction in the Cumberland Valley of Southeastern Kentucky. *Southeastern Archaeology* 15:1–28.
Johannessen, S.
1993   Farmers of the Late Woodland. In *Foraging and Farming in the Eastern Woodlands,* edited by C. M. Scarry, 57–77. Gainesville: University of Florida Press.
Johannessen, S., and L. A. Whalley
1988   Floral Analyses. In *Late Woodland Sites in the American Bottom Uplands,* edited by C. Bentz, D. McElrath, F. Finney, and R. Lacampagne, 265–288. American Bottom Archaeology FAI-270 Site Reports No. 18, University of Illinois, Champaign-Urbana.
Johnson, K.
1987   The Search for Aguacaleyquen and Cali: Archaeological Survey of Portions of Alachua, Bradford, Citrus, Clay, Columbia, Marion, Sumter, and Union Counties, Florida. Miscellaneous Project Report Series 33. Gainesville: Florida Museum of Natural History, Department of Anthropology.
1990   The Discovery of a Seventeenth-Century Spanish Mission in Ichetucknee State Park, 1986. *Florida Journal of Anthropology* 15:39–46.
Johnson, W. G.
1990   The Role of Maize in South Florida Aboriginal Societies: An Overview. *Florida Anthropologist* 43:209–214.
Johnston, F. E.
1961   Sequence of Epiphyseal Union in a Prehistoric Kentucky Population from Indian Knoll. *American Journal of Physical Anthropology* 20: 249–254.
1962   Growth of the Long Bones of Infants and Young Children at Indian Knoll. *Human Biology* 23:66–81.
Jones, B. C.
1982   Southern Cult Manifestations at the Lake Jackson Site, Leon County, Florida: Salvage Excavation of Mound 3. *Midcontinental Journal of Archaeology* 7:3–44.
Jurmain, R. D.
1977   Stress and the Etiology of Osteoarthritis. *American Journal of Physical Anthropology* 46:353–365.
1999   *Stories from the Skeleton: Behavioral Reconstruction in Human Osteology.* Amsterdam: Gordon and Breach.
Jurmain, R. D., and V. I. Bellifemime
1997   Patterns of Cranial Trauma in a Prehistoric Population from Central California. *International Journal of Osteoarchaeology* 7:43–50.

Kaplan, E. H.
1988 *Southeastern and Caribbean Seashores*. Peterson Field Guides no. 36. Boston: Houghton Mifflin.

Katzmarzyk, C.
1998 Evidence of Stress in a Precolumbian Population from Mound G at the Crystal River Site, Florida. Master's thesis, University of Florida.

Keegan, W. F.
1987 Diffusion of Maize from South America: The Antillean Connection Reconstructed. In *Emergent Horticultural Economies of the Eastern Woodlands*, edited by W. F. Keegan, 329–344. Occasional Paper no. 7. Carbondale: Center for Archaeological Investigations, Southern Illinois University.

Keegan, W. F., and M. J. DeNiro
1988 Stable Carbon and Nitrogen-Isotope Ratios of Bone Collagen Used to Study Coral-Reef and Terrestrial Components of Prehistoric Bahamian Diet. *American Antiquity* 53:320–336.

Kelly, R. C.
2000 *Warless Societies and the Origin of War*. Ann Arbor: University of Michigan Press.

Kelly, R. L.
1995 *The Foraging Spectrum: Diversity in Hunter-Gatherer Lifeways*. Washington, D.C.: Smithsonian Institution Press.

Kennedy, G. E.
1986 The Relationship Between Auditory Exostoses and Cold Water: A Latitudinal Analysis. *American Journal of Physical Anthropology* 71:401–415.

Kent, S.
1986 The Influence of Sedentism and Aggregation on Porotic Hyperostosis and Anaemia: A Case Study. *Man* 21:605–636.
1992 Anemia Through the Ages: Changing Perspectives and Their Implications. In *Diet, Demography, and Disease: Changing Perspectives on Anemia,* edited by P. Stuart-Macadam and S. Kent, 1–30. New York: Aldine De Gruyter.

Kohler, T. A.
1975 The Garden Patch Site: A Minor Weeden Island Ceremonial Center on the North Peninsular Florida Gulf Coast. Master's thesis, University of Florida.
1991 The Demise of Weeden Island, and Post–Weeden Island Cultural Stability in Non-Mississippianized Northern Florida. In *Stability, Transformation, and Variations: The Late Woodland Southeast,* edited by M. S. Nassaney and C. R. Cobb, 91–110. New York: Plenum.

Kohler, T. A., and G. M. Johnson
1986 Dixie County Archaeological Reconnaissance, Winter 1985/86. Report submitted to the Florida Bureau of Archaeological Research, Tallahassee.

Kolman, C. J., A. Centurion-Lara, S. A. Lukehart, D. W. Owsley, and N. Tuross
1999 Identification of *Treponema pallidum* Subspecies *pallidum* in a 200-Year-Old Skeletal Specimen. *Journal of Infectious Diseases* 180:2060–2063.

Konigsberg, L. W., and S. M. Hens
1998   Use of Ordinal Categorical Variables in Skeletal Assessment of Sex from the Cranium. *American Journal of Physical Anthropology* 107:97–112.
Kozuch, L.
1986   An Overview of Faunal Lists from Selected Safety Harbor Period Sites. On file, Zooarchaeology Range, Florida Museum of Natural History, Gainesville.
1998   Faunal Remains from the Palmer Site (8So2), with a Focus on Shark Remains. *Florida Anthropologist* 51:177–192.
Kreshover, S. J.
1944   The Pathogenesis of Enamel Hypoplasia: An Experimental Study. *Journal of Dental Research* 23:231–239.
1960   Metabolic Disturbances in Tooth Formation. *Annals of the New York Academy of Sciences* 85:161–167.
Kreshover, S. J., and O. W. Clough
1953a   Prenatal Influences on Tooth Development: I. Alloxan Diabetes in Rats. *Journal of Dental Research* 32:246–261.
1953b   Prenatal Influences on Tooth Development: II. Artificially Induced Fever in Rats. *Journal of Dental Research* 32:565–572.
Krogman, W. M., and M. Y. İşcan
1986   *The Human Skeleton in Forensic Medicine,* 2d ed. Springfield, Ill.: Charles C. Thomas.
Lambert, P. M.
1993   Health in Prehistoric Populations of the Santa Barbara Channel Islands. *American Antiquity* 58:509–522.
1994   War and Peace on the Western Front: A Study of Violent Conflict and Its Correlates in Prehistoric Hunter-Gatherer Societies of Coastal Southern California. Ph.D. diss., University of California, Santa Barbara.
1997   Patterns of Violence in Prehistoric Hunter-Gatherer Societies of Coastal Southern California. In *Troubled Times: Violence and Warfare in the Past,* edited by D. L. Martin and D. W. Frayer, 77–110. Amsterdam: Gordon and Breach.
2001   Auditory Exostoses: A Clue to Gender in Prehistoric and Historic Farming Communities of North Carolina and Virginia. In *Archaeological Studies of Gender in the Southeastern United States,* edited by J. M. Eastman and C. B. Rodning, 152–172. Gainesville: University Press of Florida.
Larsen, C. S.
1982   *The Anthropology of St. Catherines Island: 3. Prehistoric Human Biological Adaptation.* Anthropological Paper 57, part 3. New York: American Museum of Natural History.
1985   Dental Modifications and Tool Use in the Western Great Basin. *American Journal of Physical Anthropology* 67:393–402.

1987   Bioarchaeological Interpretations of Subsistence Economy and Behavior from Human Skeletal Remains. *Advances in Archaeological Method and Theory* 10:339–445.

1995   Biological Changes in Human Populations with Agriculture. *Annual Reviews of Anthropology* 24:185–213.

1997   *Bioarchaeology: Interpreting Behavior from the Human Skeleton.* Cambridge: Cambridge University Press.

1998   Gender, Health, and Activity in Foragers and Farmers in the American Southeast: Implications for Social Organization in the Georgia Bight. In *Sex and Gender in Paleopathological Perspective,* edited by A. L. Grauer and P. Stuart-Macadam, 165–187. Cambridge: Cambridge University Press.

2001   Bioarchaeology of Spanish Florida. In *Bioarchaeology of Spanish Florida: The Impact of Colonialism,* edited by C. S. Larsen, 22–51. Gainesville: University Press of Florida.

Larsen, C. S., and D. L. Hutchinson

1992   Dental Evidence for Physiological Disruption: Biocultural Interpretations from the Eastern Spanish Borderlands, U.S.A. *Journal of Paleopathology Monographic Publications* 2:151–169.

Larsen, C. S., and L. E. Sering

2000   Inferring Iron-Deficiency Anemia from Human Skeletal Remains: The Case of the Georgia Bight. In *Bioarchaeological Studies of Life in the Age of Agriculture: A View from the Southeast,* edited by P. M. Lambert, 116–133. Tuscaloosa: University of Alabama Press.

Larsen, C. S., R. Shavit, and M. C. Griffin

1991   Dental Caries Evidence for Dietary Change: An Archaeological Context. In *Advances in Dental Anthropology,* edited by M. A. Kelley and C. S. Larsen, 179–202. New York: Wiley-Liss.

Larsen, C. S., M. F. Teaford, and M. K. Sandford

1998   Teeth as Tools: Extramasticatory Behavior in Prehistoric St. Thomas, U.S. Virgin Islands. In *Human Dental Development, Morphology, and Pathology: A Tribute to Albert A. Dahlberg,* edited by J. R. Lukacs, 401–420. Eugene: University of Oregon Anthropological Papers no. 54.

Larsen, C. S., D. L. Hutchinson, M. J. Schoeninger, and L. Norr

2001   Food and Stable Isotopes in La Florida: Diet and Nutrition Before and After Contact. In *Bioarchaeology of Spanish Florida: The Impact of Colonialism,* edited by C. S. Larsen, 52–81. Gainesville: University Press of Florida.

Larsen, C. S., C. B. Ruff, M. J. Schoeninger, and D. L. Hutchinson

1992   Population Decline and Extinction in La Florida. In *Disease and Demography in the Americas: Changing Patterns Before and After 1492,* edited by J. W. Verano and D. H. Ubelaker, 25–39. Washington, D.C.: Smithsonian Institution Press.

Larson, L. H.
1972   Functional Considerations of Warfare in the Southeast During the Missis-
       sippian Period. *American Antiquity* 37:383–392.
Layrisse, M., and M. Roche
1964   The Relationship Between Anemia and Hookworm Infection. *American
       Journal of Hygiene* 79:279–301.
Le Page du Pratz, A. S.
1947   *The History of Louisiana or of the Western Parts of Virginia and Caro-
       lina.* New Orleans: J. W. W. Hamilton.
Leverett, D. H.
1982   Fluorides and the Changing Prevalence of Dental Caries. *Science* 217:
       26–30.
Lewis, C. M.
1978   The Calusa. In *Tacachale: Essays on the Indians of Florida and Southeast-
       ern Georgia During the Historic Period,* edited by J. T. Milanich and S.
       Proctor, 19–49. Gainesville: University Presses of Florida.
Livingston, R. J.
1990   Inshore Marine Habitats. In *Ecosystems of Florida,* edited by R. L. Myers
       and J. J. Ewel, 549–573. Orlando: University of Central Florida Press.
Lorant, S. (editor)
1965   *The New World: The First Picture of America.* Rev. ed. New York: Duell,
       Sloan, and Pearce.
Lotka, A. J.
[1924] 1956   *Elements of Mathematical Biology.* Reprint. Dover, New York.
Lovejoy, C. O.
1985   Dental Wear in the Libben Population: Its Functional Pattern and Role in
       the Determination of Adult Skeletal Age at Death. *American Journal of
       Physical Anthropology* 68:47–56.
Lovejoy, C. O., R. S. Meindl, T. R. Pryzbeck, and R. P. Mensforth
1985a Chronological Metamorphosis of the Auricular Surface of the Ilium.
       American Journal of Physical Anthropology 68:15–28.
Lovejoy, C. O., R. S. Meindl, R. P. Mensforth, and T. J. Barton
1985b Multifactoral Determination of Skeletal Age at Death: A Method and
       Blind Tests of Its Accuracy. *American Journal of Physical Anthropology*
       68:1–14.
Luer, G. M.
1977a Excavations at the Old Oak Site, Sarasota, Florida: A Late Weeden Is-
       land–Safety Harbor Period Site. *Florida Anthropologist* 30:37–55.
1977b The Roberts Bay Site, Sarasota, Florida. *Florida Anthropologist* 30:121–
       133.
1989   Calusa Canals in Southwestern Florida: Routes of Tribute and Exchange.
       Florida Anthropologist 42:89–130.
1995   The Brookside Mound, Sarasota County, Florida: Notes on Landscape,

Settlement, Scrub Habitat, and Isolated Burial Mounds. *Florida Anthropologist* 48:200–216.

Luer, G. M. (editor)

2002   *Archaeology of Upper Charlotte Harbor, Florida.* Florida Anthropological Society Publication no. 15.

Luer, G. M., and M. M. Almy

1979   Three Aboriginal Shell Middens on Longboat Key, Florida: Manasota Period Sites of Barrier Island Exploitation. *Florida Anthropologist* 32: 34–45.

1981   Temple Mounds of the Tampa Bay Area. *Florida Anthropologist* 34:127–155.

1982   A Definition of the Manasota Culture. *Florida Anthropologist* 35:34–58.

1987   The Laurel Mound (8So98) and Radial Burials with Comments on the Safety Harbor Period. *Florida Anthropologist* 40:301–320.

Luer, G. M., M. M. Almy, D. Ste. Claire, and R. Austin

1987   The Myakkahatchee Site (8So397), A Large Multi-Period Inland from the Shore Site in Sarasota County, Florida. *Florida Anthropologist* 40:137–153.

Luer, G. M., D. Allerton, D. Hazeltine, R. Hatfield, and D. Hood

1986   Whelk Shell Tool Blanks from Big Mound Key (8CH10), Charlotte County, Florida: With Notes on Certain Whelk Shell Tools. *Florida Anthropologist* 39:92–124.

Lukacs, J. R.

1995   The "Caries Correction Factor": A New Method of Calibrating Dental Caries Rates to Compensate for Antemortem Loss of Teeth. *International Journal of Osteoarchaeology* 5:151–156.

1996   Sex Differences in Dental Caries Rates with the Origin of Agriculture in South Asia. *Current Anthropology* 37:147–153.

Magoon, D. T., L. Norr, D. L. Hutchinson, and C. Ewen

2001   An Analysis of Human Skeletal Materials from the Snow Beach Site (8WA52). *Southeastern Archaeology* 20:18–30.

Manzi, G., A. Sperduti, and P. Passarello

1991   Behavior-Induced Auditory Exostoses in Imperial Roman Society: Evidence from Coeval Urban and Rural Communities near Rome. *American Journal of Physical Anthropology* 85:253–260.

Maples, W. R.

1987   Analysis of Skeletal Remains Recovered at the Gauthier Site, Brevard County, Florida. Miscellaneous Project Report Series 31. Gainesville: Florida State Museum of Natural History, Department of Anthropology.

Marquardt, W. H.

1984   The Josslyn Island Mound and Its Role in the Investigation of Southwest Florida's Past. Miscellaneous Project Report Series 22. Gainesville: Florida State Museum of Natural History, Department of Anthropology.

1986   The Development of Cultural Complexity in Southwest Florida: Elements of a Critique. *Southeastern Archaeology* 5:63–70.

1987   The Calusa Social Formation in Protohistoric South Florida. In *Power Relations and Social Formation,* edited by T. Patterson and C. Gailey, 98–116. Washington, D.C.: American Anthropological Association.

1991   Introduction. In *Missions to the Calusa,* edited and translated by J. H. Hann, xv–xix. Gainesville: University of Florida Press.

1992a   The Calusa Domain: An Introduction. In *Culture and Environment in the Domain of the Calusa,* edited by W. H. Marquardt, 1–7. Gainesville: University of Florida, Institute of Archaeology and Paleoenvironmental Studies Monograph 1.

1992b   Shell Artifacts from the Caloosahatchee Area. In *Culture and Environment in the Domain of the Calusa,* edited by W. H. Marquardt, 191–246. Gainesville: University of Florida, Institute of Archaeology and Paleoenvironmental Studies Monograph 1.

2001   The Emergence and Demise of the Calusa. In *Societies in Eclipse: Archaeology of the Eastern Woodlands Indians,* A.D. *1400–1700,* edited by D. S. Brose, C. W. Cowan, and R. C. Mainfort, 157–171. Washington: Smithsonian Institution Press.

Marquardt, W. H. (editor)

1992   *Culture and Environment in the Domain of the Calusa.* Gainesville: University of Florida, Institute of Archaeology and Paleoenvironmental Studies, Monograph 1.

1999   *The Archaeology of Useppa Island.* Gainesville: University of Florida, Institute of Archaeology and Paleoenvironmental Studies, Monograph 3.

Martin, D. L.

1997   Violence Against Women in the La Plata River Valley (A.D. 1000–1300). In *Troubled Times: Violence and Warfare in the Past,* edited by D. L. Martin and D. W. Frayer, 45–76. Amsterdam: Gordon and Breach.

Martin, D. L., and D. W. Frayer (editors)

1997   *Troubled Times: Violence and Warfare in the Past.* Amsterdam: Gordon and Breach.

McMichael, A. E.

1982   A Cultural Resource Assessment of Horr's Island, Collier County, Florida. Master's thesis, University of Florida.

Meindl, R. S., and C. O. Lovejoy

1985   Ectocranial Suture Closure: A Revised Method for the Determination of Skeletal Age at Death Based on the Lateral-Anterior Sutures. *American Journal of Physical Anthropology* 68:57–66.

Meindl, R. S., and K. F. Russell

1998   Recent Advances in Method and Theory in Paleodemography. *Annual Reviews in Anthropology* 27:275–399.

Mensforth, R. P., C. O. Lovejoy, J. W. Lallo, and G. J. Armelagos

1978   The Role of Constitutional Factors, Diet, and Infectious Disease in the

Etiology of Porotic Hyperostosis and Periosteal Reactions in Children. *Medical Anthropology* 2:1–59.

Merbs, C. F.
1989   Trauma. In *Reconstruction of Life from the Skeleton,* edited by M. Y. İşcan and K.A.R. Kennedy, 161–189. New York: A. R. Liss.

Miccozi, M. S.
1991   *Postmortem Change in Human and Animal Remains: A Systemic Approach.* Springfield, Ill.: Charles C. Thomas.

Milanich, J. T.
1972   Excavations at the Yellow Bluffs–Whitaker Mound, Sarasota, Florida. *Florida Anthropologist* 25:21–41.
1985   Field Schools, Fort Center, and the Origins of the Armadillo Roast: Reminiscences of Charles Fairbanks During the Florida Years, 1964–1975. In *Indians, Colonists, and Slaves: Essays in Honor of Charles H. Fairbanks,* edited by K. W. Johnson, J. M. Leader, and R. C. Wilson, 11–33. *Florida Journal of Anthropology* Special Publication 4.
1990   Central Peninsular Gulf Coast. In *Florida's Historic Preservation Plan (Archaeological Contexts),* edited by C. Payne and J. T. Milanich. Tallahassee: Florida Division of Historical Resources.
1994   *Archaeology of Precolumbian Florida.* Gainesville: University Press of Florida.
1995   *Florida Indians and the Invasion from Europe.* Gainesville: University Press of Florida.
1998   *Florida's Indians from Ancient Times to the Present.* Gainesville: University Press of Florida.

Milanich, J. T., and C. Hudson
1993   *Hernando de Soto and the Indians of Florida.* Gainesville: University Press of Florida.

Milanich, J. T., J. Chapman, A. S. Cordell, S. Hale, and R. A. Marrinan
1984a   Prehistoric Development of Calusa Society in Southwest Florida: Excavations on Useppa Island. In *Perspectives on Gulf Coast Prehistory,* edited by D. D. Davis, 258–314. Gainesville: University of Florida Press.

Milanich, J. T., A. S. Cordell, V. J. Knight, Jr., T. A. Kohler, and B. J. Sigler-Lavelle
1984b   *McKeithen Weeden Island: The Culture of Northern Florida, A.D. 200–900.* Orlando: Academic Press.

Miller, J. J.
1974   An Archaeological Survey of the Palmer Oaks Tract in Sarasota County. Tallahassee: Bureau of Historic Sites and Properties Miscellaneous Project Report Series 20.

Miller-Shaivitz, P.
1986   Physical and Health Characteristics of the Indians from the Fort Center Site. Master's thesis, Florida Atlantic University, Boca Raton.

Miller-Shaivitz, P., and M. Y. İşcan
1991   The Prehistoric People of Fort Center: Physical and Health Characteris-

tics. In *What Mean These Bones? Studies in Southeastern Bioarchaeology*, edited by M. L. Powell, P. S. Bridges, and A.M.W. Mires, 131–147. Tuscaloosa: University of Alabama Press.

Milner, G. R.
1984 Dental Caries in the Permanent Dentition of a Mississippian Population from the American Midwest. *Collegium Antropologicum* 8: 77–91.
1990 The Late Prehistoric Cahokia Cultural System of the Mississippi River Valley: Foundations, Florescence, Fragmentation. *Journal of World Prehistory* 4:1–43.
1991 Health and Cultural Change in the Late Prehistoric American Bottom, Illinois. In *What Mean These Bones? Studies in Southeastern Bioarchaeology*, edited by M. L. Powell, P. S. Bridges, and A.M.W. Mires, 52–69. Tuscaloosa: University of Alabama Press.
1999 Warfare in Prehistoric and Early Historic North America. *Journal of Archaeological Research* 7:105–151.

Milner, G. R., and C. S. Larsen
1991 Teeth as Artifacts of Human Behavior: Intentional Mutilation and Accidental Modification. In *Advances in Dental Anthropology*, edited by M. A. Kelley and C. S. Larsen, 357–378. New York: Wiley-Liss.

Milner, G. R., and V. G. Smith
1989 Carnivore Alteration of Human Bone from a Late Prehistoric Site in Illinois. *American Journal of Physical Anthropology* 79:43–49.
1990 Oneota Human Skeletal Remains. In *Archaeological Investigations at the Morton Village and Norris Farms 35 Cemetery*, edited by S. K. Santure, 111–148. Illinois State Museum Reports of Investigation 45.

Milner, G. R., E. Anderson, and V. G. Smith
1991 Warfare in Late Prehistoric West-Central Illinois. *American Antiquity* 56: 581–603.

Milner, G. R., D. A. Humpf, and H. C. Harpending
1989 Pattern Matching of Age at Death Distributions in Paleodemographic Analysis. *American Journal of Physical Anthropology* 80:49–58.

Milner, G. R., J. W. Wood, and J. L. Boldsen
2000 Paleodemography. In *Biological Anthropology of the Human Skeleton*, edited by M. A. Katzenberg and S. R. Saunders, 467–498. New York: Wiley-Liss.

Mitchem, J. M.
1989 Redefining Safety Harbor: Late Prehistoric/Protohistoric Archaeology in West Peninsular Florida. Ph.D. diss., University of Florida.

Mitchem, J. M., M. T. Smith, A. C. Goodyear, and R. R. Allen
1985 Early Spanish Contact on the Florida Gulf Coast: The Weeki Wachee and Ruth Smith Mounds. In *Indians, Colonists, and Slaves: Essays in Honor of Charles H. Fairbanks*, edited by K. W. Johnson, J. M. Leader, and R. C. Wilson, 179–219. *Florida Journal of Anthropology* Special Publication 4.

Montague, C. L., and R. G. Wiegert

1990   Salt Marshes. In *Ecosystems of Florida,* edited by R. L. Myers and J. J. Ewel, 481–516. Orlando: University of Central Florida Press.

Moore, C. B.

1892   A Burial Mound of Florida. *American Naturalist* 26:129–143.

1894   Certain Sand Mounds of the St. John's River, Florida. *Journal of the Academy of Natural Sciences of Philadelphia* 10:4–103, 128–246.

1900   Certain Antiquities of the Florida West-Coast. *Journal of the Academy of Natural Sciences of Philadelphia* 11:351–394.

1902   Certain Aboriginal Remains of the Northwest Florida Coast, part 2. *Journal of the Academy of Natural Sciences of Philadelphia* 12:125–358.

1903   Certain Aboriginal Mounds of the Florida Central-West Coast. *Journal of the Academy of Natural Sciences of Philadelphia* 12:361–438.

1905   Miscellaneous Investigations in Florida. *Journal of the Academy of Natural Sciences of Philadelphia* 13:406–425.

1907   Moundville Revisited: Crystal River Revisited: Mounds of the Lower Chattahoochee and Lower Flint Rivers: Notes on the Ten Thousand Islands, Florida. *Journal of the Academy of Natural Sciences of Philadelphia* 13:334–405, 406–425.

1918   The Northwest Florida Coast Revisited. *Journal of the Academy of Natural Sciences of Philadelphia* 16:513–581.

1919   Notes on the Archaeology of Florida. *American Anthropologist* 21:400–402.

Moore, J. A., A. C. Swedlund, and G. J. Armelagos

1975   The Use of Life Tables in Paleodemography. In *Population Studies in Archaeology and Biological Anthropology, a Symposium,* edited by A. C. Swedlund, 57–70. Memoirs of the Society for American Archaeology 30.

Moore, J. F.

1985   Archaeobotanical Analyses at Five Sites in the Richard B. Russell Reservoir, Georgia and South Carolina. In *Prehistoric Human Ecology along the Upper Savannah River: Excavations at the Rucker's Bottom, Abbeville, and Bullard Site Groups,* assembled by D. G. Anderson and J. Schuldenrein, vol. 2, 673–694. Atlanta: Southeast Archeological Services Branch, National Park Service.

Moran, E.

2000   *Human Adaptability: An Introduction to Ecological Anthropology.* Boulder: Westview Press.

Myers, R. L., and J. J. Ewel (editors)

1990   *Ecosystems of Florida.* Orlando: University of Central Florida Press.

Nassaney, M. S., and K. Pyle

1999   The Adoption of the Bow and Arrow in Eastern North America: A View from Central Arkansas. *American Antiquity* 64:243–263.

Neill, W. T.
1958   A Stratified Early Site at Silver Springs, Florida. *Florida Anthropologist* 11:33–48.
Neitzel, R. S.
1965   *Archaeology of the Fatherland Site: the Grand Village of the Natchez.* Anthropological Paper 51. New York: American Museum of Natural History.
Newbrun, E.
1978   *Cariology.* Baltimore: Williams and Wilkins.
1982   Sugar and Dental Caries: A Reviw of Human Studies. *Science* 217:418–423.
Newsom, L. A.
1991   Horr's Island Archaeobotanical Research. In *Final Report on Horr's Island: The Archaeology of Archaic and Glades Settlement and Subsistence Patterns*, Part II, by M. Russo, A. S. Cordell, L. A. Newsom, and S. Scudder, 591–644. Report prepared for Key Marco Developments, Marco Island, Florida, by the Department of Anthropology, Florida Museum of Natural History, Gainesville.
1998   Archaeobotanical Research at Shell Ridge Midden, Palmer Site (8So2), Sarasota County, Florida. *Florida Anthropologist* 51:207–222.
Newsom, L. A., and I. R. Quitmyer
1992   Archaeobotanical and Faunal Remains. In *Excavations on the Franciscan Frontier: Archaeology at the Fig Springs Mission*, by B. R. Weisman, 206–233. Gainesville: University of Florida Press.
Norr, L.
1984   Prehistoric Subsistence and Health Status of Coastal Peoples from the Panamanian Isthmus of Lower Central America. In *Paleopathology at the Origins of Agriculture*, edited by M. N. Cohen and G. J. Armelagos, 463–490. Orlando: Academic Press.
1990   Nutritional Consequences of Prehistoric Subsistence Strategies in Lower Central America. Ph.D. diss., University of Illinois, Urbana-Champaign.
1995   Interpreting Dietary Maize from Bone Stable Isotopes in the American Tropics: The State of the Art. In *Archaeology in the Lowland American Tropics: Current Analytical Methods and Recent Applications*, edited by P. W. Stahl, 198–223. Cambridge: Cambridge University Press.
2002   Stable Isotope Analysis and Dietary Inference. In *Foraging, Farming, and Coastal Biocultural Adaptation in Late Prehistoric North Carolina*, by D. L. Hutchinson, 178–205. Gainesville: University Press of Florida.
Norr, L., D. L. Hutchinson, K. J. Walker, L. A. Newsom, and W. H. Marquardt
n.d.   Calusa Subsistence in Southwest Florida. Manuscript in possession of authors.
Odum, E. P.
1963   *Ecology.* New York: Holt, Rinehart, and Winston.

Odum, W. E., and C. C. McIvor
1990   Mangroves. In *Ecosystems of Florida,* edited by R. L. Myers and J. J. Ewel, 517–548. Orlando: University of Central Florida Press.

O'Leary, M. H.
1988   Carbon Isotopes in Photosynthesis. *BioScience* 38:328–336.

Ortner, D. J.
1998   Male-Female Immune Reactivity and Its Implications for Interpreting Evidence in Human Skeletal Pathology. In *Sex and Gender in Paleopathological Perspective,* edited by A. L. Grauer and P. Stuart-Macadam, 79–92. Cambridge: Cambridge University Press.

Ortner, D. J., and A. C. Aufderheide (editors)
1991   *Human Paleopathology: Current Syntheses and Future Options.* Washington, D.C.: Smithsonian Institution Press.

Ortner, D. J., and W. G. J. Putschar
1985   *Identification of Pathological Conditions in Human Skeletal Remains.* Washington, D.C.: Smithsonian Institution Press.

Otterbein, K.F.
1994   *Feuding and Warfare: Selected Works of Keith F. Otterbein.* Amsterdam: Gordon and Breach.

Peebles, C. S.
1987   The Rise and Fall of the Mississippian in Western Alabama: The Moundville and Summerville Phases, A.D. 1000–1600. *Mississippi Archaeology* 22:1–31.

Pfeiffer, S.
1983   Demographic Parameters of the Uxbridge Ossuary Population. *Ontario Archaeology* 40:9–14.
1986   Morbidity and Mortality in the Uxbridge Ossuary. *Canadian Review of Physical Anthropology* 5:23–31.

Pfeiffer, S., and S. I. Fairgrieve
1994   Evidence from Ossuaries: The Effect of Contact on the Health of Iroquoians. In *In the Wake of Contact: Biological Responses to Conquest,* edited by C. S. Larsen and G. R. Milner, 47–61. New York: Wiley-Liss.

Phenice, T. W.
1969   A Newly Developed Method of Sexing the Os Pubis. *American Journal of Physical Anthropology* 30:297–302.

Pober, D.
1996   Demographics, Health, and Sociopolitical Organization of Ross Hammock, Florida (8VO131a). Master's thesis, University of Florida.

Powell, M. L.
1983   Biocultural Analysis of Human Skeletal Remains from the Lubbub Creek Archaeological Locality. In *Prehistoric Agricultural Communities in West Central Alabama,* vol. 2, edited by C. S. Peebles. National Technical Information Service AD-A155048/GAR, Washington, D.C.

1985   The Analysis of Dental Wear and Caries for Dietary Reconstruction. In *The Analysis of Prehistoric Diets,* edited by R. I. Gilbert and J. H. Melke, 307–338. Orlando: Academic Press.

1988a *Status and Health in Prehistory: A Case Study of the Moundville Chiefdom.* Washington, D.C.: Smithsonian Institution Press.

1988b *The People of Nodena, a Biocultural Analysis of a Late Mississippian Community in Northeast Arkansas.* Part 2 of *Nodena, an Account of 75 Years of Archaeological Investigation in Southeast Mississippi County, Arkansas.* Fayetteville: Arkansas Archeological Survey Research Series 28.

1990   On the Eve of Conquest: Life and Death at Irene Mound, Georgia. In *The Archaeology of Mission Santa Catalina de Guale: 2. Biocultural Interpretations of a Population in Transition,* edited by C. S. Larsen, 26–35. Anthropological Paper 68. New York: American Museum of Natural History.

1991a Ranked Status and Health in the Mississippian Community at Moundville. In *What Mean These Bones? Studies in Southeastern Bioarchaeology,* edited by M. L. Powell, P. S. Bridges, and A.M.W. Mires, 22–51. Tuscaloosa: University of Alabama Press.

1991b Endemic Treponematosis and Tuberculosis in the Prehistoric Southeastern United States: Biological Costs of Chronic Endemic Disease. In *Human Paleopathology: Current Syntheses and Future Options,* edited by D. J. Ortner and A. C. Aufderheide, 173–180. Washington, D.C.: Smithsonian Institution Press.

Powell, M. L., and J. D. Rogers
1980   *Bioarchaeology of the McCutchan-McLaughlin site, Biophysical and Mortuary Variability in Eastern Oklahoma.* Oklahoma Archaeological Survey Studies in Oklahoma's Past no. 5, Norman.

Prentice, G.
1986   An Analysis of the Symbolism Expressed by the Birger Figurine. *American Antiquity* 51:239–266.

Purdy, B. A.
1996   *Indian Art of Ancient Florida.* Gainesville: University Press of Florida.

Quitmyer, I. R.
1998   Zoological Indicators of Habitat Exploitation and Seasonality from the Shell Ridge Midden, Palmer Site (8So2), Osprey, Florida. *Florida Anthropologist* 51:193–205.

Reeves, M.
2000   Dental Health at Early Historic Fusihatchee Town: Biocultural Implications of Contact in Alabama. In *Bioarchaeological Studies of Life in the Age of Agriculture: A View from the Southeast,* edited by P. M. Lambert, 78–95. Tuscaloosa: University of Alabama Press.

Reinhard, K. J.
1992   Pattern of Diet, Parasitism, and Anemia in Prehistoric Western North

America. In *Diet, Demography, and Disease: Changing Perspectives on Anemia,* edited by P. Stuart-Macadam and S. Kent, 219–258. New York: Aldine de Gruyter.

1996 Parasite Ecology of Two Anasazi Villages. In *Case Studies in Environmental Archaeology,* edited by E. J. Reitz, L. A. Newsom, and S. J. Scudder, 175–189. New York: Plenum Press.

Reitz, E. J.
1982 Availability and Use of Fish along Coastal Georgia and Florida. *Southeastern Archaeology* 1:65–88.

1988 Evidence for Coastal Adaptations in Georgia and South Carolina. *Archaeology of Eastern North America* 16:137–158.

Reitz, E. J., and E. S. Wing
1999 *Zooarchaeology.* Cambridge: Cambridge University Press.

Robb, J.
1997 Violence and Gender in Early Italy. In *Troubled Times: Violence and Warfare in the Past,* edited by D.L. Martin and D.W. Frayer, 111–144. Amsterdam: Gordon and Breach.

Roberts, C. A., and K. Manchester
1995 *The Archaeology of Disease,* 2d ed. Ithaca: Cornell University Press.

Roberts, C. A., M. E. Lewis, and P. Boocock
1998 Infectious Disease, Sex, and Gender: The Complexity of It All. In *Sex and Gender in Paleopathological Perspective,* edited by A. L. Grauer and P. Stuart-Macadam, 93–113. Cambridge: Cambridge University Press.

Robertson, J. A.
1993 The Account by a Gentleman from Elvas. In *The De Soto Chronicles: The Expedition of Hernando de Soto to North America in 1539–1543,* vol. 2, edited by L. A. Clayton, V. J. Knight, Jr., and E. C. Moore, 19–220. Tuscaloosa: University of Alabama Press.

Rogers, J., and T. Waldron
1995 *A Field Guide to Joint Disease in Archaeology.* Chichester: John Wiley and Sons.

Rose, J. C., M. K. Marks, and L. L. Tieszen
1991 Bioarchaeology and Subsistence in the Central and Lower Portions of the Mississippi Valley. In *What Mean These Bones? Studies in Southeastern Bioarchaeology,* edited by M. L. Powell, P. S. Bridges, and A.M.W. Mires, 7–21. Tuscaloosa: University of Alabama Press.

Russo, M.
1993 The Archaic Period. In *Florida's Cultural Heritage: A View of the Past,* edited by C. Payne and J. T. Milanich. Tallahassee: Florida Division of Historical Resources (www.dos.state.fl.us/dhr/bar/hist_contexts).

Russo, M., and I. R. Quitmyer
1996 Sedentism in Coastal Populations of South Florida. In *Case Studies in Environmental Archaeology,* edited by E. J. Reitz, L. A. Newsom, and S. J. Scudder, 215–232. New York: Plenum Press.

Russo, M., A. S. Cordell, L. A. Newsom, and S. Scudder
1991   *Final Report on Horr's Island: The Archaeology of Archaic and Glades Settlement and Subsistence Patterns.* Report prepared for Key Marco Developments, Marco Island, Florida, by the Department of Anthropology, Florida Museum of Natural History, Gainesville.

Saunders, L. P.
1972   Osteology of the Republic Groves Site. Master's thesis, Florida Atlantic University, Boca Raton.

Saunders, S. R.
1991   Subadult Skeletons and Growth Related Studies. In *Skeletal Biology of Past Peoples: Research Methods,* edited by S. R. Saunders and M. A. Katzenberg, 1–20. New York: Wiley-Liss.

2000   Subadult Skeletons and Growth-Related Studies. In *Biological Anthropology of the Human Skeleton,* edited by M. A. Katzenberg and S. R. Saunders, 135–161. New York: Wiley-Liss.

Saunders, S. R., D. A. Herring, and G. Boyce
1995   Can Skeletal Samples Adequately Represent the Living Populations They Come From? The St. Thomas' Cemetery Site, Belleville, Ontario. In *Bodies of Evidence: Reconstructing History Through Skeletal Analysis,* edited by A. L. Grauer, 69–80. New York: Wiley-Liss.

Scarry, C. M.
1993a   Agricultural Risk and the Development of the Moundville Chiefdom. In *Foraging and Farming in the Eastern Woodlands,* edited by C. M. Scarry, 157–181. Gainesville: University of Florida Press.

1993b   Variability in Mississippian Crop Production Strategies. In *Foraging and Farming in the Eastern Woodlands,* edited by C. M. Scarry, 78–90. Gainesville: University of Florida Press.

1993c   Plant Production and Procurement in Apalachee Province. In *The Spanish Missions of La Florida,* edited by B. G. McEwan, 357–375. Gainesville: University of Florida Press.

1999   Precolumbian Use of Plants on Useppa Island. In *The Archaeology of Useppa Island,* edited by William H. Marquardt, 129–137. Gainesville: University of Florida, Institute of Archaeology and Paleoenvironmental Studies, Monograph 3.

Scarry, C. M., and L. A. Newsom
1992   Archaeobotanical Research in the Calusa Heartland. In *Culture and Environment in the Domain of the Calusa,* edited by W. H. Marquardt, 375–401. Gainesville: University of Florida, Institute of Archaeology and Paleoenvironmental Studies, Monograph 1.

Schoeninger, M. J., and M. J. DeNiro
1984   Nitrogen and Carbon Isotopic Composition of Bone Collagen from Marine and Terrestrial Animals. *Geochimica et Cosmochimica Acta* 48:625–639.

Schoeninger, M. J., and K. Moore
1992   Bone Stable Isotope Studies in Archaeology. *Journal of World Prehistory* 6:247–296.

Schoeninger, M. J., M. J. DeNiro, and H. Tauber
1983   Stable Nitrogen Isotope Ratios of Bone Collagen Reflect Marine and Terrestrial Components of Prehistoric Human Diet. *Science* 220:1381–1383.

Schoeninger, M. J., N. J. van der Merwe, K. Moore, J. Lee-Thorpe, and C. S. Larsen
1990   Decrease in Diet Quality between the Prehistoric and Contact Periods. In *The Archaeology of Mission Santa Catalina de Guale: 2. Biocultural Interpretations of a Population in Transition,* edited by C. S. Larsen, 78–94. Anthropological Paper 68. New York: American Museum of Natural History.

Schultz, M., C. S. Larsen, and K. Kreutz
2001   Disease in Spanish Florida: Microscopy of Porotic Hyperostosis and Cribra Orbitalia. In *Bioarchaeology of Spanish Florida: The Impact of Colonialism,* edited by C. S. Larsen, 207–225. Gainesville: University Press of Florida.

Sears, E. O.
1982   Pollen Analysis. In *Fort Center: An Archaeological Site in the Lake Okeechobee Basin,* by W. H. Sears, 118–129. Gainesville: University Presses of Florida.

Sears, W. H.
1959   *Two Weeden Island Period Burial Mounds, Florida.* Gainesville: Contributions of the Florida State Museum, Social Sciences 5.

1960   *The Bayshore Homes Site, St. Petersburg, Florida.* Gainesville: Contributions of the Florida State Museum, Social Sciences 6.

1967   The Tierra Verde Burial Mound. *Florida Anthropologist* 20:25–73.

1971   The Weeden Island Site, St. Petersburg, Florida. *Florida Anthropologist* 24:51–60.

1982   *Fort Center: An Archaeological Site in the Lake Okeechobee Basin.* Gainesville: University Presses of Florida.

Shearer, G., and D. H. Kohl
1994   Information Derived from Variation in the Natural Abundance of 15N in Complex Biological Systems. In *Isotopes in Organic Chemistry: Heavy Atom Isotope Effects,* edited by E. Buncel and W.H.J. Saunders, 191–237. Amsterdam: Elsevier Science Press.

Simpson, J. C.
1939   Notes on Two Interesting Mounds Excavated in Hillsborough County. In *Third Biennial Report to the State Board of Conservation, Biennium Ending Dec. 31, 1938,* 56–62. Tallahassee: Florida State Board of Conservation.

Skinner, M., and A. H. Goodman
1992   Anthropological Uses of Developmental Defects of Enamel. In *Skeletal Biology of Past Peoples: Research Methods,* edited by S. R. Saunders and M. A. Katzenberg, 153–174. New York: Wiley-Liss.

Smith, B. D.
1986   The Archaeology of the Southeastern United States: From Dalton to de Soto, 10,500–500 B.P. In *Advances in World Archaeology,* vol. 5, edited by F. Wendorf and A. E. Close, 1–91. New York: Academic Press.
1992   Prehistoric Plant Husbandry in Eastern North America. In *The Origins of Agriculture: An International Perspective,* edited by C. W. Cowan and P. J. Watson, 101–119. Washington, D.C.: Smithsonian Institution Press.

Smith, B. (translator)
1966   *Relation that Alvar Nuñez Cabeza de Vaca Gave of What Befel the Armament in Indias.* Reprint. Ann Arbor: University Microfilms March of America Series 9.

Smith, B. N., and S. Epstein
1971   Two Categories of $^{13}C/^{12}C$ Ratios in Plants. *Botanical Gazette* 137: 99–104.

Smith, M. O.
1996   "Parry" Fractures and Female-Directed Interpersonal Violence: Implications from the Late Archaic Period of West Tennessee. *International Journal of Osteoarchaeology* 6:84–91.
1997   Osteological Indicators of Warfare in the Archaic Period of the Western Tennessee Valley. In *Troubled Times: Violence and Warfare in the Past,* edited by D. L. Martin and D. W. Frayer, 241–266. Amsterdam: Gordon and Breach.
2001   Temporal Change in the Patterns and Frequency of Warfare in the Chickamauga Reservoir. Paper presented at the annual meeting of the Southeastern Archaeological Conference, Chattanooga.

Smith, S. D.
1971   Excavations at the Hope Mound with an Addendum to the Safford Mound. *Florida Anthropologist* 24:107–134.

Snow, C. E.
1962   *Indian Burials from St. Petersburg, Florida.* Gainesville: Contributions of the Florida State Museum 8.

Solís de Merás, G.
1964   *Pedro Menéndez de Avilés, Adelantado, Governor, and Captain-General of Florida.* Translated by Jeannette Thurber Connor. Gainesville: University of Florida Press.

St. Hoyme, L. E., and M. Y. İşcan
1989   Determination of Sex and Race: Accuracy and Assumptions. In *Reconstruction of Life from the Skeleton,* edited by M. Y. İşcan and K.A.R. Kennedy, 53–94. New York: A. R. Liss.

Standen, V., M. Allison, and B. Arriaza
1985   Osteoma del conducto auditivo externo: Hipótesis en torno a una Posible
        Patología Laboral Prehispánica. *Revista Chungará* 15:197–209.
Standen, V., V. T. Arriaza, and C. M. Santoro
1997   External Auditory Exostosis in Prehistoric Chilean Populations: A Test of
        the Cold Water Hypothesis. *American Journal of Physical Anthropology*
        103:119–130.
Steinbock, R. T.
1976   *Paleopathological Diagnosis and Interpretation.* Springfield, Ill.: C. C.
        Thomas.
Steponaitis, V. P.
1986   Prehistoric Archaeology in the Southeastern United States, 1970–1985.
        Annual Reviews of Anthropology 15:363–404.
Stewart, T. D.
1979   *Essentials of Forensic Anthropology.* Springfield, Ill.: C. C. Thomas.
Stirling, M. W.
1930   Prehistoric Mounds in the Vicinity of Tampa Bay, Florida. *Explorations
        and Fieldwork of the Smithsonian Institution in 1929,* 183–186.
1931   Mounds of the Vanished Calusa Indians of Florida. *Explorations and
        Fieldwork of the Smithsonian Institution in 1930,* 167–172.
1935   Smithsonian Archeological Projects Conducted under the Federal Emer-
        gency Relief Administration, 1933–1934. *Annual Report of the Smith-
        sonian Institution 1934,* 371–400.
Stojanowksi, C. M.
1997   Descriptive Analysis of the Prehistoric Bird Island (8DI52) Skeletal Popu-
        lation. Master's thesis, Florida State University.
Stone, T. T., D. N. Dickel, and G. H. Doran
1990   The Preservation and Conservation of Waterlogged Bone from the Wind-
        over Site, Florida: A Comparison of Methods. *Journal of Field Archaeol-
        ogy* 17:177–186.
Storey, R.
1998   The Mothers and Daughters of a Patrilineal Civilization: The Health of
        Females among the Late Classic Maya of Copan, Honduras. In *Sex and
        Gender in Paleopathological Perspective,* edited by A. L. Grauer and P.
        Stuart-Macadam, 133–148. Cambridge: Cambridge University Press.
Storey, R., and K. Hirth
1997   Archaeological and Paleodemographic Analyses of the El Cajón Skeletal
        Population. In *Integrating Archaeological Demography: Multidisciplin-
        ary Approaches to Prehistoric Population,* edited by R. R. Paine, 131–
        149. Occasional Paper no. 24. Carbondale: Center for Archaeological
        Investigations, Southern Illinois University.
Stuart-Macadam, P.
1985   Porotic Hyperostosis: Representative of a Childhood Condition. *Ameri-
        can Journal of Physical Anthropology* 66:391–398.

1987a A Radiographic Study of Porotic Hyperostosis. *American Journal of Physical Anthropology* 74:511–520.

1987b Porotic Hyperostosis: New Evidence to Support the Anemia Theory. *American Journal of Physical Anthropology* 74:521– 526.

Stuiver, M., and P. J. Reimer

1993 Calib 4.3. Extended 14C Data Base and Revised CALIB Radiocarbon Calibration Program. *Radiocarbon* 35:215–230.

Suchey, J. M., S. T. Brooks, and D. Katz

1988 *Instructional Materials Accompanying Female Pubic Symphyseal Models of the Suchey-Brooks System.* Bellvue, Colo.: Distributed by France Casting.

Suckling, G., D. C. Elliot, and D. C. Thurley

1983 The Production of Developmental Defects of the Enamel in the Incisor Teeth of Penned Sheep Resulting from Induced Parasitism. *Archives of Oral Biology* 28:393–399.

1986 The Macroscopic Appearance and Associated Histological Changes in the Enamel Organ of Hypoplastic Lesions of Sheep Incisor Teeth Resulting from Induced Parasitism. *Archives of Oral Biology* 31:427–439.

Sullivan, L. P. (editor)

1995 *The Prehistory of the Chickamauga Basin in Tennessee.* Knoxville: University of Tennessee Press.

Swedlund, A. C. (editor)

1975 *Population Studies in Archaeology and Biological Anthropology: A Symposium.* Society for American Archaeology Memoir no. 30.

Teaford, M. F.

1986 Dental Microwear and Diet in Two Species of Colobus. In *Primate Ecology and Conservation,* edited by J. Else and P. Lee, 63–66. Cambridge: Cambridge University Press.

1988 Scanning Electron Microscope Diagnosis of Wear Patterns Versus Artifacts on Fossil Teeth. *Scanning Microscopy* 2:1167–1175.

1991 Dental Microwear: What Can It Tell Us about Diet and Dental Function? In *Advances in Dental Anthropology,* edited by M. A. Kelley and C. S. Larsen, 341–356. New York: Wiley-Liss.

1994 Dental Microwear and Dental Function. *Evolutionary Anthropology* 3: 17–30.

2002 Dental Microwear. In *Foraging, Farming, and Coastal Biocultural Adaptation in Late Prehistoric North Carolina,* edited by D. L. Hutchinson, 169–177. Gainesville: University Press of Florida.

Teaford, M. F., and K. E. Glander

1996 Dental Microwear and Diet in a Wild Population of Mantled Howlers *Alouatta palliata.* In *Adaptive Radiations of Neotropical Primates,* edited by M. Norconk, A. Rosenberger, and P. Garber, 433–449. New York: Plenum Press.

Teaford, M. F., and J. D. Lytle
1996   Diet Induced Changes in Rates of Human Tooth Microwear: A Case Study Involving Stone-Ground Maize. *American Journal of Physical Anthropology* 100:143–147.

Teaford, M. F., and J. G. Robinson
1989   Seasonal or Ecological Differences in Diet and Molar Microwear in *Cebus nigrivittatus*. *American Journal of Physical Anthropology* 80:391–401.

Teaford, M. F., and A. Walker
1984   Quantitative Differences in Dental Microwear Between Primate Species with Different Diets and a Comment on the Presumed Diet of Sivipithecus. *American Journal of Physical Anthropology* 64:191–200.

Teaford, M. F., C. S. Larsen, R. F. Pastor, and V. E. Noble
2001   Pits and Scratches: Microscopic Evidence of Tooth Use and Masticatory Behavior in La Florida. In *Bioarchaeology of Spanish Florida: The Impact of Colonialism*, edited by C. S. Larsen, 82–112. Gainesville: University Press of Florida.

Tieszen, L. L.
1991   Natural Variations in the Carbon Isotope Values of Plants: Implications for Archaeology,Ecology, and Paleoecology. *Journal of Archaeological Science* 18:227–248.

Torrence, C. McP.
1999   The Archaic Period on Useppa Island: Excavations on Calusa Ridge. In *The Archaeology of Useppa Island*, edited by W. H. Marquardt, 23–76. Gainesville: University of Florida, Institute of Archaeology and Paleoenvironmental Studies, Monograph 3.

Tucker, B. K., D. L. Hutchinson, M.F.G. Gilliland, H. J. Daniel, C. M. Thomas, and L. D. Wolfe
2001   Microscopic Observations of Hacking Trauma. *Journal of Forensic Sciences* 46:234–240.

Turner, C. G., and J. D. Cadien
1969   Dental Chipping in Aleuts, Eskimos, and Indians. *American Journal of Physical Anthropology* 31:303–310.

Tuross, N., M. L. Fogel, L. Newsom, and G. H. Doran
1994   Subsistence in the Florida Archaic: The Stable Isotope and Archaeobotanical Evidence from the Windover Site. *American Antiquity* 59:288–303.

Ubelaker, D. H.
1989   *Human Skeletal Remains,* 2d ed. Washington, D.C.: Taraxacum.
1992   Porotic Hyperostosis in Ecuador. In *Diet, Demography, and Disease: Changing Perspectives on Anemia,* edited by P. Stuart-Macadam and S. Kent, 201–217. Amsterdam: Aldine de Gruyter.

Ubelaker, D. H., T. W. Phenice, and W. M. Bass
1970   Artificial Interproximal Grooving of the Teeth in American Indians. *American Journal of Physical Anthropology* 30:145–150.

van der Merwe, N. J., and J. C. Vogel

1978 ^{13}C Content of Human Collagen as a Measure of Prehistoric Diet in Woodland North America. *Nature* 276:815–816.

Van Gilse, P.

1938   Des observations ultérieures sur las genese des exostoses du conduit externe par l'irrigation d'eau froide. *Acta Otolaryngology* 26:343–352.

Velasco-Vazquez, J., A. Betancor-Rodriguez, M. Arnay-de-La-Rosa, and E. Gonzalez-Reimers

2000   Auricular Exostoses in the Prehistoric Population of Gran Canaria. *American Journal of Physical Anthropology* 112:49–56.

Velleman, P. F., and D. C. Hoaglin

1981   *Applications, Basics, and Computing of Exploratory Data Analysis.* Boston: Duxbury Press.

Vogel, J. C., and N. J. van der Merwe

1977   Isotopic Evidence for Early Maize Cultivation in New York State. *American Antiquity* 42:238–242.

Vradenburg, J. A., R. A. Benfer, and L. Sattenspiel

1997   Evaluating Archaeological Hypotheses of Population Growth on the Central Coast of Peru. In *Integrating Archaeological Demography: Multidisciplinary Approaches to Prehistoric Population,* edited by R. R. Paine, 150–174. Center for Archaeological Investigations Occasional Paper no. 24. Center for Archaeological Investigations, Southern Illinois University.

Wada, E.

1980   Nitrogen Isotope Fractionation and Its Significance in Biogeochemical Processes Occurring in Marine Environments. In *Isotope Marine Geochemistry,* edited by E. D. Goldberg, Y. Horibe, and K. Saruhaski, 375–398. Tokyo: Uchida Rokakuho.

Walker, K. J.

1989   Artifacts of a Fishy Nature: Charlotte Harbor's Prehistoric Estuarine Fishing Technology. Paper presented at the 46th Annual Southeastern Archaeological Conference, Tampa.

1990   The Caloosahatchee Region. In *Florida's Historic Preservation Plan (Archaeological Contexts),* edited by C. Payne and J. T. Milanich. Tallahassee: Florida Division of Historical Resources.

1992a   The Zooarchaeology of Charlotte Harbor's Prehistoric Maritime Adaptation: Spatial and Temporal Perspectives. In *Culture and Environment in the Domain of the Calusa,* edited by W. H. Marquardt, 265–366. Gainesville: University of Florida, Institute of Archaeology and Paleoenvironmental Studies, Monograph 1.

1992b   Bone Artifacts from Josslyn Island, Buck Key Shell Midden, and Cash Mound: A Preliminary Assessment for the Caloosahatchee Area. In *Cul-*

ture and Environment in the Domain of the Calusa, edited by W. H. Marquardt, 229–246. Gainesville: University of Florida, Institute of Archaeology and Paleoenvironmental Studies, Monograph 1.

Walker, K. J., and W. H. Marquardt

2003   *The Archaeology of Pineland: A Coastal Southwest Florida Village Complex, ca. A.D. 100–600.* Gainesville: University of Florida, Institute of Archaeology and Paleoenvironmental Studies, Monograph 4.

Walker, P. L.

1986   Porotic Hyperostosis in a Marine-Dependent California Indian Population. *American Journal of Physical Anthropology* 69:345–354.

1989   Cranial Injuries as Evidence of Violence in Prehistoric Southern California. *American Journal of Physical Anthropology* 80:313–323.

1997   Wife Beating, Boxing, and Broken Noses: Skeletal Evidence for the Cultural Patterning of Interpersonal Violence. In *Troubled Times: Violence and Warfare in the Past,* edited by D. L. Martin and D. W. Frayer, 145–180. Langhorne, Pa.: Gordon and Breach.

Walker, P. L., and P. M. Lambert

1989   Skeletal Evidence for Stress During a Period of Change in Prehistoric California. In *Advances in Paleopathology,* edited by L. Capasso. Journal of Paleopathology Monographic Publication 1:207–212.

Walker, P. L., D. C. Cook, and P. M. Lambert

1997   Skeletal Evidence for Child Abuse: A Physical Anthropological Perspective. *Journal of Forensic Sciences* 42:196–207.

Walker, S. T.

1880   Preliminary Explorations among the Indian Mounds in Southern Florida. *Annual Report of the Smithsonian Institution for 1879,* 392–413. Washington, D.C.: Smithsonian Institution.

Walsh-Haney, H.

1999   Skeletal Evidence of Health, Disease, Subsistence, and Settlement at Two Archaic Florida Sites. Master's thesis, University of Florida.

Warren, L., F. Bushnell, and G. Spence

1965   Six Contributions to the Hand Motif from the Safety Harbor Burial Mound on Cabbage Key, Pinellas County, Florida. *Florida Anthropologist* 18:235–238.

Watson, P. J.

1989   Early Plant Cultivation in the Eastern Woodlands of North America. In *Foraging and Farming: The Evolution of Plant Exploitation,* edited by D. R. Harris and G. C. Hillman, 555–571. London: Unwin Hyman.

Weaver, D. S.

1998   Osteoporosis in the Bioarchaeology of Women. In *Sex and Gender in Paleopathological Perspective,* edited by A. L. Grauer and P. Stuart-Macadam, 27–44. Cambridge: Cambridge University Press.

Weinberg, E.
1992   Iron Withholding in Prevention of Disease. In *Diet, Demography, and Disease: Changing Perspectives on Anemia,* edited by P. Stuart-Macadam and S. Kent, 105–150. Amsterdam: Aldine de Gruyter.

Weisman, B. R.
1986   The Cove of the Withlacoochee: A First Look at the Archaeology of an Interior Florida Wetland. *Florida Anthropologist* 39:4–23.
1989   *Like Beads on a String: A Culture History of the Seminole Indians in North Peninsular Florida.* Tuscaloosa: University of Alabama Press.
1992   *Excavations on the Franciscan Frontier: Archaeology at the Fig Springs Mission.* Gainesville: University of Florida Press.
1995   *Crystal River: A Ceremonial Mound Center on the Florida Gulf Coast.* Tallahassee: Florida Archaeology 8.

Weiss, K. M.
1973   *Demographic Models for Anthropology.* Society for American Archaeology Memoirs 27.

Welch, P.
1990   Mississippian Emergence in West-Central Alabama. In *The Mississippian Emergence,* edited by B. D. Smith, 197–225. Washington, D.C.: Smithsonian Institution Press.

Wharton, B., G. Ballo, and M. Hope
1981   The Republic Groves Site, Hardee County, Florida. *Florida Anthropologist* 34:59–80.

Wheeler, R. J.
2000   *Treasure of the Calusa: The Johnson/Willcox Collection from Mound Key, Florida.* Monographs in Florida Archaeology 1. Tallahassee: Rose Printing.

White, G. E.
1975   *Dental Caries: A Multifactorial Disease.* Springfield, Ill.: C. C. Thomas.

Widmer, R. J.
1988   *The Evolution of the Calusa: A Nonagricultural Chiefdom on the Southwest Florida Coast.* Tuscaloosa: University of Alabama Press.

Wilkinson, R. G.
1997   Violence Against Women: Raiding and Abduction in Prehistoric Michigan. In *Troubled Times: Violence and Warfare in the Past,* edited by D. L. Martin and D. W. Frayer, 21–44. Amsterdam: Gordon and Breach.

Willey, G. R.
1948   Culture Sequence in the Manatee Region of West Florida. *American Antiquity* 13:209–218.
1949   *Archeology of the Florida Gulf Coast.* Washington: Smithsonian Miscellaneous Collections 113.

Williamson, M. A.
1998   Regional Variation in Health and Lifeways among Late Prehistoric Georgia Agriculturalists. Ph.D. diss., Purdue University, West Lafayette, Ind.

Wilson, C. J.

1982   *The Indian Presence: Archeology of Sanibel, Captiva, and Adjacent Islands in Pine Island Sound.* Sanibel, Fla.: Sanibel-Captiva Conservation Foundation.

Woodward, M., and A.R.P. Walker

1994   Sugar Consumption and Dental Caries: Evidence from 90 Countries. *British Dental Journal* 176:297–302.

Worth, J. E.

1993   Account of the Northern Conquest and Discovery of Hernando De Soto by Rodrigo Rangel. In *The De Soto Chronicles: The Expedition of Hernando de Soto to North America in 1539–1543,* vol. 1, edited by L. A. Clayton, V. J. Knight, Jr., and E. C. Moore, 247–306. Tuscaloosa: University of Alabama Press.

Wymer, D. A.

1987a Paleoethnobotanical Record of the Lower Tennessee–Cumberland Region. *Southeastern Archaeology* 6:124–129.

1987b The Middle Woodland–Late Woodland Interface in Central Ohio: Subsistence Continuity Amid Cultural Change. In *Emergent Horticultural Economies of the Eastern Woodlands,* edited by W. F. Keegan, 201–216. Occasional Paper no. 7. Carbondale: Center for Archaeological Investigations, Southern Illinois University.

Yarnell, R. A., and M. J. Black

1985   Temporal Trends Indicated by a Survey of Archaic and Woodland Plant Food Remains from Southeastern North America. *Southeastern Archaeology* 4:93–106.

Zimmerman, L. J., T. Emerson, P. Willey, M. Swegle, J. B. Gregg, P. Gregg, E. White, C. Smith, T. Haberman, and M. P. Bumstead

1981   *The Crow Creek Site (39BR11) Massacre: A Preliminary Report.* Omaha: U.S. Army Corps of Engineers.

Zimmerman, M. R., and M. A. Kelley

1982   *Atlas of Paleopathology.* New York: Praeger.

Zubillaga, F. (editor)

1946   Monumenta Antiquae Floridae (1566–1572). *Monumenta Missionum Societatis Iesu* 3. Rome.

Index

References in *italics* refer to figures and tables.

Burial Mound (Palmer site): description of, 43, 51–52, 53; excavation of, 46, 47, 48
Burial mounds in central Gulf coast region, 36, 37, 37–39, 40
Button osteomas, 79

Cabeza de Vaca, 29, 34
Caloosahatchee region, 22–29, 23
Calusa: in Caloosahatchee region, 22–24; social organization of, xvii, 6, 28; Tocobaga and, 41, 157; wealth items and, 158
Calusa Ridge, 28–29
Canton Street, 21
Captiva Mound, 28–29
Carbon isotopic variation, 88
Carious lesions: in comparison populations, 100–104, 101, 102, 103, 135, 136, 142–143; dietary focus and, 134–135, 135; etiology of, 104; example of, 63; in Gulf coast populations, 129, 130, 148; maize consumption and, 103–104; Palmer site and, 62–63, 64; sex comparisons of, 152
Casey Key, 16
Cash Mound, 24–25
Cedar Key, 29
Ceramics, 32
Change, evidence for, 156–158
Charlotte Harbor region: description of, 16; dietary focus of, 147; settlements in, 5. See also Calusa
Charnel houses, 2, 41
Civil Works Administration, 36
Coastal region, definition of, 92
Cockrell, W. A., 93, 95
Comparative populations, overview of, 92–99, 93, 94
Conflict, 154–156. See also Violence; Warfare
Coonti, 27
Corn. See Maize
Cove of the Withlacoochee, 29, 30–31, 32. See also Tatham Mound
Cranial blunt trauma: coastal vs. noncoastal populations, 140; in comparison populations, 123, 124, 125,

144; at Palmer site, 82–83, 85, 86, 87; reduction in, 156
Crystal River: burial complex at, 32, 33, 96–97; description of, 29–30; mound at, 28
Culture, guiding principles of, 6

DeBry, engravings by, 155, 157
Dental caries. See Carious lesions
Dental chipping: in comparison populations, 107, 107–108, 143; in Gulf coast populations, 129, 148; at Palmer site, 63–64, 65; sex comparisons of, 152
Dental microwear: in comparison populations, 108; at Palmer site, 89–90; Palmer site compared to eastern U.S. sites, 185–190, 186, 188, 189, 190
De Soto expedition, 34
Destruction: of archaeological sites, 159; of bone, causes of, 54; lytic, of skeleton, 71
Dietary focus: adaptation and, 153–154; of Gulf coast populations, 10–11, 146–148; of interior compared to coastal populations, 11–12; population comparisons, 132–140, 133, 135, 137, 138, 139; sex and, 12; trends in, 129; Windover Pond, 21. See also Maritime resources
Dietary reconstruction: apatite carbonate analysis, 173, 178, 179, 180; apatite vs. collagen carbon values, 132; carious lesions, 62–63, 63, 64, 100–104, 101, 102, 103; comparative isotope signatures, 133; in comparison populations, 126–128, 127, 128, 181–182; dental chipping, 63–64, 65; of Gulf coast populations, 147, 148; interpretation of results, 178–182; methods and materials, 171; overview of, 10; populations north of Charlotte Harbor, xvii; sample quality, 172; stable isotope analysis, 87–89, 169–171; stable isotope results, 173, 173–178

Emergent Mississippian stage, 3, 42
Enamel hypoplasias: coastal vs. noncoastal populations, 137, 137–138, 149–150; in

Dale L. Hutchinson is an associate professor of anthropology at the University of North Carolina at Chapel Hill. He specializes in human osteology, forensic anthropology, and bioarchaeology, with an emphasis on paleopathology and dietary reconstruction in the southeastern and mid-Atlantic United States and in Bolivia. His publications include *Foraging, Farming, and Coastal Biocultural Adaptation in Late Prehistoric North Carolina*, also published by the University Press of Florida.

Ripley P. Bullen Series
Florida Museum of Natural History
Edited by Jerald T. Milanich

Tacachale: Essays on the Indians of Florida and Southeastern Georgia during the Historic Period, edited by Jerald T. Milanich and Samuel Proctor (1978); first paperback edition, 1994

Aboriginal Subsistence Technology on the Southeastern Coastal Plain during the Late Prehistoric Period, by Lewis H. Larson (1980)

Cemochechobee: Archaeology of a Mississippian Ceremonial Center on the Chattahoochee River, by Frank T. Schnell, Vernon J. Knight, Jr., and Gail S. Schnell (1981)

Fort Center: An Archaeological Site in the Lake Okeechobee Basin, by William H. Sears, with contributions by Elsie O'R. Sears and Karl T. Steinen (1982); first paperback edition, 1994

Perspectives on Gulf Coast Prehistory, edited by Dave D. Davis (1984)

Archaeology of Aboriginal Culture Change in the Interior Southeast: Depopulation during the Early Historic Period, by Marvin T. Smith (1987); first paperback edition, 1992

Apalachee: The Land between the Rivers, by John H. Hann (1988)

Key Marco's Buried Treasure: Archaeology and Adventure in the Nineteenth Century, by Marion Spjut Gilliland (1989)

First Encounters: Spanish Explorations in the Caribbean and the United States, 1492–1570, edited by Jerald T. Milanich and Susan Milbrath (1989)

Missions to the Calusa, edited and translated by John H. Hann, with an introduction by William H. Marquardt (1991)

Excavations on the Franciscan Frontier: Archaeology at the Fig Springs Mission, by Brent Richards Weisman (1992)

The People Who Discovered Columbus: The Prehistory of the Bahamas, by William F. Keegan (1992)

Hernando de Soto and the Indians of Florida, by Jerald T. Milanich and Charles Hudson (1993)

Foraging and Farming in the Eastern Woodlands, edited by C. Margaret Scarry (1993)

Puerto Real: The Archaeology of a Sixteenth-Century Spanish Town in Hispaniola, edited by Kathleen Deagan (1995)

Political Structure and Change in the Prehistoric Southeastern United States, edited by John F. Scarry (1996)

Bioarchaeology of Native American Adaptation in the Spanish Borderlands, edited by Brenda J. Baker and Lisa Kealhofer (1996)

A History of the Timucua Indians and Missions, by John H. Hann (1996)

Archaeology of the Mid-Holocene Southeast, edited by Kenneth E. Sassaman and David G. Anderson (1996)

The Indigenous People of the Caribbean, edited by Samuel M. Wilson (1997); first paperback edition, 1999

Hernando de Soto among the Apalachee: The Archaeology of the First Winter Encampment, by Charles R. Ewen and John H. Hann (1998)

The Timucuan Chiefdoms of Spanish Florida, by John E. Worth: vol. 1, *Assimilation;* vol. 2, *Resistance and Destruction* (1998)

Ancient Earthen Enclosures of the Eastern Woodlands, edited by Robert C. Mainfort, Jr., and Lynne P. Sullivan (1998)

An Environmental History of Northeast Florida, by James J. Miller (1998)

Precolumbian Architecture in Eastern North America, by William N. Morgan (1999)

Archaeology of Colonial Pensacola, edited by Judith A. Bense (1999)

Grit-Tempered: Early Women Archaeologists in the Southeastern United States, edited by Nancy Marie White, Lynne P. Sullivan, and Rochelle A. Marrinan (1999); first paperback edition, 2001

Coosa: The Rise and Fall of a Southeastern Mississippian Chiefdom, by Marvin T. Smith (2000)

Religion, Power, and Politics in Colonial St. Augustine, by Robert L. Kapitzke (2001)

Bioarchaeology of Spanish Florida: The Impact of Colonialism, edited by Clark Spencer Larsen (2001)

Archaeological Studies of Gender in the Southeastern United States, edited by Jane M. Eastman and Christopher B. Rodning (2001)

The Archaeology of Traditions: Agency and History Before and After Columbus, edited by Timothy R. Pauketat (2001)

Foraging, Farming, and Coastal Biocultural Adaptation in Late Prehistoric North Carolina, by Dale L. Hutchinson (2002)

Windover: Multidisciplinary Investigations of an Early Archaic Florida Cemetery, edited by Glen H. Doran (2002)

Archaeology of the Everglades, by John W. Griffin (2002)

Pioneer in Space and Time: John Mann Goggin and the Development of Florida Archaeology, by Brent Richards Weisman (2002)

Indians of Central and South Florida, 1513–1763, by John H. Hann (2003)

Bioarchaeology of the Florida Gulf Coast: Adaptation, Conflict, and Change, by Dale L. Hutchinson (2004)

Presidio Santa Maria de Galve: A Struggle for Survival in Colonial Spanish Pensacola, edited by Judith A. Bense (2004)